Learning C++
A Hands-On Approach

Eric Nagler
University of California Santa Cruz Extension

book is Borland C++ oriented book

PWS Publishing Company
I(T)P™ *An International Thomson Publishing Company*

Boston • Albany • Bonn • Cincinnati • Detroit • London • Madrid • Melbourne • Mexico City
New York • Pacific Grove • Paris • San Francisco • Singapore • Tokyo • Toronto • Washington

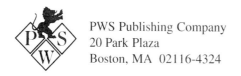

PWS Publishing Company
20 Park Plaza
Boston, MA 02116-4324

Reprinted in 1997 by PWS Publishing Company, a division of International Thomson Publishing Inc.
Originally copyright 1993 and 1997 by West Publishing Company.

I(T)P™

International Thomson Publishing
The trademark ITP is used under license.

Library of Congress Cataloging-in-Publication Data

Nagler, Eric P.
  Learning C++ : a hands-on approach / Eric
    Nagler. — 2nd ed.
    p. cm.
  Includes bibliographical references and index.
  ISBN 0-314-20039-8 (pbk. : alk. paper)
  1. C++ (Computer program language) I. Title.
QA76.73.C15N33   1997
005.13'3—dc20   96-20162
                                              CIP
British Library Cataloguing-in-Publication Data.
A catalog record for this book is available from
the British Library.

Sponsoring Editor: *David Dietz*
Marketing Manager: *Nathan Wilbur*
Prepress Services: *Carlisle Communications*
Printing & Binding: *West Publishing Company*

TRADEMARKS
ANSI is a registered trademark of American National
Standards Institute.
AT&T is a registered trademark of AT&T.
Borland C++ is a registered trademark of Borland
International, Inc.
CompuServe is a registered trademark of CompuServe, Inc.
X3J16 is a technical committee that operates under X3
procedures and policies. X3 is an Accredited Standards
Committee that operates under the procedures of ANSI.

Printed and bound in the United States of America.
  99 00 01 02 — 10 9 8 7 6 5 4

 THIS TEXT IS PRINTED ON 10% POST CONSUMER RECYLCED PAPER

For more information, contact:
PWS Publishing Company
20 Park Plaza
Boston, MA 02116

International Thomson Publishing Europe
Berkshire House
168–173 High Holborn
London WC1V 7AA
England

Thomas Nelson Australia
102 Dodds Street
South Melbourne, 3205
Victoria, Australia

Nelson Canada
1120 Birchmont Road
Scarborough, Ontario
Canada M1K 5G4

International Thomson Editores
Campos Eliseos 385, Piso 7
Col. Polanco
11560 Mexico D.F., Mexico

International Thomson Publishing GmbH
Königswinterer Strasse 418
53227 Bonn, Germany

International Thomson Publishing Asia
221 Henderson Road
#05-10 Henderson Building
Singapore 0315

International Thomson Publishing Japan
Hirakawacho Kyowa Building, 31
2-2-1 Hirakawacho
Chiyoda-ku, Tokyo 102
Japan

Contents

Chapter 1
Moving from C to C++

Chapter 2
Introduction to iostream Methods

Chapter 6
Classes

Chapter 8
More Class Features

Chapter 9
Function Overloading

Chapter 10
Inheritance

Chapter 11
Templates

Chapter 12
Exception Handling

Chapter 13
Namespaces

Chapter 14
Runtime Type Information

Chapter 15
Iostream Output

Chapter 16
Iostream Input

Chapter 17
Manipulators

Chapter 18
File Input/Output

List of Tables

Acknowledgments

Writing a book is not an easy thing to do. In isolation, it's just about an impossible task. Many people, including a good number of my students, spent a great deal of time reading the proof pages in order to offer their insights and find typos, all in the name of making this a better book. I would especially like to express my gratitude to all of the manuscript reviewers who worked on either the first edition and/or this revised edition:

- Thomas J Ahlborn, West Chester University
- Farrokh Attarzadeh, University of Houston
- Bonnie Bailey, Morehead State University
- Gary Blaine, software consultant
- Marian Corcoran, University of California Santa Cruz Extension
- Edmund I Deaton, San Diego State University
- H E Dunsmore, Purdue University
- Carl F Eckberg, San Diego State University
- Mary Edgington, Wichita State University
- Rhonda Ficek, Moorhead State University
- John J Forsyth, Michigan State University
- Peter Isaacson, University of Northern Colorado
- Bob Koss, Robert Koss & Associates
- Grant Larkin, De Anza Community College
- Daniel Masterson, Utah Valley Community College
- Robert A McDonald, East Stroudsburg University
- Mike Michaelson, Palomar College
- Allan Miller, College of San Mateo
- Michael Mohlé, Princeton-Galax Systems
- William Muellner, Elmhurst College
- Richard J Reid, Michigan State University
- Arline Sachs, Northern Virginia Community College
- Cliff Sherrill, Yavapai College
- Jerrold Siegel, University of Missouri at St. Louis
- Al Stevens, Dr. Dobbs' Journal

Scott Meyers also was gracious enough with his time to review parts of this book for technical accuracy. John Dlugosz, whose knowledge of C++ is unsurpassed, also assisted me tremendously in my understanding of templates. In addition, I wish to thank the technical staff at Borland International and the people who participate in the Borland forums on CompuServe for answering many of my questions.

The design and layout of this book were done in FrameMaker 5.0 on a Macintosh with help from Linda Kuester. Nell Angelo also assisted greatly with the copy-edit.

Finally, I would like to acknowledge the support that I have continually been receiving for the past five years from West Educational Publishing, in particular from Richard Mixter and Lauren Fogel.

About the Author...

Eric Nagler received his B.A. in mathematics from the University of Michigan in 1963, went to work for the federal government as a computer programmer, and has been working in the field of data processing ever since. He first started teaching computer languages in 1980, C in 1987, C++ in 1990, and Java in 1997. He has taught these languages at numerous companies in the San Jose, California Bay Area, and is currently on the staff of the University of California Santa Cruz Extension.

Preface

This book first appeared on the market in June 1993, and covered those aspects of the C++ programming language that were incorporated into Borland C++ version 3.1. I am very pleased that it has been adopted in many colleges and universities. Since the first edition, there have been many changes and additions to C++, and I felt that a completely revised edition of this book was long overdue.

The second edition covers the most recent version of the Borland compiler, 5.0. Borland C++ was chosen over other compilers because it has consistently been in the forefront in terms of implementing the ANSI/ISO C++ Standard, and I wanted to make this book as up-to-date and compatible with the Standard as possible. Nevertheless, the vast majority of other C++ compilers on the market today (including prior versions of Borland C++) can be used with this book provided that they are fairly recent. For Borland, this would mean at least version 4.0, and for Microsoft, it would mean at least Visual C++ 4.0.

If you compile any of the programs in this book, and don't get the expected result (e.g., compiler or linker error, or different run-time results), then I encourage you to contact me so that we can come up with an answer.

What's Inside

This book presents a complete introductory course in the C++ programming language, and also includes some topics that one might consider to be "advanced." It is designed to be used either on your own or in a classroom setting, in which case it serves as your notes for the various topics covered in your course.

The level of detail in this book goes beyond what most other books on C++ have to say on any particular topic. This means that in a classroom the amount of note-taking that you will have to do should be kept to a minimum. The advantage of this approach to learning is that (1) if you are constantly taking notes, you are not devoting complete attention to what the instructor or another student is saying, and (2) it is very easy to copy code incorrectly, thereby resulting in a program that either will not compile or has a bug. Instead, you may want to keep a marking pen handy to highlight certain passages. Nevertheless, at the end of the book there are several blank pages that you may use to jot down any new material.

What's New in the Second Edition

This second edition retains all of the strengths of the first edition such as depth of coverage, accuracy, and readability, that were so enthusiastically received by instructors and students alike. Comments and suggestions from students, instructors, and reviewers have helped me to revise this text, making it even more useful and accessible. The second edition reflects the considerable changes in the C++ language and incorporates several new features. For example, Chapter 1 has been completely updated to cover the most important new features of the C++ language (especially the new styles of casting) to help you make the transition from C to C++. The chapters on inheritance and polymorphism in the first edition have now been combined into one chapter (Chapter 10), and the section on multiple inheritance (10.18) has been rewritten. Chapter 11 covering templates (perhaps the most important chapter in the book) was revamped to incorporate the numerous changes that have occurred in the past several years. In addition, you will find new chapters covering namespaces (Chapter 13) and runtime type information (Chapter 14).

The most important change, however, is in the realm of input and output. In the first edition, all of the examples up to Chapter 12 relied on the stdio library. This was done in order to avoid the extra burden of having to learn iostream methods in order to perform simple input and output tasks. However, the response from students and other readers indicated that they wanted these iostream methods to be introduced much earlier in order to start thinking in an object-oriented fashion as soon as possible. On the other hand, they did not want to be bothered with the intricate detail that accompanies iostream methods, such as formatting, error handling, overloading the insertion and extraction operators, etc. Therefore, I tried to strike a balance in this edition by introducing a very simplified version of iostream methods in Chapter 2 that covers just the essential items that are needed to perform input and output operations. The aforementioned details of iostream methods are deferred until the final four Chapters, 15 through 18. Feel free to jump ahead and refer to these chapters if you want to explore iostream methods in more detail.

The second edition has a completely revised design. All examples now have a signature icon, making them easier to locate. Implementing the requests of reviewers, more examples now demonstrate practical programming situations. In addition, you will find two new features in this book — Tip boxes and Caution boxes.

A Tip box will be highlighted by this icon:

 Tip

and a Caution box uses this icon:

 Caution

A Tip grabs your attention to alert you to an important aspect of the C++ language, and adherence to a Caution could save you precious time in testing and debugging.

I feel that these changes in organization, content, and design clearly strengthen the book. The second edition of *Learning C++: A Hands-on Approach* is now pedagogically stronger and reflects the many changes in the C++ language.

Supplements

In keeping with PWS Publishing's commitment to exploring the resources of new technology, qualified adopters of this text can now use the Internet to access supplements.

Examples

Qualified users will find all of the code examples used in the text via PWS Publishing's home page at http://www.pws.com

Solutions Manual

The solutions for the exercises in each chapter are available to qualified users via PWS Publishing's home page at http://www.pws.com

Prerequisites

In order to get the maximum benefit from this book, you should have a thorough working knowledge of the C language. This means, in particular, that your knowledge of C syntax, the various constructs, structures, arrays, functions, pointers, etc. is current. A knowledge of advanced C programming is helpful but not mandatory.

Unfortunately, some people believe that C++ is just C with a couple of extra keywords and the ability to write classes. They could not be more wrong. In terms of difficulty, I have polled many of my former students and overwhelmingly they agree that the material covered in C++ was much more difficult than they had anticipated. I would estimate that it is at least twice as hard to move from C to C++ as it is to go from another language, say Pascal, to C.

Nothing Explains Like an Example

Over 400 examples of C++ programs (or parts of programs) are included in this book. The reason that there are so many is simply my belief that nothing can explain a C++ concept as well as a good example with the output shown (where applicable). In fact, many of the examples in this book were created as a direct result of questions asked by students in previous classes. An old saying goes, "The only way to learn programming is to program". It has never been more true than it is with C++.

All of the programs shown are "flat file". This means that when the program involves more than one file, e.g., a header and a definition, they are shown as though they physically are one file on disk, even though a header and definition should be maintained as two physically separate files. If you were to compile one of these programs, then the compiler would probably complain that it cannot include a particular user-defined header file. One solution is to create several dummy empty header files in some directory that satisfy the preprocessor, or merely comment out the appropriate preprocessor include directives.

When output is shown, it is commented out so that it does not interfere with the compilation process.

How to Obtain the Examples on Diskette

All of the examples in this book are available on 3 1/2" diskette in text format. An order form can be found in the back of the book.

Other Sources of Information

I would also like to note that no matter how good a given book on C++ may be, no single book can possibly teach you everything that you might want or need to know. Therefore, I highly encourage you to purchase as many books on C++ as you can afford so that you may see what a variety of authors have to say on a given topic. Then you should contrast and compare their views (and perhaps even find inconsistencies).

There are also several good magazines on the market that deal exclusively with the C and C++ languages, such as The C++ Report and The C/C++ Users Journal.

What About Object-oriented Programming?

I also assume that many of you are studying C++ because you have heard that it has the capability to do object-oriented programming. The reason that C++ has become so popular is that it is a natural extension of the C language, which has become one of the most widely used programming languages. Therefore, people feel it is quite natural to migrate into C++ once they have mastered C. This is fine, but you should also be aware that there are many other object-oriented languages in use today, such as Object Pascal, Smalltalk, Modula 2, Objective-C, and Eiffel.

The transition from C to C++ can logically be categorized into three phases. Phase 1 would be the use of C++ as a "better C". This might entail the usage of reference variables, the new style of commenting, new ways to dynamically allocate memory, function overloading, etc. Phase 2 would involve the creation of classes and data encapsulation. Phase 3 would introduce derivation and polymorphism to make full use of C++ as an object-oriented programming language (OOPL). Please be aware that while certain areas of object-oriented design will be mentioned (indeed, it's impossible to ignore), a complete course in object-oriented programming, including analysis, design, implementation, message passing, client-server relationships, and so forth, is beyond the scope of this book.

Where Things Now Stand

In order to provide some kind of standardization process, a committee called ANSI/ISO C++, with the number X3J16, started its work in 1990 to hammer out a C++ standard to which all compilers must eventually conform. This committee has been meeting three times a year, in March, July and November. The first public draft was made available in April 1995, and second is due to come out in July 1996.

When the committee first met, it was decided that the C++ standard would be based upon two documents: (1) The Annotated C++ Reference Manual by Bjarne Stroustrup and Margaret Ellis, and (2) the ISO Standard for the C Programming Language. As of today (May 1996), the standard has for the most part been completed, except for certain details that still need to be ironed out (particularly in the area of templates). Unfortunately, by the time the standard is completed, and the various compiler vendors implement it, we may very well be in the next century.

Nobody is Perfect

If you encounter any errors in this book, grammatical or technical, I would appreciate hearing from you. I can be contacted at the following address:

Eric Nagler
P O Box 2483
Santa Clara, California 95055-2483

epn@eric-nagler.com
http://www.eric-nagler.com

Chapter 1

Moving from C to C++

1.1   Introduction

The C++ language was invented as an extension and enhancement of the C language by Bjarne Stroustrup of AT&T Bell Laboratories in 1979, and has evolved into a unique language. In some ways C++ is no longer a "better" C but can prove to be rather frustrating and inconvenient for a C programmer.

For the sake of backward compatibility, you can take your existing C programs and compile them successfully using a C++ compiler. Maybe. Unfortunately, it's not quite that simple, as there are some subtle differences that you must be aware of. This chapter will cover those differences. In addition, C++ adds some very useful miscellaneous features to C that are also covered in this chapter. This is sometimes called "using C++ as a better C". So let's get started.

1.2   Source Program Names

Because many C++ compilers can compile a program written in either C or C++, they must have a way to determine the type of code that they are processing. If the source code extension is .CPP, then the compiler assumes that you want to do a C++ compilation. Otherwise, unless the extension is something that is recognizable, such as .LIB, .OBJ, .ASM, .DEF, etc., any other extension implies that a C compilation will be done. So if your first C++ program produces, say, several dozen error messages, you'll know where to look first!

On the other hand, if you are doing a command-line compilation, then the Borland option -P will force the compiler to do a C++ compilation regardless of the program's extension. It is up to you to ensure that the compiler you are using interprets your code in the way you intend.

1.3   C++-style of Commenting

C++ defines a new comment that consists of two forward slashes (/ /). Whenever the compiler encounters this token, it will ignore everything that follows it to the end of the current line. It does *not* extend across different lines like a C-style comment.

1.3.1   Comments, Please?

The token / / itself is ignored if it is encountered as part of a C-style comment, and the token / * is ignored if it is part of a C++-style comment. In addition, the token / / is *not* part of a macro, so that in the following example the line declaring the variable x has no trouble being compiled because False is defined to be 0, *not* 0 followed by a C++-style comment.

 Example 1.1

```
/*   C comment using
        2 lines              */

//   C++ comment to the end of the current line

/*   C comment -     // is ignored  */

//   C++ comment -   /* is ignored

#define False 0          // A macro
int x = False + 1;       // OK; x will be 1
```

By the way, some C++ purists insist that it's bad style, if not downright ugly, to write a C++ program and include C-style comments. This author does not share that opinion, and in fact will be using C-style comments in the book where they are appropriate.

 Tip

Needless to say (but I'll say it anyway), your program should always use enough comments to explain to the reader (and to yourself!) what it is trying to accomplish.

1.4 Implicit Use of Type `int`

Ever since its creation, C++ has honored the C tradition of assuming type `int` in situations where a type name would normally be written, but in fact is absent.

 Example 1.2

```
main(void)                  // int main(void)
{
    const limit = 10;       // const int limit = 10;
    typedef integer;        // typedef int integer;
    return 0;
}
```

However, this style of coding has been made invalid, so someday it may not compile. Therefore, you should always explicitly specify type `int` where appropriate.

 Tip

The C++ Draft Working Paper (DWP) allows the `main()` *function to omit a* `return` *statement, in which case a return value of 0 is implied. Because this feature is not implemented in Borland 5.0, each* `main()` *function in this book will continue to show an explicit* `return` *statement.*

1.5 Is It C or C++?

Occasionally the preprocessor needs to ask the question, "Am I running in a C or C++ environment?" The answer can be found by looking at the preprocessor symbol `__cplusplus` (*two* leading underscores). This macro will always be on whenever you are compiling a C++ program. If you are compiling a C program using a C++ compiler, it will be off.

For example, a header file unique to C++ is called `iostream.h` (discussed in more detail in Chapter 2). The first few lines in this header file are:

 Example 1.3

```
#ifndef __cplusplus
#error Must use C++ for type iostream.h
#endif
```

Consequently, if you are doing a C compilation and include this header file, the Boolean condition then gets evaluated to 'true', the error message appears on the terminal screen, and it's the end of the line for you!

1.6   Declaring and Defining Functions

OK, all you K & R programmers out there, no more cheating on your function prototypes. When you write C++ code, you *must* use ANSI-style function prototyping in your programs. (The word "prototype" is not strictly a C++ term, and has been replaced by the word "declaration".)

A function definition implies the declaration, but the opposite is not true. The declaration or definition of a function must precede an actual call of that function and specify the correct number and type of formal arguments. If a type does not match exactly, it is a fatal error only if the compiler *cannot* do an implicit type conversion. Remember: the compiler is very smart, and knows how to convert *any* fundamental type into *any other* fundamental type (except, of course, that most pointer types cannot be converted to any other pointer type, nor can a `double`, for example, be converted to a pointer type).

  Example 1.4

```
void foo(int x);    // Function declaration

void g()
{
    foo(3);         // OK; call matches declaration exactly
    foo(4.37);      // OK; converts from double to int
}

void foo(int x)     // Function definition
{
    // Do something
}
```

  Tip

Like C, formal argument names in function declarations are always optional, and serve only to provide documentation to someone reading the code.

Since a function *definition* consists of the complete function itself, if it precedes the call to that function, it negates the need for an additional function *declaration*.

Example 1.5

```
void foo(int x)      // Function definition
{
    // Do something
}

void g()
{
    foo(3);          // OK; call matches definition exactly
    foo(4.37);       // OK; converts from double to int
}
```

Arguments passed in to an ellipsis (e.g., the second argument to `scanf()` and `printf()`) will undergo default promotions, i.e., `char` to `int`, and `float` to `double`.

 Caution

Some C++ compilers may give you a warning message if the implicit type conversion of an actual argument causes significance to be lost, e.g., the conversion of a `double` *to a* `char`*.*

1.7   Functions Taking No Arguments

In the C language, if you declare a function such as:

 Example 1.6

```
void foo();      /* A function declaration in C */
```

then you really have not said anything one way or the other about the number or types of arguments that can be passed in. In other words, such a declaration does *not* constitute a function prototype.

If you want to specify that the function cannot be called with any arguments whatsoever, then the declaration can be turned into a prototype by writing the keyword `void` in the formal argument list.

 Example 1.7

```
void foo(void);      /* A function prototype in C */
```

Because all functions in C++ *must* be declared before they are used, Example 1.6 would seem to be meaningless in C++. However, C++ has said that it really has the same meaning as that of Example 1.7. In other words, to declare a function that takes no arguments, you may write the keyword `void` between the parentheses (as you would in C), or simply write empty parentheses.

1.8 Formal Argument Names in Function Definitions

As mentioned earlier, in both C and C++, formal argument names in function declarations are always optional since they really do not provide any useful information to the compiler. But if you want to write them for the sake of good documentation, then it's perfectly acceptable to do so.

 Example 1.8

```
void foo(int arg);   // Same as...
void foo(int);
```

However, when it comes time to write the function *definition*, C requires you to provide the formal argument names, which just makes sense. C++, however, does away with this restriction because of the concept of *function overloading* in which more than one function can exist at the same scope and have the same name.

For example, the following is perfectly valid C++ code.

Example 1.9

```
#include <stdio.h>

void foo(int)    // No formal argument name
{
   puts("int got called");
}

void foo(char)  // Overloaded function
{
   puts("char got called");
}

void foo(double)  // Overloaded function
{
   puts("double got called");
}

int main()
{
   foo(0);               // Call foo(int)
   foo('A');             // Call foo(char)
   foo(1.234);           // Call foo(double)
   return 0;
}

/* The output of this program is:

int got called
char got called
double got called

*/
```

Since you are only interested in which function got called, there is no need to provide formal argument names, and in fact this would generate warning messages about names being defined but never used.

 Tip

Function overloading is discussed in greater detail in Chapter 9.

1.9   Initialization vs. Assignment

Before proceeding any farther, it is critical that you understand the difference
between the processes of initialization and assignment. This has important ramifications in C++, and you will pay a handsome price in terms of time and space if you
don't know which is which.

First, *initialization* is the process in which an object is declared and given some initial value. It is essentially a one-step process. For example, here the variable `data` is
being declared and initialized with the value 1.

 Example 1.10

```
int data = 1;    // Declaration and initialization
```

On the other hand, *assignment* is the process in which an existing object is overwritten with the contents of some other object. Nothing is being created. For example,
here `data` is being assigned the value 2, which replaces the previous value of 1.

 Example 1.11

```
data = 2;    // Assignment
```

Despite the fact that an equal sign appears in both initialization and assignment
statements, the compiler can easily differentiate one from the other by asking if the
statement begins with a *type* (excluding modifiers such as `const`). If the answer is
yes, then it's initialization; if no, it's assignment. Example 1.10 begins with the type
`int`, so it's initialization; Example 1.11 does not begin with a type, so it's assignment. Never forget this simple rule later on when dealing with user-defined types.

 Tip

*It's an excellent idea to get into the habit of preferring initialization over
assignment whenever you can. This topic will be revisited in Chapter 7
when you will learn how to initialize (not assign) the data members of a
class.*

1.10   Placement of Variable Declarations

In C, whenever you write a block of code, the variables must be declared at the
beginning, before any executable statements. If you want to create a new variable,
you must start a new block (scope) by writing an open brace.

For example, in the program below, a number, n1, is declared and printed, after which the same operation is performed on another integer, n2. Because n2 is declared after the call to printf(), a new block is required. This is OK, provided that n2 does not need to be referenced outside the block (since it is an auto variable and will go out of scope when the block ends).

 Example 1.12

```
/* A C language program */

#include <stdio.h>

int main(void)
{
    int n1 = 1;
    printf("n1 = %d\n", n1);
    {
        int n2 = 2;
        printf("n2 = %d\n", n2);
    }  /* n2 goes out of scope here */
    return 0;
}  /* n1 goes out of scope here */

/* The output of this program is:

n1 = 1
n2 = 2

*/
```

The only other approach would be to declare n2 at the same time that n1 is declared.

However, in C++ this restriction disappears because declaration statements are treated the same as executable statements, which means that they may be freely mixed.

Here is a repeat of Example 1.12 now written in C++.

Example 1.13

```
// a C++ language program

#include <stdio.h>

int main()
{
   int n1 = 1;
   printf("n1 = %d\n", n1);
   int n2 = 2;   // No braces needed!
   printf("n2 = %d\n", n2);
   return 0;
} // Both n1 and n2 go out of scope here

/* The output of this program is:

n1 = 1
n2 = 2

*/
```

One advantage of this feature is that it allows you to declare a variable closer to its actual use in the program. On the other hand, some people may prefer to have all of the variables declared in only one place, e.g., at the beginning of a function.

But when you get to the point of creating user-defined objects, you must first have available the values that will be used in the creation process itself. This implies that you first need to execute statements, and then declare that an object is coming into existence *without* starting a new scope. Thus, it's mandatory that you have the capability to freely mix the two types of statements.

1.11   Variable Declaration Within a `for` Loop

C++ also lets you declare the counting variable of a `for` loop as part of the initialization syntax. This allows you to prefer initialization of the variable to assignment into the variable, and could be very important if a user-defined type is involved.

In addition, the `for` loop *creates its own scope,* so that if another variable with the same name happens to already exist, then there is no naming conflict. When the `for` loop ends, the counting variable then *goes out of scope.*

Because this scoping rule is a fairly recent change to the language, Borland compilers prior to 5.0 work exactly the opposite way, so that the counting variable remains *in scope* after the loop ends. You should experiment with your compiler to see how it's implemented.

This is how a `for` loop is supposed to act under the C++ language standard, and how in fact it does act under Borland 5.0.

 Example 1.14

```
void foo()
{
   int i = 9;
   for(int i = 0; i < 5; ++i)      // OK; hides first 'i'
   {
       // Body of loop
   }
   ++i;      // OK; i becomes 10
}

// Equivalent to...

void foo()
{
   int i = 9;
   {
      for(int i = 0; i < 5; ++i)    // OK; hides first 'i'
      {
          // Body of loop
      }
   }
   ++i;      // OK; i becomes 10
}
```

1.12   Initialization of Global Variables

In C, global variables may be initialized only to constant values, i.e., values whose addresses are known at compilation time. In C++, however, they may be initialized to the value of an expression, provided that the expression can be computed.

 Example 1.15

```
#include <stdio.h>
/* At the global scope... */
int a = 1; /* legal in both C and C++ */
int b = a; /* legal only in C++ */
int c = puts("Ready to start"); /* legal only in C++ */
```

 Tip

This capability is more than just a "nice feature". It's really a necessity, as

1.13   Initialization of Arrays

In C, all of the initializers in an array declaration must be known to the compiler. For example, a list of constants works just fine. An array of pointers-to-characters is also a good example because the compiler knows the address of each string as it is stored in global memory, not on the stack or the heap, when `main()` is called. Therefore, the following program works just fine in both C and C++.

 Example 1.16

```
/* A C language program */

#include <stdio.h>

int main(void)
{
    const char* array[] = { "Some", "string", "data" };
    const int size = sizeof(array) / sizeof(*array);
    int i;
    for(i = 0; i < size; ++i)
        puts(array[i]);
    return 0;
}

/* The output of this program is:

Some
string
data

*/
```

 Tip

Whenever the compiler encounters an array, it automatically generates a pointer to the first element. However, the one exception to this rule occurs in the case of sizeof *which always yields the number of bytes, not a pointer to the first element.*

On the other hand, the following somewhat similar program does *not* compile in C because the compiler has no idea where the `auto` integers will be on the stack at execution time. C++, however, does not impose this restriction, and instead computes the addresses of the initializing elements at execution time. This feature is especially useful when you must initialize an array of pointers with heap-space addresses.

Example 1.17

```
// A C++ language program

#include <stdio.h>

int main()
{
   int n1 = 1;
   int n2 = 2;
   const int* array[] = {&n1, &n2};  // Error in C, OK in C++
   const int size = sizeof(array) / sizeof(*array);
   for(int i = 0; i < size; ++i)
      printf("array[%d] = %d\n", i, *array[i]);
   return 0;
}

/* The output of this program is:

array[0] = 1
array[1] = 2

*/
```

1.14 Character Constants

In C, all character constants are stored in either 2 or 4 bytes, depending upon the compiler and memory model. Therefore, the sizeof a character constant, e.g., 'A', is either 2 or 4. But in C++, the sizeof a character constant is always 1. In both C and C++ the sizeof keyword applied to type char is always 1.

Example 1.18

```
#include <stdio.h>

int main(void)
{
  printf("size of 'A' = %d\n", sizeof('A'));
  printf("size of char = %d\n", sizeof(char));
  return 0;
}

/* In C the output of this program is:

size of 'A' = 2
size of char = 1

In C++ the output of this program is:

size of 'A' = 1
size of char = 1

*/
```

1.15   Empty Initializer Clause

When you initialize an array in C, you must provide at least one entry as part of the initializer list between the braces. If you choose to specify the dimension, and the number of initializing values is less than this dimension, then the extra elements are guaranteed to be initialized to the proper default value of 0 for the fundamental types.

 Example 1.19

```
int array1[3] = { 1, 2 };    // OK; last element is 0
double array2[3] = { };      // Error in C, OK in C++
```

However, C++ now allows an empty pair of braces, in which case each element of the array is initialized to its default value.

 Caution

Borland C++ 5.0 does not yet support this feature.

1.16 Conversion of `void*` Pointers

In both C and C++, the conversion from any pointer type *into* type `void*` is considered to be standard conversion, and is therefore done implicitly for you by the compiler.

The conversion *from* `void*` into a different pointer type is also a standard conversion in C. But in C++, to enforce the stronger type-checking mechanism and ensure that you know what you are doing, a cast is mandatory. Therefore, this program compiles in C but not in C++.

 Example 1.20

```
void foo(void)
{
    char* c = "test string";
    void* v = c;    /* standard conversion */
    int* i = v;     /* OK in C, error in C++ */
}
```

Congratulations. You now have a pointer of type `int` pointing to an array of characters. When you use pointer arithmetic on your newly created pointer, you will get some very interesting results. This is why the code is not type-safe in C and fails to compile in C++.

But if you're a glutton for punishment, and determined to make it work in C++, you must write a cast.

 Example 1.21

```
void foo(void)
{
    char* c = "test string";
    void* v = c;
    int* i = (int*)v;       // OK in both C and C++
}
```

 Caution

Borland 5.0 produces a "suspicious pointer conversion" warning message without the cast, whereas prior versions produced a fatal error message.

1.17   **Use 0, Not** NULL

C++ guarantees that a constant expression that evaluates to 0 will be converted to a pointer type whenever a pointer is expected. So there is really no problem using 0 whereas, in C, you would use the macro NULL. As you just saw in the previous paragraph, you could have a problem if NULL were defined as ((void*)0). The only exception is when 0 is passed as an unchecked argument (e.g., as the second argument in a printf() or scanf() statement that uses ellipses). In this case the 0 requires a cast to a pointer type.

 Example 1.22

```
int* p1 = 0;        // OK
void* p2 = 0;       // OK
if(p2 == 0)         // OK
    // ...
```

1.18   **Using the Tag Name as the Type Name**

Suppose, in C, you have a structure definition called Person to be used in some linked list application, and later wish to create an instance of this definition called student. You could write:

 Example 1.23

```
/* A C language structure */

struct Person
{
    char name[25];
    long ssn;
    struct Person* next;
};

struct Person student;
```

and the job would be done. However, you can shorten this process by using a typedef:

Example 1.24

```
/* A C language structure using a typedef */

typedef struct Person
{
   char name[25];
   long ssn;
   struct Person* next;      /* Cannot say Person* next */
} Person;

Person student;
```

Note that the word `Person` used as the tag name for the structure in the first line is required because it's needed to declare the `next` field.

Fortunately, in C++ the need to `typedef` a structure is no longer necessary because the tag name of a structure automatically becomes the type name as soon as it's encountered by the compiler. In other words, in C++ you can simply write:

 Example 1.25

```
// A C++ language structure

struct Person
{
   char name[25];
   long ssn;
   Person* next;
};

Person student;   // Keyword struct not needed
```

 Tip

This lack of a need to do a `typedef` also applies to the keywords `enum` and `union`, and to the C++ keyword `class`. Of course, the `typedef` keyword is still valid, and may be used in other contexts to simplify your code.

1.19   The `const` Keyword

By definition, in ANSI C, a variable declared with the modifier `const` is one that cannot be modified. In C, a variable may be declared `const` without being initialized (thereby serving no useful purpose), whereas in C++, all constants *must* be initialized.

 Example 1.26

```
const int x;        // OK in C, error in C++
const int y = 0;    // OK in both C and C++
y = 1;              // Always an error
```

1.19.1   `const` Keyword when Calling a Function by Value

With regard to the use of a `const`-qualified formal argument when you pass an actual argument into a function by value, it's OK to use but it is not required. The reason is that even without using it, a constant value can be used as the actual argument, and still be received by a non-constant formal argument. In other words, any combination of `const` and non-`const` arguments works.

 Example 1.27

```
void foo(const int x);
void bar(int y);

void g(const int a, int b)
{
    foo(a);    // OK
    foo(b);    // OK
    bar(a);    // OK
    bar(b);    // OK
}
```

1.19.2   `const` Keyword when Returning a Value from a Function

Similarly, when a function returns a fundamental type by value, it buys you nothing to qualify the return type with `const` since what's being returned is always a temporary object that cannot be modified.

Example 1.28

```
const int foo();
int bar();

void g()
{
    int a = foo();              // OK
    const int b = foo();        // OK
    int c = bar();              // OK
    const int d = bar();        // OK
}
```

 Tip

> *When a* **user-defined** *type is returned from a function by value, the* `const` *qualifier does make a difference.*

1.19.3   `const` **Keyword with Pointers**

When dealing with pointers, the situation is a little more confusing because now there are two objects involved: the pointer itself and the object to which the pointer points. If the word `const` follows the asterisk, then the pointer itself cannot be changed. However, this has nothing to do with the object being pointed at.

 Example 1.29

```
void foo(char* const ptr)
{
    ptr = "A";      // Error; ptr's address cannot be changed
    *ptr = 'A';     // OK; where ptr points can be changed
}
```

On the other hand, if the word `const` appears immediately in front of the type, then the object being pointed at cannot be changed. Similarly, the word `const` has nothing to do with the pointer itself.

 Example 1.30

```
void foo(const char* ptr)
{
    ptr = "A";      // OK; ptr's address can be changed
    *ptr = 'A';     // Error; where ptr points cannot be changed
}
```

Of course, you may write the keyword `const` in both places.

Example 1.31

```
void foo(const char* const ptr)
{
  ptr = "A";     // Error; ptr's address cannot be changed
  *ptr = 'A';    // Error; where ptr points cannot be changed
}
```

1.19.4   `const` **Keyword with Pointers using a** `typedef`

Be very careful when using a `typedef` with a pointer. In the following example, `Pointer` is a pseudonym for type `char*`, but a `const Pointer` means that the variable being declared is constant, not the string that is being pointed at.

Example 1.32

```
typedef char* Pointer;
void foo(const Pointer ptr)
// Same as... void foo(Pointer const ptr)
{
  ptr = "A";     // Error; ptr's address cannot be changed
  *ptr = 'A';    // OK; where ptr points can be changed
}
```

To make both the pointer `ptr` and the string to which it points constant, you would have to write:

Example 1.33

```
typedef const char* Pointer;
void foo(const Pointer ptr)
{
  ptr = "A";     // Error; ptr's address cannot be changed
  *ptr = 'A';    // Error; where ptr points cannot be changed
}
```

1.19.5   **Support Constant Objects!**

In C++, it is crucial that you write code with the capability to support constant objects. If you don't, then users of your functions (and later on of your classes) will be very unhappy with you.

To see why, suppose you decide to write a function called `display()` that receives a `char*` pointer and displays the string to which this pointer points. The user then decides to invoke your function with an object of type `const char*`.

 Example 1.34

```
#include <stdio.h>

void display(char* p)     // Should be const char*
{
    puts(p);
}

int main()
{
    const char* ptr = "test string";
    display(ptr);   // Error; no conversion to char*
    return 0;
}
```

The compiler complains about the call to `display()` because there is no implicit conversion from `const char*` to `char*`, thereby forcing the user to cast `ptr` into type `char*` before invoking the function. Boo! The solution, of course, is to write the `display()` function properly by declaring the formal argument to be type `const char*`. Now your function can support arguments of type `char*` as well as type `const char*`.

1.19.6   How to Support `char**` and `const char**` Types

While it's always safe to do a conversion from type `char*` into type `const char*`, it is an error to convert from type `char**` into type `const char**`. The correct declaration is `const char* const*`. Since type `const char**` can implicitly be converted to type `const char* const*`, a function with an argument of type `const char* const*` can accommodate either type `char**` or `const char**`.

Example 1.35

```
void foo(const char**);
void bar(const char* const*);

void g()
{
   char* names[] = { "Tom", "Dick", "Harry" };
   const char* places[] = { "San Jose", "Sunnyvale" };

   foo(names);    // Error
   bar(names);    // OK
   foo(places);   // OK
   bar(places);   // OK
}
```

1.19.7   How C and C++ Handle const Differently

The big difference between how C and C++ handle constants is that, in C++, the fundamental (built-in) type constant values are kept in a separate compiler-only table and substituted into the code as literal constants, very similar to how #define works. On the other hand, if you were to take the address of a constant object in C++ and store this address into a pointer variable, then storage for the constant itself must be reserved. In C, the value of a const is not determined until execution time.

One good use of the way C++ handles const variables is when you need to specify the dimension of some array that will exist on the stack or in the global space. Of course, in C this would cause a compilation error because, as was just stated, the variable does not get its value until execution time.

 Example 1.36

```
void foo()
{
   const int dim = 10;
   int array[dim + 1];     // Error in C, OK in C++
}
```

On the other hand:

Example 1.37

```
void foo()
{
    int n = 10;
    const int dim = n;
    int array[dim];    // Error in both C and C++
}
```

does *not* work in C++ (and, obviously, not in C) because there is no way that the compiler can determine the value of dim since the value of n is not determined until execution time.

1.19.8   Use const **in Lieu of** #define

In C++, whenever you would normally use a #define to symbolically declare a value, use the const keyword if you can. It preserves type checking, and the variable follows the normal scoping rules.

For example, the following code will not compile because the #define, although written within the function foo(), affects the remainder of the program, including the max in bar().

Example 1.38

```
void foo()
{
    #define max 10
    int array[max];
}

void bar()
{
    double max = 10.0;    // Error; double 10 = 10.0;
}
```

Changing the #define to a const works because max is now localized to the function foo().

Example 1.39

```
void foo()
{
   const int max = 10;
   int array[max];
}

void bar()
{
   double max = 10.0;     // OK
}
```

1.20   Linkage of `const` **Variables**

By default, `const` values in C at global scope have *external* linkage. This means that the linker sees them and may use them in a file that has an `extern` declaration. In C++, however, the default is *internal*.

Example 1.40

```
// At global scope...

const int x = 1;           // Internal in C++, external in C
extern const int y = 1;    // External in both C++ and C
static const int z = 1;    // Internal in both C++ and C
```

The implication in C++ is that if several different compilation modules each include a header file that has a constant defined at global scope, the linker will *not* produce a duplicate definition error message because it knows nothing about the constants.

Example 1.41

```
// File header.h

#ifndef HEADER_H
#define HEADER_H

const int x = 1;

#endif

// File a.cpp

#include "header.h"        // OK; x is internal

// File b.cpp

#include "header.h"        // OK; x is internal
```

Of course, if two header files each have a constant at global scope with the same name, and a compilation unit includes both header files, then the compiler will issue a redefinition error, as shown in the following example.

 Example 1.42

```
// File header1.h

#ifndef HEADER1_H
#define HEADER1_H

const int x = 1;

#endif

// File header2.h

#ifndef HEADER2_H
#define HEADER2_H

const int x = 1;

#endif

// File a.cpp

#include "header1.h"
#include "header2.h"        // Error; duplicate definition of x
```

1.21   Enumerated Types

Enumerated types in C++, while having an underlying integral representation, are their own distinct types. Using integral promotion, they may be converted to type `int`, `unsigned int`, `long`, or `unsigned long` implicitly. However, unlike C, you cannot modify enumerated types by assignment or initialization with an object that is not a member of the specific enumeration. Also, arithmetic operators (such as `++` and `--`) that attempt to modify the enumerated variable cannot be used.

    Example 1.43

```
void foo()
{ .
   enum color { red, blue };
   color c = red;     // OK
   c = blue;          // OK
   c = 1;             // OK in C, error in C++
   ++c;               // OK in C, error in C++
   int x = c;         // OK; promotion to type int
}
```

1.22   Type `bool`

A language such as Pascal has a built-in Boolean type to represent the values 'true' and 'false', whereas the C language does not. Therefore, in both C and C++ it is quite common to attempt to create a Boolean type, and just about everyone does it differently. Even so, inherent problems still remain.

For example, using a `typedef` of an `int` to create a Boolean type doesn't work too well because the two types are really identical and therefore cannot be used to achieve function overloading.

Example 1.44

```
#include <stdio.h>

typedef int Boolean;

void foo(Boolean)
{
   puts("Boolean got called");
}

void foo(int)    // Duplicate definition error
{
   puts("int got called");
}
```

Furthermore, using an enumeration to create a Boolean type does not work because of the requirement to be able to freely convert back and forth between this type and type int and, as mentioned earlier, there is no implicit conversion from an int to an enum).

Example 1.45

```
enum Boolean { False = 0, True };
Boolean foo()
{
   return 1;  // Error; can't convert int to Boolean
}
```

To solve these problems, the C++ language has added a new integral Boolean type called bool with the corresponding literals false and true. All three are now keywords in the language. Displaying the values of false and true using printf() shows the values 0 and 1, respectively.

Non-zero integral and pointer values are implicitly converted to true, and true is implicitly converted to 1. Zero integral and pointer values are implicitly converted to false, and false is implicitly converted to 0.

nonzero values → true → 1
zero → false → 0

Example 1.46

```
#include <stdio.h>

int main()
{
    printf("false = %d\n", false);
    printf("true = %d\n", true);
    bool b1 = 9;
    printf("b1 = %d\n", b1);
    const char* ptr = "test string";
    bool b2 = ptr;
    printf("b2 = %d\n", b2);
    return 0;
}

/* The output of this program is:

false = 0
true = 1
b1 = 1
b2 = 1

*/
```

The language definition has also been changed so that the following three Boolean operators take arguments of type `bool` and yield an answer of type `bool`.

Table 1-1   Boolean Operators and type `bool`

&&	And
||	Or
!	Not

Also, the following six relational operators always produce `bool` results.

Table 1-2   Relational Operators and type `bool`

<	Less than
>	Greater than
<=	Less than or equal to
>=	Greater than or equal to
==	Equal to
!=	Not equal to

Finally, each of the following keywords and the conditional operator will have its Boolean expression automatically converted to type `bool`.

Table 1-3   Constructs and type `bool`

if(Boolean_expression)
for(Boolean_expression)
while(Boolean_expression)
do...while(Boolean_expression)
Boolean ? true-expression : false-expression

For purposes of backward compatibility, you may want to include the following header file when compiling under Borland 5.0 or any previous Borland version in order to ensure that the type `bool` is defined properly.

 Example 1.47

```
// File bool.h

#ifndef BOOL_H
#define BOOL_H

#ifndef __BOOL__
typedef int bool;
const bool false = 0;
const bool true = 1;
#endif

#endif
```

Borland C++ 5.0 has the macro __BOOL__ defined, so when running under a Borland version prior to 5.0, the `typedef` and constants will take effect, but if you subsequently convert to 5.0, then no harm is done if you do not remove the `#include` statement.

 Tip

The effect of displaying and getting a variable of type `bool` *is discussed in Chapters 15 and 16, respectively.*

1.23   New Styles of Casting

Bjarne Stroustrup, the creator of C++, has called the C-style of casting a "sledge-hammer", and he's right. This is because it can be very unclear to someone reading your code why you are performing a cast. For example, given this code segment with generic types T and U:

Example 1.48

```
T data = 0;
const T* ptr1 = &data;
// ...
U* ptr2 = (U*)ptr1;
```

does the programmer intend to obtain a pointer to type U that is unrelated to T? Cast away the `const` attribute? Both? Perhaps navigate a class hierarchy?

This confusion has been solved by the new style of casting that C++ provides. Stroustrup maintains that the goal of the new casts is to minimize and localize unsafe and error-prone programming practices.

1.23.1   A Cast vs. a Conversion

First, let's make sure the terminology is correct, and that you understand the difference between a cast and a conversion. A *conversion* occurs when the compiler changes the type of an object. This can involve changing the bits that represent the object (e.g., the conversion from a `double` to an `int`), or it can mean simply reinterpreting the same bits (as in a conversion from a `int` to an `unsigned`), or the conversion from an `enum` to an `int`. There are some conversions that the compiler is allowed to do whenever they are needed. These are called *implicit conversions,* e.g., the `double` to the `int`.

On the other hand, there are some conversions that the compiler is allowed to do only when you give it "permission". These are known as *explicit conversions,* e.g., the conversion from a `void*` to a `char*`, or the conversion of a pointer-to-a-constant-object to a pointer-to-a-non-constant-object. You give the compiler "permission" to do an explicit conversion by using a *cast*.

1.23.2   Generic Format of a Cast

The generic format for the new style of casting is always:

 Example 1.49

```
type_of_cast<new_type>(expr)
```

where `type_of_cast` represents one of four new types:

- `static_cast`
- `reinterpret_cast`
- `const_cast`
- `dynamic_cast`

Each type is a keyword in the language. `new_type` represents the new type that you wish the cast to produce, and must be enclosed within angle brackets. `expr` is the expression that is to be cast, and must be enclosed within parentheses.

A brief description of the first three casts follows.

Tip

> `dynamic_cast` *is part of run-time type information, and will be discussed in Chapter 14.*

1.23.3 `static_cast` Keyword

The `static_cast` keyword is how C++ performs a conversion that requests an "equivalent" value in a different representation. For example, you would use a `static_cast` to find the equivalent type `int` value of a `double` value. In effect, it is a "safe" cast because it can "replace" what the compiler would consider to be an implicit type conversion. In addition, a `static_cast` can convert to type `void`.

For example, the addition of two `int`s produces a type `int`, which could overflow, so in order to perform `long` addition, a `static_cast` would be used (in lieu of storing one of the `int`s into a `long`).

Example 1.50

```
int a = 30000;
int b = 30000;
long c = a + b;    // Erroneous results
long c = static_cast<long>(a) + b;   // Correct
```

Similarly, in order to perform floating point (not integer) division, a `static_cast` is required if both operands are integral types:

Example 1.51

```
int a = 7;
int b = 4;
float c = static_cast<float>(a) / b;
```

1.23.4 `reinterpret_cast` Keyword

The `reinterpret_cast` keyword is how C++ performs conversions that demand that a bit pattern of an object be reevaluated without the approval of the type system. In essence, it is an "unsafe" cast, and is meant to replace the old-style cast of

(T) expr for conversions (such as int* to char*) and a non-pointer to a pointer which are inherently unsafe and implementation dependent. For example, the conversion of an int* to a char*, and a double to a double* both require a reinterpret_cast.

 Example 1.52

```
int x = 1;
int* p1 = &x;
char* p2 = reinterpret_cast<char*>(p1);

double d = 1.23;
double* p3 = reinterpret_cast<double*>(d);
```

Do you remember that the implicit conversion from void* to any other pointer type is not implicitly done in C++? Therefore, it requires a reinterpret_cast.

 Example 1.53

```
#include <stdlib.h>
char* ptr = reinterpret_cast<char*>(malloc(10));
```

Note that the compiler will enforce that you are using the correct cast, so that you are not allowed to use a reinterpret_cast where a static_cast is called for, and vice-versa.

 Example 1.54

```
int a = 7, b = 4;
float c = reinterpret_cast<float>(a) / b;      // Error

int* p_int;
char* p_char = static_cast<char*>(p_int);      // Error
```

The decision whether to use a static_cast or a reinterpret_cast can be made by asking this simple question: Would the code compile if no cast whatsoever were present? If the answer is yes, then use a static_cast; if the answer is no, then use a reinterpret_cast.

1.23.5   const_cast **Keyword**

The const_cast keyword is how C++ explicitly casts away the const-ness or volatile-ness of an object. It is meant to replace the old-style cast of (T) expr for conversions used to gain access to data specified const or volatile. The type of the argument T must be identical to the type of the argument expr except for the const and volatile modifiers. The result is identical to expr except that its type is now T. Neither a `static_cast` nor a `reinterpret_cast` may be used in this situation. The `const_cast` keyword may also be used to add a `const` or `volatile` qualifier to a pointer.

For example, refer back to Example 1.34 in which the `display()` function fails to support constant strings. The only way the user can invoke the function is to use a `const_cast` (in lieu of a C-style cast).

 Example 1.55

```
#include <stdio.h>

void display(char* p)      // Oops -- forgot to use const
{
    puts(p);
}

int main()
{
    const char* ptr = "test string";
    display(const_cast<char*>(ptr));    // OK
    return 0;
}

/* The output of this program is:

test string

*/
```

1.24   Wide Characters

The C++ keyword `wchar_t` describes a new type called a *wide character*. It is used to represent character sets with more than 256 elements.

A character or string literal can use an `L` prefix to make it into a wide character.

 Example 1.56

```
wchar_t ch = L'ab';
wchar_t* ptr = L"Test";
```

 Tip

`wchar_t` *is also a* `typedef` *in the file* `stddef.h`.

1.25   Trigraphs

Trigraphs are three consecutive characters (with two '?'s being the first two characters) that can be used where special characters are not available on the keyboard.
They were introduced in ANSI C in order to accommodate non-ASCII systems that
used nine C characters not present in the ISO 646 character set.

Trigraphs are processed very early, even before macros. They may also be used in
string literals.

Table 1-4   Trigraphs

Existing Character	Trigraph Representation
#	??=
[	??(
]	??)
\	??/
{	??<
}	??>
|	??!
^	??'
~	??-

 Example 1.57

```
??=define array(a,b) a??(b??) ??!??! b??(a??)
// becomes...
#define array(a,b) a[b] || b[a]
```

 Caution

*In order to process trigraphs using any Borland C++ compiler, you need to
run the program TRIGRAPH.EXE against your source code before you
compile it.*

1.26   Digraphs

Similar to trigraphs, C++ supports digraphs to replace all of the symbols that one might expect to find on a typical keyboard, and supports new keywords as alternate spellings for some of the commonly used symbols. The digraphs are recognized as preprocessing tokens and each is converted to the corresponding primary representation.

Table 1-5   Digraphs

Existing Spelling	Alternate Spelling
[	<:
]	:>
{	<%
}	%>
#	%:
&	bitand
&&	and
|	bitor
||	or
^	xor
~	compl
&=	and_eq
|=	or_eq
^=	xor_eq
!	not
!=	not_eq

  Example 1.58

```
%:define array(a,b) a<:b:> or b<:a:>
// becomes...
#define array(a,b) a[b] || b[a]
```

  Caution

Borland C++ 5.0 does not yet support digraphs.

1.27   C and C++ Keywords

Here are all of the 73 keywords used in C++, including digraphs. Those in bold-face type are specific to C++.

Table 1-6   C++ Keywords

and	**and_eq**	asm
auto	**bitand**	**bitor**
bool	break	case
catch	char	**class**
compl	const	**const_cast**
continue	default	**delete**
do	double	**dynamic_cast**
else	enum	**explicit**
extern	**false**	float
for	**friend**	goto
if	**inline**	int
long	**mutable**	**namespace**
new	**not**	**not_eq**
operator	**or**	**or_eq**
private	**protected**	**public**
register	**reinterpret_cast**	return
short	signed	sizeof
static	**static_cast**	struct
switch	**template**	**this**
throw	**true**	**try**
typedef	**typeid**	**typename**
union	unsigned	**using**
virtual	void	volatile
wchar_t	while	**xor**
xor_eq		

Exercise 1.1

Write a C++ program that allocates an array of `size` integers on the heap, where `size` has been declared as a constant. Then declare a variable called `value` and prompt the operator to enter a number into `value` which is subsequently used to fill each element of the array. Finally, print the array using a `for` loop and the same counting variable that was used to fill the array. Be sure to include some C++-style comments.

 Exercise 1.2

Given the structure:

```
struct Student
{
    char name[20];
    long ssn;
    int grades[5];
    float average;
};
```

write a `main()` function that:

■ Creates an object of type `Student`;

■ Passes the *address* of this object to a function called `GetData()`;

■ Passes this object by *value* to a function called `WriteData()`.

Then write a function called `GetData()` that:

■ Receives the address of the structure object as its one formal argument;

■ Prompts the terminal operator and receives the `name` field;

■ Prompts the terminal operator and receives the `ssn` field;

■ Prompts the terminal operator and loops 5 times to receive all entries in the `grades` array;

■ Computes the floating point average of the 5 grades and stores it into the field `average`;

■ Returns control back to `main()`.

Finally, write a function called `WriteData()` that:

■ Prints a title line to identify the NAME, SSN, and AVERAGE;

■ Prints the name, ssn, and the average (to an accuracy of 2 decimal positions);

■ Returns control back to `main()`.

Chapter 2

Introduction to iostream Methods

2.1   Introduction

Well, I hate to be the bearer of bad news, but it's time for you to say good-bye to your old friends `scanf()`, `printf()`, `gets()`, `puts()`, and the rest of the stdio gang. In this chapter you will learn how to use the basic capabilities of a new library called *iostream*. This library will serve you well once you start dealing with user-defined objects. And besides, you don't *really* like `scanf()` and `printf()` that much, do you?

2.2   Why Switch to Something New?

Perhaps you are wondering about the justification for abandoning the stdio library and switching to something new. There are several good reasons for doing so.

■ The iostream library is object-oriented in the sense that when you perform input and output, you are really sending messages to your keyboard and screen, which are just objects in the real world.

■ While `scanf()`, `printf()` and the rest of the functions in the stdio library can handle fundamental types just fine, they cannot be modified to accommodate user-defined types. On the other hand, the methods in iostream are extensible, so that the input or output of an instance of some class can be written *exactly* the same way as that for a fundamental type. The implementation of this feature will be shown in Chapter 9.

■ The functions `scanf()` and `printf()` are very error-prone (in case you hadn't noticed). With `scanf()` you have to remember to write an ampersand in front of a variable name. With `printf()` you have to remember that if you're printing an `int`, then the conversion mask must be `"%d"`, and if you're printing a `long`, then it must be `"%ld"`. For floating point types, both a `float` and a `double` are displayed with `"%f"`, whereas a `long double` is displayed with `"%Lf"`. On the other hand, when using `scanf()` a `float` is described with `"%f"` and a `double` with `"lf"`. If you make a mistake, then you may get incorrect input or output. Fortunately, this problem goes away when you use iostream methods because the argument type itself determines how it is to be displayed.

2.3   Include `iostream.h`

The first step to using iostream methods is to include a new header file called `iostream.h`.

 Example 2.1

```
#include <iostream.h>
```

This is essentially the equivalent of including the header file `stdio.h`. It contains the definitions for several classes, and provides you with what's called a *public interface* to the methods of the classes. If all this object-oriented terminology sounds a bit confusing, don't worry about it now. It will all become a lot clearer in Chapter 6.

2.4   The Instance `cout`

As mentioned above, your terminal screen is just an object, and in object-oriented programming you send messages to objects. With iostream methods, the screen (or wherever the standard output has been routed) has been "attached" to an object called `cout` ("console output"). This object lives in the global space so that it is accessible by any function, and exists as soon as your program starts. Furthermore, this object has been *instantiated* from a class whose name is `ostream`. Therefore, within the header file `iostream.h`, you will find this statement.

 Example 2.2

```
extern ostream cout;
```

The statement declares (not defines) the object cout to be of type ostream, and makes its name available to anyone including the header file. (cout is actually defined in a definition file that has already been compiled into object format.)

2.5   The Insertion Operator   <<

The most important message you can send to the cout object is called *insert*, and it is written using an overloaded bitwise left-shift operator (<<). (Operator function overloading is discussed in much more detail in Chapter 9.) Following this operator, you write the data that you wish to be displayed on your screen. The type of this data can be anything that was handled previously by printf().

For example, this is how you would display the value of a simple variable of type int. The compiler is smart enough to know that the left-shift operator in this context means "insert" into the cout object, and not left-shift. Of course, if you really do want to perform a bitwise left-shift operation, then you must use parentheses.

Example 2.3

```
#include <iostream.h>

int main()
{
    int data = 123;
    cout << data;
    cout << '\n';
    cout << (data << 1);
    cout << '\n';
    return 0;
}

/* The output of this program is:

123
246

*/
```

2.5.1   Chaining Calls Together

Do I hear you saying how nice it would be to have the capability to display more than one value of any type using just a single statement? Fortunately, this can be done very easily by "chaining" calls to the insertion operator.

Example 2.4

```
#include <iostream.h>

int main()
{
   int data = 123;
   cout << "The answer is " << data << '\n';
   return 0;
}

/* The output of this program is:

The answer is 123

*/
```

All expressions of any fundamental type (including pointers) can be chained together in this fashion to make your code more readable.

 Tip

In looking at C++ coding examples, you may very well come across the symbol endl. *This simply means a newline character and a guaranteed flush of the output buffer. It is really a* manipulator, *and will be discussed further in Chapter 17.*

While there is no law that says you have to use chaining, look at how awkward and disjointed the same program appears when chaining is *not* used.

 Example 2.5

```
#include <iostream.h>

int main()
{
   int data = 123;
   cout << "The answer is ";
   cout << data;
   cout << '\n';
   return 0;
}

/* The output of this program is:

The answer is 123

*/
```

Tip

> *The use of* `'\n'` *to produce a newline is slightly more efficient than using the string literal* `"\n"`*. When the last item to be inserted into the output stream is a string literal, then it's better to include a newline as part of the literal itself instead of sending another insertion message.*

2.6   Be Aware of Precedence

As noted earlier, the usage of the left-shift operator with iostream methods is called *operator function overloading*. What you need to know here is that one of the fundamental rules associated with operator function overloading is that you cannot change the precedence of the operator when you extend its meaning. (You also cannot change its associativity, nor its unary/binary characteristics.)

The importance of precedence comes into play when you output an expression using an operator with precedence *lower* than left-shift. The bitwise 'and' and conditional operators are excellent examples, as shown in the following program which displays the low-order bit of the variable x and then determines if x is true or false.

Example 2.6

```
#include <iostream.h>

int main()
{
    int x = 9;
    cout << "last bit is " << x & 1 << '\n';          // Error
    cout << "x is " << x ? "true\n" : "false\n";      // Error
    return 0;
}
```

The problem with this code is that the compiler will use the left-shift operator to bind the cout object to the string literal, and then to the variable x, *before* evaluating the result of the bitwise 'and' operator. The net result will be a compilation error because now you are asking the compiler to apply the bitwise 'and' operator to the cout object, and this it cannot do. A similar problem exists with the conditional operator.

The solution, of course, is to use parentheses to override the built-in precedence.

Example 2.7

```
#include <iostream.h>

int main()
{
   int x = 9;
   cout << "last bit is " << (x & 1) << '\n';      // OK
   cout << "x is " << (x ? "true\n" : "false\n"); // OK
   return 0;
}

/* The output of this program is:

last bit is 1
x is true

*/
```

Obviously, if the precedence of an operator is higher than left-shift, then the use of parentheses is optional.

 Caution

Borland C++ may give you a warning message saying "Ambiguous opera-tors need parentheses" even when there is no ambiguity present. You may safely ignore this message.

2.7   Formatting the Output

How the output gets formatted to look presentable will be discussed in great detail in Chapter 15. For now it's enough to use iostream methods in their simplest form.

2.8   The Instance `cin`

In a manner very similar to that of `cout`, your computer's keyboard has been "attached" to an object called `cin` ("console input") which also lives in the global space. Sending messages to the `cin` object thus achieves the goal of getting terminal operator input.

`cin` is an instance of the class `istream`, and, like `cout`, is also declared in the header file `iostream.h`.

Example 2.8

```
extern istream cin;
```

2.9   The Extraction Operator

The most important message you can send to the `cin` object is called "extract", and is written using an overloaded bitwise right-shift operator (>>). Following this operator you write the name of the variable into which the data from the keyboard is to be stored. The type of this data can be any type that is handled by `scanf()`.

For example, this is how you would enter and display the value of some variable.

 Example 2.9

```
#include <iostream.h>

int main()
{
   cout << "Enter an integer value: ";
   // cout.flush();
   int data;
   cin >> data;
   cout << data << '\n';
   return 0;
}

/* A typical run of this program is:

Enter an integer value: 5
5

*/
```

 Tip

Since the iostream library does not guarantee that an output message will appear on the screen prior to the output of a newline character, you can ensure this happens by including the line that is commented out in the previous example.

2.9.1   Chaining Calls Together

As with the insertion operator, extraction messages can be chained together using the same or different types of data.

 Example 2.10

```
#include <iostream.h>

int main()
{
    cout << "Enter an integer and a double: ";
    int data1;
    double data2;
    cin >> data1 >> data2;
    cout << data1 << " and " << data2 << '\n';
    return 0;
}

/* A typical run of this program would yield:

Enter an integer and a double: 5 7.34
5 and 7.34

*/
```

The iostream methods separate one input value from another by the occurrence of (1) at least one whitespace character (blank, tab or newline), or (2) a character that cannot be part of the variable being formed (e.g., reading 123ABC as a number will stop when the character 'A' is seen, and the characters "ABC" will remain in the system stream). Your program will not resume execution until all variables have received values, and the <ENTER> key has been pressed.

 Tip

> *If you get confused between the insertion and extraction operators, just think of the angle brackets as pointing in the direction of the flow of data. The insertion operator points to the left toward the* cout *object (the terminal screen), while the extraction operator points from the* cin *object (the keyboard) toward the variable into which the data is to be stored.*

2.10   Checking for End-of-File

The termination of input data is usually denoted when an end-of-file character is encountered. In DOS and Windows, this is done by pressing <CTRL>-Z on the keyboard. (In Unix environments and on Macintosh computers, it's done by pressing <CTRL>-D.)

Class `istream` has a method called `eof()` (inherited from class `ios`) that returns `true` if end-of-file was entered, and `false` if not. If end-of-file is found, then the content of the variable is *not* modified.

Like data members inside a structure object, methods are accessed by writing the object's name (`cin`), the dot operator, and the method name (`eof()`).

 Example 2.11

```
if(cin.eof())
    // end-of-file was entered
else
    // end-of-file was not entered
```

If you wish to set up a loop to enter some data, and iterate until the operator enters end-of-file, then the code would be:

 Example 2.12

```
#include <iostream.h>

int main()
{
    cout << "Enter an integer: ";
    int data;
    while(!(cin >> data).eof())
    {
        cout << "You entered: " << data << '\n';
        cout << "Next integer: ";
    }
    cout << "End-of-file\n";
    return 0;
}

/* A typical run of this program would yield:

Enter an integer: 123
You entered: 123
Next integer: 456
You entered: 456
Next integer: ^Z
End-of-file

*/
```

relates to classes (similar to struct)

Note that the parentheses surrounding the extraction operation itself are mandatory to prevent the 'not' operator from being applied to the `cin` object and to avoid "sending the message `eof()`" to the (supposed) object called `data`.

Caution

> *If you input into a string buffer, be aware that the extraction operator acts like* scanf() *in the sense that embedded whitespace will stop the transfer of characters from the system stream into your buffer area. Also, you still have the possibility for buffer overflow.*

2.11   Checking for Errors

Can something go wrong when the terminal operator enters data from the keyboard? Of course it can! But how you detect input errors, and recover from them, is not something that you need to worry about at this time. Until this topic is discussed in Chapter 16, you will just have to assume that the world is a perfect place, and that terminal operators never make mistakes.

Review Questions

1. Why are iostream methods better than those of stdio?
2. What is the object `cout`?
3. What is the insertion operator?
4. What is the object `cin`?
5. What is the extraction operator?
6. How do you check for end-of-file when using the `cin` object?

 Exercise 2.1

Write a C++ program that reads an `int`, `char`, and `double` from the keyboard and echoes them back to the terminal operator. Terminate the program when end-of-file is encountered.

 Exercise 2.2

Write a C++ program that reads in numbers from the keyboard. When end-of-file is encountered, display the highest, lowest, and average of all of the numbers read.

 Exercise 2.3

Write a C++ program that computes and prints the first 20 Fibonacci numbers. A Fibonacci number is a number that is computed by adding the two previous numbers in the sequence.

Prompt the terminal operator for the starting two numbers (typically 0 and 1), so that the first few numbers should be 1, 2, 3, 5, 8, 13, 21, 34, 55, etc. Then display the newly computed number and its predecessor, and the ratio of this new number divided by the predecessor. You should observe the convergence to the Golden Mean (also known as the Golden Ratio) of 1.61803.

Be sure to test with different starting numbers. When end-of-file is entered, terminate the program.

Chapter 3

Reference Variables

3.1   Introduction

A reference variable is something that is brand new in C++, and fills a big void in
the C language. It allows you to create *aliases* to variables and objects, thereby sim-
plifying your coding job, and providing a more intuitive interface for the users of
your functions and classes.

3.2   What's the Problem?

Recall from the previous chapter that the way to enter data from the keyboard is to
write code similar to this.

 Example 3.1

```
#include <iostream.h>

void foo()
{
    int data;
    cin >> data;
    // etc.
}
```

It should be obvious that the extraction operator function is responsible for modifying the variable `data` with whatever the terminal operator enters from the keyboard. But it's also obvious that you do *not* need to write an ampersand in front of

the variable name in order to generate its address. This is a good thing because it makes your (coding) life a lot easier, even though I'm sure you've *never* forgotten the ampersand whenever you wrote a `scanf()`. In addition, it's obvious that the variable is not being passed into the extraction operator function by value, because that defeats the whole purpose.

Given this situation, just how *does* the extraction function modify the variable `data`? You guessed it — by using a reference variable.

3.3   How to Create a Reference Variable

The creation of a reference variable in C++ is nothing more than the creation of an alias. This is done by appending an ampersand (&) to the end of some existing type name. But since an alias, by definition, must refer (or bind) to some "real" object, the C++ compiler will insist that your reference variable be *initialized* at the same time that it's created. If you fail to do this, you will get a compilation error.

 Example 3.2

```
int& ref;    // Error; ref is not initialized
```

Of course, the solution is to initialize (bind) `ref` to some variable of type `int`.

 Example 3.3

```
int num = 0;
int& ref = num;   // OK; ref is an alias for num
```

Since `ref` is just an alias for `num`, then whenever `ref` is referenced, `num` is really the variable being used.

3.3.1   Reference Variables Cannot Be "Reassigned" or "Reinitialized"

Note also that once a reference variable is initialized with some existing variable, it cannot be "reassigned" or "reinitialized" to some other variable as long as it (the reference variable) remains in scope.

Example 3.4

```
int num = 0;
int& ref = num;
int data = 1;
ref = data;   // Assigns 1 to num
```

3.3.2 Reference Variables Must Bind to the Same Type

The type of the reference variable must correspond to the type of the object for which it is an alias. (User-defined types in an inheritance hierarchy are an exception to this rule.)

 Example 3.5

```
int num = 0;
float& ref = num;   // Error; cannot mix types
```

 Caution ex: int & ref [10] ;// not possible

Unlike an array of pointers, you cannot create an array of references.

while num [0] = ref ; is posible

3.4 References to Constant and Non-constant Objects

If an object is modifiable, then you can always create a simple reference to it. In addition, this reference can be a reference-to-`const` (*not* a "constant reference") to prevent the object from being modified through the reference itself. This is done by writing the word `const` in front of the type. On the other hand, if the object is either constant or `const`-qualified, then you can *only* create a reference to it of type reference-to-`const`.

 Example 3.6

```
int x = 0;
const int y = 0;
int& ref = y;         // Error
int& ref = 0;         // Error
int& ref = x;         // OK
const int& ref = x;   // OK
const int& ref = 0;   // OK
const int& ref = y;   // OK
```

There really is no such thing as a "constant reference" because unlike a pointer, writing the keyword const *after* the ampersand and before the variable name is an error since the actual object can still be modified and the name is already "constant" in the sense that you cannot bind the variable to anything else. While such code may compile successfully, it has been deemed invalid by the C++ Draft.

 Example 3.7

```
int x = 0;
int& const ref = x;     // Error; deemed invalid
```

3.5   Reference Variables Used as Formal Arguments

The declaration of reference variables up to now has not really served a very useful purpose. After all, if a variable and an alias for that variable are both defined within the same scope, then why bother to use the alias? Why not just use the name of the variable itself?

The real usefulness of a reference variable occurs when it is created in a scope that is *different* from the scope of the variable for which it is an alias. For example, a function sets up a brand new scope whenever it is called. If a reference variable is used as a formal argument, then it merely becomes an alias for the corresponding actual argument. This means that whenever the formal argument is used within the body of the function, the actual argument in the calling function is the one that is really being manipulated. This is exactly what was demonstrated in the example at the start of this chapter.

For example, note how the variable number in the function foo() is just an alias for the "real" object num in main(). This style of coding is much cleaner than the C-style of passing an address and receiving it into a pointer variable, which then must be dereferenced.

Example 3.8

```cpp
#include <iostream.h>

void foo(int& number)
{
    ++number;      // Add 1 to num
}

int main()
{
    int num = 0;
    foo(num);
    cout << "num = " << num << '\n';
    return 0;
}

/* The output of this program is:

num = 1

*/
```

number is an alias for the "real" fixed num

After looking at this example, you should now understand how the extraction operator modifies variables that are declared in a different scope.

Note that if the variable num is *not* to be changed, then you should continue to use the C-style pass-by-value, even though you could pass it by reference-to-const and achieve the same end result. In other words, when a fundamental type of variable needs to be used in a function, and no changes need to be made to that variable, then pass it in by value. One benefit of this is that the executable code will be slightly more efficient.

Example 3.9

```
#include <iostream.h>

void foo(int number)
// Same result as... void foo(const int& number)
{
   cout << "number = " << number << '\n';
}

int main()
{
   int num = 0;
   foo(num);
   return 0;
}

/* The output of this program is:

number = 0

*/
```

3.6   Making a Reference to a Pointer

As noted earlier, there is no problem in making a reference to a pointer. This saves you from having to create a pointer-to-pointer in a function if that function needs to modify a pointer variable that is passed in.

    Example 3.10

```
#include <iostream.h>

void foo(char*& ref_ptr)
{
    ref_ptr = "Hello C++";
}

int main()
{
    char* ptr;
    foo(ptr);    ial̵l
    const char quote = '"';
    cout << quote << ptr << quote << '\n';
    return 0;
}

/* The output of this program is:

"Hello C++"

*/
```

    Tip

It buys you nothing to make a reference to a pointer if that pointer was created by specifying the name of an array. The reason is that this kind of pointer is constant, *and cannot be changed anyway.*

3.7   Making a Reference to a Structure

In addition to creating references to fundamental (and pointer) types, you may also create references for structures. This has the benefit of passing a hidden pointer to the structure object instead of passing the entire structure object on the stack (which can be quite inefficient). In addition, if you want to ensure that the structure object is a "read-only" object in the sense that it cannot be modified by a function, then its declaration must be reference-to-`const`. You do this by preceding the reference type with the keyword `const`.

In the following example, the object `Author` is passed to the function `change()` by reference in order to fill the data field `name`. Then it is passed by reference-to-`const` to the function `display()` in order to display the `name`.

 Example 3.11

```
#include <iostream.h>

struct Person
{
   const char* name;
};

// Non-constant reference to allow changes to occur
void change(Person& p)
{
   p.name = "Bjarne Stroustrup";
}

// Reference-to-const to support constant objects
void display(const Person& p)
{
   cout << p.name << " is the author of C++\n";
}

int main()
{
   Person Author;
   change(Author);
   display(Author);
   return 0;
}

/* The output of this program is:

Bjarne Stroustrup is the author of C++

*/
```

3.8   Returning from a Function by Reference

A function may also return a variable by reference, or reference-to-`const`. Without the use of a const-qualifier, the function then returns an lvalue, and its output can be modified.

For example, the following program uses `foo()` to add 1 to the variable `num`, and then 1 is added to the output of `foo()` itself by the increment operator. Since `foo()` returns `num` by reference, the net result is that `num` gets incremented twice.

 Example 3.12

```
#include <iostream.h>

int& foo(int& number)
{
    ++number;
    return number;
}

int main()
{
    int num = 0;
    cout << "num = " << ++foo(num) << '\n';
    return 0;
}

/* The output of this program is:

num = 2

*/
```

Of course, if the function `foo()` had returned `number` *by value* instead of by reference, then a compilation error would have resulted because the increment operator is no longer being applied to an 'lvalue'.

 Caution

> *Never return a local stack-based variable from a function by reference or by pointer. If you do, then you will be referring or pointing to stack space that you no longer own.*

Review Questions

1. Explain what a reference variable is.

2. Why would you use a reference variable?

3. What are the advantages and disadvantages of reference variables in comparison to pointers?

4. Why can't a reference variable be "reassigned" to another variable after being created?

5. Why do reference variables have to be initialized?

6. What happens when a value is passed into a function by reference and the type of the reference variable is incompatible with the argument?

7. What is the difference between passing a structure object into a function by reference vs. by constant reference?

 Exercise 3.1

Write a function called `swap()` that uses pointer variables to swap the contents of two integer variables in the calling routine, and test your function. Then modify it so that it does the same thing, but now use reference variables. Test this function to ensure that it also works.

 Exercise 3.2

Given the `main()` function:

```
#include <iostream.h>

int main()
{
    const int array[] = { 5, -6, 21, 15, -8 };
    const int length = sizeof(array) / sizeof(*array);
    int max;
    int min;
    find(array, length, max, min);
    cout << "max = " << max << '\n';
    cout << "min = " << min << '\n';
    return 0;
}
```

write the function called `find()` that finds the maximum and minimum values in the array. Be sure to use reference variables only where applicable.

Exercise 3.3

Write a program that computes the minimum number of quarters, dimes, nickels, and pennies that are contained within a specified amount of money. For example, given $1.18, the answer would be 4 quarters, 1 dime, 1 nickel, and 3 pennies. Given $0.31, the answer would be 1 quarter, 1 nickel and 1 penny.

Use the following structure to describe a coin type:

```
struct Coin
{
    int denom;            // 1 or 5 or 10 or 25
    long count;           // Count of occurrences
    const char* single;   // Text for 1 occurrence, e.g.,
                          // "penny"
    const char* multiple; // Text for more than 1 occurrence,
                          // e.g., "pennies"
};
```

- In the `main()` function, create and initialize an array of four `Coin` objects.

- Prompt the terminal operator to enter a money amount (use a `long int` to avoid precision problems, e.g., 123 would represent $1.23). If end-of-file is entered, terminate the program.

- For each amount, create a `for` loop that traverses the array and, for each element, calls the functions `change()` and `print()`.

- The first argument in `change()` is the money amount received by reference, and the second is a reference to the array element. This function computes the number of coins, and adjusts the money amount accordingly. Note that it can be written in just *two* statements.

- The only argument to `print()` is the array element passed in by reference-to-`const`. Do not print any output for a coin whose count is zero.

Chapter 4

Default Function Arguments

4.1   Introduction

In many cases, a C++ function needs to be *overloaded* so that it can be called with no arguments, one argument, two arguments, etc. Normally this would entail your having to write separate function bodies that can accommodate the varying number of arguments. But by using default function arguments, only one such function needs to be written.

For example, you may want to construct a complex number that requires both a real and an imaginary part. There are three ways in which this can be done: (1) by specifying no arguments whatsoever, in which case both the real and imaginary parts of the number will default to some fixed value, (2) by specifying only the real part, in which case the imaginary part will default to some fixed value, and (3) by specifying both the real and the imaginary parts. Normally this scenario would require three distinct types of construction, but by employing the power of default function arguments, only *one* such type of construction needs to be written. Exactly how this is accomplished will be discussed in detail in Chapter 7.

4.2   Mandatory and Default Arguments

A function's formal argument list now contains two types of formal arguments: mandatory and default. The order of these arguments is easy to remember—the mandatory arguments, if present, are written first, followed by any default arguments. A function may thus contain all mandatory arguments, all default arguments, or some combination thereof.

4.3   How to Specify Default Arguments

If you are declaring or defining a function, then you specify a default argument value by writing:

- The type of the formal argument;

- The formal argument name (always optional);

- An '=' sign;

- The default value itself as an expression. This expression is evaluated when the function is called, but any variables used are bound at the point where the expression is written. Thus, it may use any variable that is in scope at the point of its appearance in the source code. There is one exception to this rule: the default argument expression is prohibited from using other formal arguments in the function, even though those that precede it are in scope. This is because when the function is called, the order of evaluating the arguments is unspecified, and the other arguments may be uninitialized even though they are in scope.

For example, all of these miscellaneous function declarations are valid.

Example 4.1

```
void foo1(int n = 0);

void foo2(int n, char ch = '\0');

void foo3(int n = 0, char ch = '\0');

int x = 1;    // At global scope
int g(double = 0.0);
void foo4(int n = x + g());
```

On the other hand, this function declaration is invalid because the default argument precedes the mandatory argument.

Example 4.2

```
void foo5(int n = 0, char ch);    // Error
```

4.4   Where to Specify Default Arguments

A default function argument may appear in either a function declaration or in a definition. Normally, it will appear in the declaration which will be part of some header file. By including the header file in your program, you ensure that the compiler knows all there is to know about the function and its arguments. Presumably the function definition has already been compiled into object format, and that's all there is to it.

On the other hand, if you provide the function definition as part of your source code, then you have two options. First, you may write the function declaration before any calls to the function occur. If you do this, then this is where any default function arguments must appear. When you write the function definition, it is written just as you normally would, and you may *not* repeat the default argument(s).

  Example 4.3

```
#include <iostream.h>

// Function declaration; assume 'number' has a default of 0
void print(int number = 0);

int main()
{
   print();
   print(1);
   return 0;
}

// Function definition
void print(int number)    // Default is not repeated
{
   cout << number << '\n';
}

/* The output of this program is:

0
1

*/
```

The second option is for you to *define* the function before you use it. In this case the definition implies the declaration, so you have no choice except to specify the default arguments in the function definition line. Thus, the program above may be written as:

Example 4.4

```
#include <iostream.h>

// Function definition
void print(int number = 0)
{
   cout << number << '\n';
}

int main()
{
   print();
   print(1);
   return 0;
}

/* The output of this program is:

0
1

*/
```

Next is a program that needs to do exponentiation, i.e., raise a number to a certain power. However, let's assume that most of the time the number has to be squared, so it makes sense to use a default value of 2 for the exponent in the function power() that will be called to do the computation.

Example 4.5

```cpp
#include <iostream.h>

// Function declaration. The second argument defaults
// to the value 2
long power(int base, int exp = 2);

int main()
{
   cout << "Enter a base value: ";
   int base;
   while(!(cin >> base).eof())
   {
      // Use the default value
      cout << base << " squared = " << power(base) << '\n';
      // Override the default value
      cout << base << " cubed = " << power(base, 3) << '\n';
      cout << "Next base: ";
   }
   cout << "End-of-file\n";
   return 0;
}

long power(int base, int exp)
{
   return (exp == 0) ? 1L : base * power(base, exp - 1);
}

/* A typical run would yield:

Enter a base value: 3
3 squared = 9
3 cubed = 27
Next base: -2
-2 squared = 4
-2 cubed = -8
Next base: ^Z
End-of-file

*/
```

4.5   How to Call a Function With More Than One Default Argument

When the function is called, you must first specify all of the mandatory actual arguments, if present, in the order in which they are declared. Next, you may override the default arguments, if any, but only in the order in which they were declared. That is, if there are three default arguments, then you may override the first, the first and the second, or all three. You *cannot* override the first and the third, or just the second, or just the third. (If this were not so, then how would the compiler know which formal argument to match with an actual argument?) You also cannot simply write a comma to "skip over" a default argument.

Here is an example where a default function argument would be useful. Suppose you want to write a function that clears an array of 256 characters to some value. Most of the time you decide that the array should be entirely cleared to blanks, so this is what you would specify for the default function arguments. But there is also no problem in overriding the default length with a new length of 100, and the default clearing character with that of the null character. Note that if you wish to take the default value of the length, but override the clearing character, then the default length value must be explicitly written.

 Example 4.6

```
const int dim = 256;

void clear(char* ptr, int length = dim, char ch = ' ')
{
   for(int i = 0; i < length; ++i)
      ptr[i] = ch;
}

void foo()
{
   char buffer[dim];
   clear(buffer);               // Take both defaults
   clear(buffer, 100);          // Override first default
   clear(buffer, dim, '\0');    // Override second default
   clear(buffer, 100, '\0');    // Override both defaults
}
```

4.6 Objects Used as Default Arguments

The default value in a function declaration may involve a user-defined object, provided that the address of that object is known to the compiler. For example, the screen object cout (introduced in Chapter 2) may be used as a default argument if you think that most of the time a function would want to display its output to the screen. However, if you want to display to another output device, then it would be no problem to do so. (cerr is the error logging device, which defaults to the screen. If the output of this program is redirected to a disk file, then that is where its output would appear.)

 Example 4.7

```
#include <iostream.h>

void display(ostream& = cout);

int main()
{
   display();
   display(cerr);
   return 0;
}

void display(ostream& str)
{
   str << "Some nice data\n";
}

/* The output of this program is:

Some nice data
Some nice data

*/
```

4.7   Expressions Used as Default Arguments

As mentioned earlier, the default value in a function may also consist of some expression. The compiler just needs to know the address of any global variables, and must have already seen the declaration of any function that may be called. The actual default value that is pushed onto the stack is computed at run-time.

 Example 4.8

```
#include <iostream.h>

int n = 0;      // Global definition

int foo()
{
   return 1;
}

int g(int x = foo() + n)
{
   return x;
}

int main()
{
   n = 2;
   cout << "answer = " << g() << '\n';
   return 0;
}

/* The output of this program is:

answer = 3

*/
```

4.8   Redeclaration of a Function

Suppose you include a header file which contains the declaration for a function that displays all of the prime numbers between a starting and ending range provided by the user. Such a declaration might appear as:

 Example 4.9

```
// File header.h

void display_primes(int, int);
```

This is fine, except that one day you decide that the ending value of 1000 is something that you frequently specify, so it would certainly be nice if that could be a default value. Fortunately, C++ allows you to do this by redeclaring a function and specifying a default argument, provided that all arguments to the right of this default (if any) also have default values. Thus, you would write:

 Example 4.10

```
#include <header.h>

void display_primes(int, int = 1000);

void foo()
{
   display_primes(2, 500);  // OK
   display_primes(2);       // OK; display from 2 to 1000
}
```

Furthermore, you decide that you would like to start displaying prime numbers most of the time starting with 2. Then you can add yet another declaration with 2 as the default value for the first argument. (But you cannot respecify a default value for the second argument since it already has a default value.)

Example 4.11

```
#include <header.h>

void display_primes(int, int = 1000);
void display_primes(int = 2, int);

void foo()
{
   display_primes(2, 500); // OK
   display_primes(100);    // OK; display from 100 to 1000
   display_primes();       // OK; display from 2 to 1000
}
```

The net result is the same as though the function `display_primes()` had been originally declared as:

 Example 4.12

```
void display_primes(int = 2, int = 1000);
```

Review Questions

1. Why are default function arguments useful?

2. What is the difference between a mandatory and a default function argument?

3. Why must default function arguments be specified last in a function's formal argument list?

4. Is this a valid declaration of a function whose one argument is a pointer that defaults to the value 0?

```
void foo(int*= 0);
```

 Exercise 4.1

Write a function that takes three input arguments: (1) a starting number, (2) an ending number, and (3) a number representing the number of integers to be output per line. This last value should default to 5. Display all of the numbers in the specified range in the format specified by the third argument.

Then write a `main()` function that tests the function by:

- Reading in three integer numbers (start, end, and number-per-line) within a while loop. If end-of-file is entered, then the program should terminate;

- Ensuring that the starting number is less than or equal to the ending number;

- Ensuring that the number-per-line is greater than or equal to 1;

- Calling the function using all three actual arguments;

- Calling the function using only the first two arguments;

- Returning to the top of the while loop for more data.

 Exercise 4.2

Write a function that prints a specified number of blank lines on the screen. This number should default to 1. If it's zero or negative, assume the number 1. Then write a program to test the function.

Exercise 4.3

Given the `main()` function:

```cpp
#include <iostream.h>

int main()
{
   int array[] = { 4, 6, -3, -9, 10 };
   const int length = sizeof(array) / sizeof(*array);

   cout << "Original sequence:\n";
   print(array, length);

   cout << "Ascending sequence:\n";
   sort(array, length);
   print(array, length);

   cout << "Descending sequence\n:";
   sort(array, length, 'D');
   print(array, length);

   return 0;
}
```

write the function `sort()` that sorts the array into either ascending or descending sequence. By default, this function should use ascending sequence. If necessary, be sure to use the `swap()` routine from Chapter 3, Exercise 3.1. In addition, write a `print()` function that iterates through the array and displays each element.

Chapter 5

Dynamic Memory Allocation

5.1   Introduction

C++ has introduced a new (pun intended!) method for you to allocate and release dynamic memory. As you will soon see, the C method of handling this task via the functions `malloc()` and `free()` must now be abandoned. The main reason is that you are about to enter the world of user-defined types, and `malloc()` and `free()` will not be able to handle the tasks that need to be done.

5.2   Dynamic Memory Allocation in C

Let's take a moment to review how memory is allocated and released dynamically in C. There are four functions that handle this:

■   `malloc()` takes one argument: an unsigned integral value (of type `size_t`) representing the number of bytes that is to be obtained. In order to ascertain the exact number of bytes, the `sizeof` keyword is typically used, especially where structure objects are involved. If the function successfully finds the requested amount of contiguous space, it returns an address of type `void*` that points to the first byte of this space. If an error occurred, or if no more space is available, then the address zero (NULL) is returned;

■   `calloc()` takes two arguments: a number representing the number of elements that are to be allocated, and a number specifying the size of each element. In addition, all of the allocated space is automatically initialized to binary zero;

■   `realloc()` takes two arguments: a pointer to existing space, and a number representing the total amount of new space. The data from the existing space is copied into the new space, the existing space is deallocated, and the pointer to the new space is returned;

- free() takes one argument: a pointer to existing space. It then releases this space so that it may be reused. If this pointer is equal to zero, then no operation is performed.

5.3   C++ Keyword new

Like the malloc() function in C, the C++ keyword new is used to allocate contiguous, unnamed memory at execution time. In its simplest form, you write the keyword new followed by whatever type of data you want to allocate. This is called a *new-expression*, and is a unary operator.

  Example 5.1

```
// An expression to allocate one char
new char

// An expression to allocate one int
new int

// An expression to allocate one double
new double

// An expression to allocate one pointer-to-float
new float*
```

Unlike malloc(), you no longer need to use the sizeof keyword to specify the exact number of bytes needed. Instead, you merely specify a particular type, either fundamental or user-defined. The fact that different types occupy different amounts of storage is handled automatically by the compiler.

5.3.1   The Function operator new()

The new-expression automatically invokes a call to the function operator new(). When allocating an object of type T, a first argument of sizeof(T) is automatically supplied to this function. If the value of this argument is zero, then a value of 1 is assumed.

If operator new() cannot allocate the requested amount of heap space, it returns a pointer whose value is zero. If this is the case, and the user has decided not to handle allocation failures, then operator new() will throw an exception. On the other hand, if the user has decided to handle allocation failures (by calling the function set_new_handler()), then the user's function will be invoked. Presumably, this function will release some heap space before returning; otherwise, it should abort the program.

If `operator new()` successfully allocates the heap space, then it returns the address of this space which is converted to a pointer to the type being allocated.

While various compiler vendors are free to write their own implementations of `operator new()`, a typical scenario would be as follows.

 Example 5.2

```
void* operator new(size_t size)
{
   if(size == 0)
      size = 1;
   while(1)
   {
      void* p = malloc(size);   // Try to get space
      if(p)   // If space allocated OK...
         return p;      // then return the address
      if(!_new_handler)      // If no new_handler...
         // throw an exception (and function exits)
      _new_handler();        // Handle the error by calling the
                             // the user's function, and repeat

   }
}
```

The example above uses exception handling, which is not covered until Chapter 12, so don't worry about it for now. Until then we will just have to cross our fingers and assume success!

 Tip

> *C++ does not provide functions analogous to* `realloc()` *and* `calloc()`. *Therefore, should you want to emulate what these functions do, you will have to write your own versions (in lieu of using a variable-sized array class from a library).*

5.4   Allocating a Single Instance of a Fundamental Type

To get memory using the new keyword for a single instance of some fundamental type, write the keyword new followed by the type. Then initialize (or assign to) a pointer with the resultant address. An open parenthesis following the keyword new is part of the syntax, and everything that follows until the closing parenthesis is considered to be the type. For any complicated type specification, you can put parentheses around the whole type.

 Example 5.3

```
// One char
char* ptr_char = new char;

// One int
int* ptr_int = new int;

// One double
double* ptr_double = new double;

// One pointer to a float
float** ptr_ptr_float = new float*;

// One pointer-to-function taking no arguments and
// returning an int. Parentheses surrounding the type are
// mandatory.
int (**ptr_func)() = new (int(*)());

// Are you kidding? The preceding example with a typedef
typedef int (*Ptr)();
Ptr* ptr_func = new Ptr;
```

5.5   How to Initialize a Fundamental Type

Because it's so important to be able to initialize variables and objects in C++, fundamental types allocated from the heap via new can be initialized with some value by enclosing the value within parentheses immediately after the type name.

 Example 5.4

```
// An 'int' from the heap initialized to 65
int* ptr_int = new int(65);

// A 'char' from the heap initialized to 'A'
char* ptr_char = new char('A');
```

ptr_int

Note the difference between the following two lines.

 Example 5.5

```
int* ptr_int = new int;      // Uninitialized space
int* ptr_int = new int();    // Initialized to 0
```

In the first case, an `int` is created on the heap, and its value is unknown. But in the second case, the value will be initialized to whatever value an `int` at the global space would have. And since all global fundamental types have their initial values set to zero by default, a zero is placed into that location on the heap.

 Caution

Borland C++ 5.0 does not yet support this feature.

5.6 Memory for an Array of a Fundamental Type

Perhaps your program needs to allocate not just one object, but rather an array of objects of some type. To get memory for an array of some fundamental type, write the keyword `new`, the type name, and the number of array elements enclosed within square brackets (*not* parentheses!). This number can be either a constant or some expression whose value is determined at execution time (but see the restrictions associated with multidimensional arrays). The return type is identical to that of a single instance, and the actual value returned is a pointer to the first element of the array.

If the value of the expression between the square brackets is zero, an array with no elements is allocated, and the pointer returned by the new-expression is non-zero and distinct from the pointer to any other object. If the value is determined to be invalid at execution time, then the results are unpredictable.

 Caution

It is not possible to provide initializing values for the individual elements of an array created when using new. *The best you can do is assign into them after the creation has occurred (even though you could legitimately say that you are "initializing" the array since it is getting a meaningful value for the first time).*

Here are some examples of allocating arrays of some fundamental types.

Example 5.6

```
int dim = 5;

// An array of 1 char
char* ptr_char = new char[1];

// An array of 5 floats
float* ptr_float = new float[dim];

// An array of 5 pointers to char
char** ptr_ptr_char = new char*[dim];

// An array of 5 pointers-to-function taking no
// arguments and returning an int
int (**ptr_func)() = new (int(*[dim])());

// Please! The preceding example with a typedef
typedef int (*Ptr)();
Ptr* ptr = new Ptr[dim];
```

You must be very careful *not* to use parentheses around the type to be allocated.

 Example 5.7

```
int dim = 10;
int** ptr;
ptr = new int*[dim];        // OK
ptr = new (int*[dim]);      // OK; entire type is parenthesized
ptr = new (int*)[dim];      // Error; result is type int*
```

On the erroneous line above, the new-expression is `new (int*)` and nothing more. Therefore, it will allocate an object of type `int**`, which is then subscripted by `[dim]`, thereby producing a result of type `int*`. Obviously this result cannot be stored into `ptr` because of the incompatibilities in the types.

You should note that the allocation of a single object, and the allocation of an array of one object, are *not* the same. This has important ramifications when the `delete` operator is used.

 Caution

Be very careful that you don't use parentheses when you want brackets, and vice versa. The compiler does not know that the value between parentheses really represents some array dimension, and will be quite happy to initialize a single object using this value.

5.7   The C++ Keyword `delete`

The `delete` keyword in C++ is used to release the space that was reserved by `new`. It is analogous to the function `free()` in C, which takes as its one argument a pointer to the space. The content of the pointer itself is not modified by `delete`.

 Caution

> *You should not commingle C and C++ styles of dynamic memory allocation. That is, if you* `malloc()` *some space, then you should* `free()` *it. Similarly, if you* `new` *some space, then you should* `delete` *it. Do not use* `delete` *with* `malloc()`, *nor* `free()` *with* `new`.

5.7.1   How to Delete a Single Instance from the Heap

To delete a single instance from the heap (including a pointer), write the keyword `delete` followed by the name of the pointer that points to the heap space. This keyword invokes a hidden function call to `operator delete()`.

 Example 5.8

```
int* ptr1 = new int;
int** ptr2 = new int*;
// process...
delete ptr1;
delete ptr2;
```

5.7.2   How to Delete an Array of Instances from the Heap

To delete an array of instances from the heap (including an array of pointers), write the keyword `delete` followed by a pair of empty brackets and the name of the pointer variable. This keyword invokes a hidden function call to `operator delete[]()`.

 Example 5.9

```
int* ptr1 = new int[ /* any value */ ];
int** ptr2 = new int*[ /* any value */ ];
// process...
delete [] ptr1;
delete [] ptr2;
```

The brackets are required to tell the compiler to expect an array of objects on the heap. This has important ramifications when you need to delete an array of user-defined objects.

 Caution

Don't forget this simple rule: if you used brackets in new, *then use brackets in* delete. *If you didn't use brackets in* new, *then don't use brackets in* delete.

5.7.3   Deleting a Zero-based Pointer

If the content of a pointer given to delete contains the value zero, it is perfectly permissible since this situation is guaranteed *not* to do anything harmful. This comes in handy in a program that initializes a pointer to zero, and then eventually terminates by deleting whatever space happens to be pointed at by this pointer. If the terminal operator is prompted for some number representing the amount of space desired, but immediately enters end-of-file, then the program will simply issue a delete on a pointer whose value is zero.

 Caution

You should **never** *attempt to release space via* delete *that was not allocated via* new, *and never attempt to release the same space twice. If you do, the results are unpredictable.*

5.7.4   Using new **and** delete **to Store Strings on the Heap**

In the following example, the user is asked to enter string data from the keyboard. The input is captured into a buffer area of some fixed length, after which it is copied onto the heap. Note that exactly the right amount of heap space is allocated to store each string. After all strings have been entered, they are printed and their heap space released via delete.

The key data element is pointer, which is a pointer-to-pointer so that the array of pointers needed to keep track of the strings can grow dynamically on the heap. Note the use of the reference type in the function input() to avoid a triple dereferencing situation.

Example 5.10

```cpp
#include <iostream.h>
#include <string.h>

typedef char* Ptr_char;
typedef Ptr_char* Ptr_ptr_char;

void input(Ptr_ptr_char& ptr, int& counter);
void output(Ptr_ptr_char ptr, int counter);
void release(Ptr_ptr_char ptr, int counter);

int main()
{
   Ptr_ptr_char pointer = 0;
   int counter = 0;
   input(pointer, counter);
   output(pointer, counter);
   release(pointer, counter);
   return 0;
}

void input(Ptr_ptr_char& ptr, int& counter)
{
   cout << "Enter your string: ";
   const int dim = 256;
   char buffer[dim];
   while(!(cin >> buffer).eof())
   {
      // Get the exact amount of space
      Ptr_char ptr_heap = new char[strlen(buffer) + 1];
      strcpy(ptr_heap, buffer);
      // Array of pointers grows dynamically
      Ptr_ptr_char temp_ptr = new Ptr_char[counter + 1];
      for(int i = 0; i < counter; ++i)
         temp_ptr[i] = ptr[i];
      temp_ptr[counter++] = ptr_heap;
      // Release old space for array of pointers
      delete [] ptr;
      // Update pointer to current array of pointers
      ptr = temp_ptr;
      cout << "Next string: ";
   }
}
```

(Continued)

```
void output(Ptr_ptr_char ptr, int counter)
{
   if(counter > 0)
   {
      const char quote = '"';
      cout << "The strings:\n";
      for(int i = 0; i < counter; ++i)
         cout << quote << ptr[i] << quote << '\n';
   }
   else
      cout << "Empty list\n";
}

void release(Ptr_ptr_char ptr, int counter)
{
   for(int i = counter - 1; i >= 0; --i)
      delete [] ptr[i];
   delete [] ptr;
}

/* The output of a typical run is:

Enter a string: This
Next string: is
Next string: a
Next string: test
Next string: ^Z

The strings:
"This"
"is"
"a"
"test"

*/
```

5.8   How to Allocate and Delete Multidimensional Arrays

Instead of allocating space for a 1-dimensional array, you can allocate space for an array of any dimension. For example, to allocate space for a 2-dimensional 3 x 5 array of int's, you would write:

Example 5.11

```
int rows = 3;
const int cols = 5;
int (*ptr)[cols] = new int[rows] [cols];
// ...
delete [] ptr;

// Using a typedef...
typedef int One_dim[cols];
One_dim* ptr = new One_dim[rows];
// ...
delete [] ptr;
```

The preceding example requires a bit of explanation. First, the elements of a 2-dimensional array are just a collection of 1-dimensional arrays (the rows). Consequently, the parentheses surrounding *ptr are *mandatory* in order to create just *one* pointer that points to the first 1-dimensional array which is 5 integers long (the number of columns). In other words, the array above consists of 3 *elements*, not 15. To prove this, if you were to add 1 to the content of ptr, its address would increase by 10 bytes (5 * sizeof int). This represents the start of the second 1-dimensional array (row 1, column 0), *not* the second int (row 0, column 1).

Second, when allocating an array from the heap using new, *all* dimensions must be known by the compiler *except* the first, and they must be positive. That's why rows could be determined at execution time, but cols must be constant so that the compiler knows its value. This means that for a 2-dimensional array, you *cannot* write a program that prompts the operator for the number of rows and columns, and then proceeds to allocate this array on the heap using new. The best you can do is to prompt *only* for the number of rows. (Note: Exercise #5 in Chapter 9 asks you to write a program that circumvents this problem.)

When it is time to delete the array from the heap, note that the format of the delete statement is the same as that of a 1-dimensional array. In other words, the number of columns does *not* need to be specified.

5.9   How to Detect Memory Leakage

When writing large programs that are constantly allocating and releasing memory from the heap, it is very easy to "forget" to release some of the space. If a particular function has this bug, and is executed many times, then it is quite possible that your program will run out of heap space before it finishes.

If you suspect that your program has this problem, then the following Borland-specific function called HeapSize() might prove useful. It returns the number of bytes on the heap that are currently in use. By checking this value at both the start and end of your program, or at the start and end of a particular function, you can easily detect if some memory is not being released.

 Example 5.12

```
// Borland-specific heap size function

#include <iostream.h>
#include <stdlib.h>
#include <alloc.h>

long HeapSize()
{
    int result;
    if((result = heapcheck()) != _HEAPOK)
    {
        cout << "Corrupted heap: " << result << '\n';
        exit(1);
    }
    long size = 0L;
    heapinfo info;
    info.ptr = 0;
    while(heapwalk(&info) == _HEAPOK)
        if(info.in_use)
            size += info.size;
    return size;
}
```

 Tip

The Borland function coreleft() *in the small data models returns (as an* unsigned int*) the amount of unused memory between the top of the heap and the stack. If heap memory is fragmented, then this figure is not a true representation of the amount of heap space left.*

5.10   How to Refer to the Heap Space

If desired, you may create a reference to an object allocated from the heap space. After allocating the space on the heap, either bind a reference to the resultant dereferenced pointer, or simply pass the dereferenced pointer to some function, and bind a reference to it in the formal argument list.

Example 5.13

```
#include <iostream.h>

int& input(int& value)
{
   cout << "Enter an integer: ";
   cin >> value;
   return value;
}

int main()
{
   int* ptr = new int;
   cout << "Value = " << input(*ptr) << '\n';
   delete ptr;
   return 0;
}

/* A typical run of this program would yield:

Enter an integer: 65
Value = 65

*/
```

Be very careful, though, with your use of reference variables. Can you predict the output of the following program?

 Example 5.14

```
#include <iostream.h>

int main()
{
   int* ptr = new int(1);
   int& ref = *ptr;
   cout << ref << '\n';
   ptr = new int(2);
   cout << ref << '\n';
   delete &ref;
   delete ptr;
   return 0;
}
```

Since `ref` is an alias for a location on the heap, subsequent changes to `ptr` do not affect `ref`, so a 1 is displayed both times.

By way of contrast, what is the output of the next program?

Example 5.15

```
#include <iostream.h>

int main()
{
   int* ptr = new int(1);
   int*& ref = ptr;
   cout << *ref << '\n';
   delete ref;
   ptr = new int(2);
   cout << *ref << '\n';
   delete ref;
   return 0;
}
```

Since ref is now an alias for ptr, any uses of ref are identical to using ptr, so a 1 and then a 2 are displayed.

If you got both answers correct, then congratulations! You now have a very good understanding of reference variables.

Review Questions

1. How does `operator new()` differ from `malloc()`?
2. What is the advantage of using `new` rather than `malloc()`?
3. How do you initialize an object allocated from the heap?
4. How do you allocate an array of instances from the heap?
5. Why can't you initialize each element of an array of instances allocated from the heap?
6. What is the difference between deleting a single instance and an array of instances?
7. How would you allocate a 3-dimensional array of `doubles` from the heap?

Exercise 5.1

Write a program that asks the user to specify the size of an integer array. Then allocate this array from the heap via `new` and prompt the operator for all of the values. Then print the array and release the space it occupies.

Exercise 5.2

Write a program that uses `new` and `delete` to dynamically allocate exactly enough free memory to hold string input data. That is, instead of allocating a fixed array of characters from the stack (which may be too big or too small), you will receive one character at a time and emulate the function `realloc()` by continually allocating, copying, and releasing space so that the physical and logical lengths of the input buffer area are always the same.

Since the extraction operator ignores the <ENTER> key, use the pseudo character '!' to signify that the end of one line of data has been encountered. At this time, display the data, and get ready for the next line of data. When end-of-file is encountered, terminate the program. (If you want the <ENTER> key to terminate a line of data, then use the named function `istream::get(char)` to input a character from the keyboard. This function honors all whitespace characters, and can be chained. See Chapter 16 for more details.)

Be sure to use separate functions to perform the tasks of initialization, adding a character, processing the end of a line, etc., and pass variables into these functions by reference where applicable.

Chapter 6

Classes

6.1 Introduction

Now that you have completed Chapters 1 through 5, you are ready for the "main event" — classes. Without a doubt, the ability to create a class in C++ is the most important enhancement that was made to the C language. As a matter of fact, C++ was originally called 'C with classes'. In the realm of top-down procedural design, the focus is on the function. In the realm of data structures, the focus is on the data. But in the realm of object-oriented programming, the focus is on the class and how it can be used to model real world abstract types.

6.2 Thinking About Structures

Let's start by thinking about a structure object in C. It consists of individual data elements whose types may be different. For example, a circle can be abstracted by envisioning a center point and a radius (using Cartesian coordinates), and can then be defined by using an appropriate structure type to describe these data elements. Here is one way to do it.

Example 6.1

```
typedef struct
{
   int x;
   int y;
} Point;

typedef struct
{
   Point center;
   int radius;
} Circle;

void f(void)
{
   Circle obj = { {50, 60}, 10 };
}
```

In order to perform operations on the circle object `obj`, you need global functions that have knowledge of the object, which is usually passed to the functions by address. This is certainly preferable to passing it by value, which incurs a lot of overhead. And if you need to make changes to the object, you have to pass its address. But as with any pointer, to prevent the function from making changes, you can add a `const` qualifier.

For example, here are several functions to perform manipulations on a `Circle` object.

Example 6.2

```
void store_radius(Circle* c, int r)
{
   c->radius = r;
}

int get_radius(const Circle* c)
{
   return c->radius;
}

void move(Circle* c, const Point* p)
{
   c->center = *p;
}

double get_area(const Circle* c)
{
   return 3.1416 * c->radius * c->radius;
}
```

6.2.1   The Problem with C

Note the loose connection between the global functions and the `Circle` object itself. That is, they live in different scopes, which means that the object somehow has to be "passed" to the function. In addition, there is nothing to prevent a new function from modifying the circle object in some disastrous way, such as storing a negative radius. And things just keep getting worse. Suppose that you change your mind and decide that it would be better to represent the circle object using polar coordinates (a radius and an angle) instead of Cartesian coordinates. Or perhaps you want to change just the name of the radius variable. Now all the functions in a big project that have abstracted a circle using Cartesian coordinates, or have hard-coded the name of the radius, will have to be painstakingly modified.

Looked at from another viewpoint, it should be obvious that the `Circle` object is completely passive in nature; it has no life of its own and is essentially "brain-dead". Thus, any action that needs to be done involving the `Circle` object ("move", "get area", "draw", "report your coordinates", etc.) cannot be performed because there is nothing inherent within the `Circle` structure to perform these actions. That's why you need to write global functions. A program written in C, therefore, consists of a series of global functions, designed in some top-down fashion, that pass fundamental data and structure objects back and forth in order to get the problem solved. This is also known as *procedural* programming.

The implication is that modeling a circle object with a structure in C is not a good idea because in the "real" world, objects are not dependent upon outside "forces" to make them "do something", and should not have to be tossed around like ping-pong balls. Instead, objects contain *within themselves* the wherewithal to perform the necessary actions to accomplish some goal or task. As another example, consider an automobile. It inherently "knows" how to start, stop, turn left, turn right, speed up, slow down, etc., provided it receives the appropriate message. These operations are "built in", and no external forces are required. (If they were, we would all literally be pushing and steering our cars down the road!)

6.3   A First Look at Encapsulation

The big difference between C and C++ in how a structure object is handled is that in C++ the object can contain functions as well as data elements. Thus, by sending messages to the object, it will respond in some predetermined way. Combining member data and the *functions* that operate upon this data into one composite type is called *data encapsulation*. That is, the data and functions are encapsulated (packaged together) in one nice, neat bundle called a C++ structure. The result is that an object no longer needs to be dependent upon any "outside" (global) functions to alter its state or behavior since these functions are already part of the object itself. That is, it can receive messages (function calls) and act upon these messages via its methods (function bodies). The structure object may also send messages to other structure objects.

This is what the `Circle` structure looks like after the global functions have all been encapsulated with the data members `center` and `radius`. Note carefully that the functions no longer need to take a pointer to a `Circle` object in their formal argument lists because they are in direct communication with the data that comprises the abstraction of the `Circle` object itself. In addition, recall from Chapter 1 that there is no longer a need for a `typedef` because both `Point` and `Circle` are inherently valid type names.

 Example 6.3

```
struct Point
{
   int x;
   int y;
};

struct Circle
{
   Point center;
   int radius;

   void store_radius(int r)
   {
      radius = r;
   }

   int get_radius()
   {
      return radius;
   }

   void move(const Point* p)
   {
      center = *p;
   }

   double get_area()
   {
      return 3.1416 * radius * radius;
   }
};
```

6.4 A Structure vs. a Class

Perhaps you are getting confused over the terms "structure" and "class". Just be aware that in C++ a structure is identical to a class, with two small exceptions. The first of these two differences will be discussed shortly when we get to the default access category of class and structure members. The second difference won't occur until Chapter 10 during inheritance. Consequently, the big change from C to C++ lies in the enhancements that were made to what a structure can contain and what it can do.

6.5 What is a Type in C++?

Before continuing the discussion of structures and classes, it's important to understand the concept of a *type* in C. When you buy a C++ compiler, it comes with some built-in, or fundamental, data types, such as int, char, float, double, etc. In and of themselves, these types do not do you any good until you *instantiate* them, i.e., create variables of a particular type.

So what is the actual definition of a type? *A type in C++ defines a range of values, and the operators that act upon these values.* For example, the type int (assuming 2 bytes) defines the integer values in the range -32768 to +32767, and the corresponding operators +, -, /, *, and %.

Notice how much more flexible a type in C++ is, as opposed to a "derived" type in C such as a structure, array, or pointer. You cannot define new operators for these types, and as a result they really are inferior to the fundamental types.

6.6 The Purpose of a Class

The concept of a *class* allows you to define a new type of data according to the needs of the problem to be solved, and to define operators to act upon this type. (This is also called *abstract data typing,* or ADT.) For example, a string in C is not one of the pre-defined types; instead, it is made up of various characters followed by the null character. It logically follows that the operators '=', '+', '-', etc., have absolutely no meaning with regard to string handling, which is why you need a function such as strcpy() in order to copy one string into another, as opposed to using the '=' operator.

But with C++ it's now possible to define a new type (which is really a class) called String (or whatever name you may want to give it) that contains the data and requisite operators (functions) to accomplish the normal tasks associated with string handling. Therefore, the user of the class no longer needs to be concerned with the intricacies of the string.h library functions, and instead merely has to manipulate

`String` objects just like objects of the fundamental types. In point of fact, we will be doing exactly this in Chapter 9.

There are many reasons to use classes in your C++ programs. For example, they encapsulate design decisions that might involve machine dependencies, e.g., how a floating point number is represented internally. In addition, classes represent well known data structures or algorithms that are of general use when writing programs, such as complex numbers and dates. They also allow the user to write in a more convenient notation by using infix rather than functional notation to imply concepts such as addition, assignment, etc. Finally, classes have the capability to provide automatic construction and destruction of their variables (discussed in the next chapter).

6.7   Components of a Class

A class can contain these different types of information:

- Member data consisting of these types:
    - Nonstatic (also known as *instance variables*)
    - Static (also known as *class variables*) (discussed in Chapter 8)
- Member functions (also called methods) consisting of these types:
    - Nonstatic, consisting of these types:
        - Named functions
        - Overloaded operator functions (discussed in Chapter 9)
        - Operator conversion functions (discussed in Chapter 8)
    - Static (discussed in Chapter 8)
- Other types used internally (such as enumerations) (discussed in this chapter)

A structure in C may not have a data member declared as static. However, this is perfectly legal in C++. Static data members and static function members will be discussed in Chapter 8.

Also note that a class may contain no data or functions, data only, functions only, or both data and functions.

6.8   How to Write a Class Definition

A class definition is written very similarly to the way in which you write a structure definition, with the keyword `class` replacing the keyword `struct`. Also, the structure tag is now called the class name. If desired, you may also create an instance of the class by writing its name after the closing brace and before the semicolon.

For example, a very high-level view of some class called `Circle` would appear as:

 Example 6.4

```
class Circle
{
    // all class members
};
```

Note that this class definition (like a structure definition) reserves *no memory* and is usually located at global scope so that all functions within a program can have access to it. Also, as with a structure definition, no direct initialization of the data members is possible for the simple reason that no memory exists that can store the value of a hypothetical initialization statement. This means that you *cannot* write:

 Example 6.5

```
class Circle
{
    int radius = 10;    // Error; no memory reserved yet
};
```

Tip

The proper way to initialize variables within a class will be shown in Chapter 7.

6.8.1   Class Declaration vs. Definition

By the way, note that the creation of a structure or class is called a *definition*, whereas a structure or class *declaration* involves writing only the keyword `struct` or `class`, followed by the name, and then a semicolon. This is different from C in which the term "definition" usually means that space has been allocated.

Example 6.6

```
class Circle;     // This is a class declaration

class Circle      // This is a class definition
{
    // All class members
};
```

A forward declaration of a class name would be needed when, for example, the name is used as an argument to a function, and the complete class definition has not yet been encountered by the compiler. Such a declaration tells the compiler that the type name is indeed valid.

 Example 6.7

```
class Circle;
class Screen
{
    void f(const Circle&);    // Circle needs to be valid
    void g(const Circle*);    // Same story here
};
```

However, when a class contains an instance of some other class, then the definition of the class must have been seen by the compiler. Otherwise, a compilation error is the result. The reason is that the compiler needs to know the cumulative size of any class it compiles, and therefore needs to know the size of the individual instance variables. If the definition of a contained instance has not yet been encountered, then it is impossible for the compiler to perform this computation.

 Example 6.8

```
class Circle;
class Screen
{
    Circle obj;   // Error; definition of Circle is not known
};
```

6.9   Principle of Data Hiding

One of the key ingredients of the C++ language is the *principle of data hiding*. (Actually, this is a misnomer, as a better term would be "data inaccessibility". You can still look at a class definition and see the data members.)

To understand the need for this principle, let's go back for a moment to the circle example, and do this:

Example 6.9

```
void f(void)
{
   Circle obj = { {50, 60}, 10 };
   obj.radius = -10;
}
```

Wow! It should be obvious that the integrity of `obj` has just been destroyed. As a matter of fact, it doesn't even have to be as severe as storing a negative number into the radius portion of the circle, because something as innocuous as:

Example 6.10

```
void f(void)
{
   Circle obj = { {50, 60}, 10 };
   obj.radius = 5;
}
```

is still a very dangerous act to allow. After all, who is to say that the designer of the `Circle` class has not deemed that the only valid radii are between 1 and 4? Fortunately, data hiding in C++ solves this problem quite nicely.

What data hiding means is simply that the data members of a class are *inaccessible* to those functions that are not part of the class. The advantage of data hiding is that once a class has been written, debugged, and placed into a library, there is no danger of a non-member function accessing the data and perhaps modifying the state of the class object in some unexpected or erroneous way. Put another way, the class object is guaranteed to be correctly manipulated by the member functions of its own class. For example, if a class member function is designed to display the object in a certain way, then such behavior will always work properly, and the user has no need to write some global function to accomplish this task. If the user of the class accidentally or intentionally tries to violate the principle of data hiding by directly addressing a class data member, then the compiler will output an error message.

Of course, all of this wonderful theory relies on the assumption that the methods of a class all do their jobs properly and without error. For example, it assumes that, indeed, there is a method within the class that is designed to change the radius. But it is then incumbent upon this method to run a validity check on the input argument (the new radius) to ensure that it is valid.

The principle of data hiding also says that how a class is represented internally is not really your concern. For example, how a floating point number is represented internally (IEEE or some other format) does not really matter to you. All that you want is the ability to manipulate floating point numbers and get the correct result. If the internal representation is subsequently changed, then your code should not be affected.

6.10   How to Manipulate a Class Object

You might very well be asking yourself, "If I, as the user of a class, cannot access the data members of that class, then how do I make changes to any object or instance of that class?" The answer is that you will always access the (public) member functions of that class in order to accomplish your task. These member functions will, in turn, access the data members for you.

Think of the data and function members of a class as living together in the same "house". Thus, they have unlimited access to each other. You, on the other hand, do not live in that house, but still need to communicate with one or more of the data members. Therefore, you must ring the doorbell and send your message to an occupant (a data member) through the sentinel (a member function) who answers. This message will then be implemented by the sentinel, and whatever results there are will be reported back to you.

6.11   Access Specifiers

The principle of data hiding, and the preceding scenario, are all very nice, except that inherently it means nothing to the compiler. In other words, you are responsible for explicitly telling the compiler which class members obey the principle of data hiding, and which do not. This is done by using three access specifiers within the class definition, each of which is a keyword in C++.

- `private`
- `public`
- `protected`

6.11.1   `private` **Keyword**

The first possibility is the specifier called `private`. This is the *default* specifier for a class, so that all members written first are automatically private. The rule with private class members is that they may be accessed *only* by the methods of that class. Consequently, you use the `private` keyword to enforce the principle of data hiding.

 Tip

Friend functions and methods of friend classes also have access to the private members of a class. This will be discussed in Chapter 8.

Unless you have an excellent reason for not doing so, *all* data members of a class should be private. Some member functions may be private if you do not want them to be accessible to non-class functions.

Also note that a class member function may access the private members of some other instance of the *same* class. This other instance would probably be passed into the member function as a formal argument.

6.11.2 `public` **Keyword**

The second access specifier is called `public`. This is the *default* specifier for a structure so that a C program that uses structures can be compiled using C++.

The rule with public class members is simple: they may be accessed by any function in your program. This is the means by which you can communicate with an object—by sending messages to the public member functions of that object.

6.11.3 `protected` **Keyword**

The third access specifier, `protected`, pertains to the member functions and data members of some new class that will be *inherited* from another class. This specifier will be discussed in more detail in Chapter 10, so you don't have to worry about it now.

6.11.4 **How to Write an Access Specifier**

To write an access specifier within the class definition, use the appropriate keyword followed by a colon before the class members to which the specifier applies. Since this specifier is very important to both you and someone reading your class, it should either be indented, outdented, or just plain "dented" so that it stands out clearly.

 Tip

> *A class or structure may repeat an access specifier any number of times, and use them in any order.*

To summarize what was just said, consider the following four ways in which to define the class/structure `Circle` so that all access privileges are identical to all of the private and public members.

Example 6.11

```
// Method #1
class Circle
{
    // private members
     public:
    // public members
};

// Method #2
class Circle
{
     public:
    // public members
     private:
    // private members
};

// Method #3
struct Circle
{
     private:
    // private members
     public:
    // public members
};

// Method #4
struct Circle
{
    // public members
     private:
    // private members
};
```

So what's your pleasure? Should you spend the rest of your (C++) life writing structures or classes? By unwritten convention, most folks in the C++ community go about their business writing classes, not structures. After all, this is C++, not C, that we're dealing with here, right? Well, OK, but at the same time no one will arrest you if you write a structure using C++, and this will be done occasionally throughout this book, particularly when all of the members are public.

The other consideration to bear in mind is whether the public or private parts of a class should be listed first. Once again, most of the C++ community prefers to write the public part first on the theory that this is what the user of the class is most interested in, so why not have it first? You can then only hope that when the user comes to the private part, he or she will avoid looking any farther. (Good luck.)

Caution

> *Don't think that you're being cute by using the preprocessor to substitute* public *every place it encounters* private. *If you do, the C++ police will encapsulate and hide you in a special class definition called* Jail.

6.12   Categories of Class Member Functions

The data members of a class describe the state of some object created, or instantiated, by that class. The member functions of a class are designed to operate upon these data members, and can typically be categorized in three different ways:

- Manager Functions. These functions are used to perform "initialization", "clean up", "copy", "assignment", and other fundamental chores associated with the class. Typically, the manager functions are the constructors, destructor, overloaded assignment operator, and operator conversion function(s).

- Constant Functions. These functions are designed to support constant instances of the class, and as a by-product cannot modify the state of the invoking object, as defined by the cumulative state of the nonstatic data members. A constant function that merely returns a value is sometimes called an *accessor*. The get_area() method of the Circle structure is an example of a constant function.

- Mutator Functions. These are the functions that make modifications to the nonstatic data members. This is how the state of an object can be changed. The move() method of the Circle structure is an example of a mutator function.

6.13   Implementation Hiding

Implementation hiding means that the class's functions (methods) can be specified in a file other than the class header file, and then compiled into object format. In other words, the implementation of the public methods is hidden since there is no need for the user of a class to know *how* the implementation of a message sent to an object is actually carried out.

Implementation hiding is not particularly new or unique to C++. To return to the analogy of a floating point number, when you add two such numbers together, you send the message "add" to an instance of type float and the correct result is returned. Exactly how the two input numbers are added is not really your problem; it just happens.

The big advantage with implementation hiding is that the author of the class is free to change the definition of the methods, and the users of that class will not have to modify their code. Instead, all that they will be required to do is re-link their object code.

6.14   Modularity

Implementation hiding is achieved by using the concept of *modularity*. This means that as you write each class, you should maintain the public interface in a header file, and maintain the implementation in a definition file. (In Borland C++, class templates are an exception to this rule.)

Header files usually end with a suffix of .h or .hpp or .hxx, while definition files usually end with a suffix of .c or .cpp or .cxx. You should use whatever convention is supported by your compiler.

Definition files should include header files only, never other definition files. Usually you should not put more than one class header or class definition into a single file. Each definition file should be a self-contained compilation unit. If you are using Borland's IDE (Integrated Development Environment), then only definition files may appear in a project file, *not* header files. If you are doing a command-line compilation, then only definition files should be specified as compilable translation units.

You must ensure that all of the necessary #include files have been specified in each definition file. In some cases, of course, only a forward declaration is needed, so do not automatically write a #include if you do not have to. Each class definition must, of course, include its own class header file.

Insofar as the order of included files is concerned, it's probably a good idea to specify the system headers before the user-defined headers (since the latter may depend upon the former, but never the other way around). Use angle brackets for system header files, and use double quotes for user-defined header files.

To ensure that a given header file is included only once in any definition file, you must enclose it within preprocessor statements that check for the existence of some variable that is unique to the class.

Example 6.12

```
// File circle.h        read file

#ifndef CIRCLE_H
#define CIRCLE_H

class Circle
{
     public:
   // public members
     private:
   // private members
};

#endif

// File circle.cpp      definition file

#include "circle.h"

// All member definitions for class Circle

// File main.cpp

#include "circle.h"

int main()
{
   // Instantiate class Circle and start sending messages
   // ...
   return 0;
}
```

6.15   How to Write a Class Using Implementation Hiding

The first step in enforcing implementation hiding is to write the declaration of the member functions within the class definition. Of course, the syntax requires that you do this anyway since you are not allowed to define a class method outside the class definition without having first declared it.

For example, here is the definition for the Circle class that contains the declarations of all of the member functions that comprise the public interface.

Example 6.13

```
// File circle.h

#ifndef CIRCLE_H
#define CIRCLE_H

#include "point.h"
class Circle
{
      public:
   void store_radius(int);
   int get_radius();
   void move(const Point*);
   double get_area();
      private:
   Point center;
   int radius;
};

#endif
```

This class is now complete enough for you to instantiate and use since the compiler only needs to encounter the declaration (not definition) of any function in order to be happy.

When the linker gains control, it will, of course, look for all of the function (and static member) definitions. If these definitions are in some object library, the linker will automatically extract them and use them to satisfy your function calls. On the other hand, you may choose to supply one or more function definitions as part of your source code.

The problem that you run across is how to inform the compiler that whatever member function you write is logically associated with its proper class. After all, there is nothing to prevent many different classes from all having the same function names, e.g., store_radius(). To make this logical association, you need to employ a brand new operator in C++ called the *scope resolution operator*.

6.16   The Scope Resolution Operator—Binary Form

The scope resolution operator, consisting of the C++ token ':', does exactly what its name implies—it resolves the scope of a member of a class. In its binary form it takes two operands, one on the left and one on the right. The one on the left is always the class name, and the one on the right is the class member name.

Therefore, to define the member functions within the `Circle` class, you would write:

 Example 6.14

```cpp
// File circle.cpp

#include "circle.h"

void Circle::store_radius(int r)
{
    radius = r;
}

int Circle::get_radius()
{
    return radius;
}

void Circle::move(const Point* p)
{
    center = *p;
}

double Circle::get_area()
{
    return 3.1416 * radius * radius;
}
```

There are several important items to note:

- You cannot define a class method in this fashion without providing its declaration within the class definition itself;

- The function, even though defined outside the class definition, still has complete and unlimited access to the class's private members. In other words, once the compiler encounters the 'Circle::', everything is considered to be in class scope. Note that this rule excludes the return type of the function;

- When the compiler attempts to resolve name binding and scope issues within a class method, it first looks to local scope, then to function scope, then to class scope, and finally to global scope. If all four searches fail to locate the specified variable, then a compilation error occurs.

 Tip

When the scope resolution operator is not used in an expression, but rather as part of a function definition, it is not an operator in the true sense of the word, but rather a punctuation mark within the syntax of the name.

It should now be obvious that it's usually a poor idea to declare a local variable within a member definition that has the same name as that of a member at class scope, as shown by the following example.

   Example 6.15

```
// File circle.h

#ifndef CIRCLE_H
#define CIRCLE_H

#include "point.h"
class Circle
{
      public:
    void store_radius(int);
    // Other declarations
      private:
    Point center;
    int radius;
};

#endif

// File circle.cpp

#include "circle.h"

void Circle::store_radius(int r)
{
    int radius;              // A locally defined 'radius'
    radius = r;              // Oops...storing into the
                             // local 'radius'
    Circle::radius = r;      // Now it's correct
}
```

The hassle of having to use scoping in order to store `r` into `Circle::radius` could have been avoided if the locally defined `radius` had been given a different name.

6.17   The Scope Resolution Operator—Unary Form

The scope resolution operator may also be used in a unary form, i.e., with just one operand to its right. This means that the named variable is to be resolved at global scope 100% of the time, bypassing local, function, and class scope. (Namespace scope, discussed in Chapter 13, is also bypassed.)

In the following example the local variable `r` is being stored into the `radius` that exists at the global, not class, scope.

 Example 6.16

```
// File global.cpp

int radius; // Global definition of 'radius'

// File circle.h

#ifndef CIRCLE_H
#define CIRCLE_H

#include "point.h"
class Circle
{
     public:
   void store_radius(int);
   // Other declarations
     private:
   Point center;
   int radius;
};

#endif

// File circle.cpp

#include "circle.h"

void Circle::store_radius(int r)
{
   ::radius = r;   // Store 'r' into the global
                   // definition of 'radius'
}
```

6.18   Constant Methods

The constant methods of a class are the opposite of the mutator methods in the sense that they support constant objects and promise not to make any changes to the state of the invoking object. That is, they may not modify any nonstatic data members of the invoking instance or of an explicit instance of the same class passed in as a formal argument.

Tip

> *The* `mutable` *keyword discussed later in this chapter provides an exception to this rule.*

You write constant methods by appending the keyword `const` as part of the function's signature in both the declaration *and* the definition. For example, the `Circle::get_radius()` and `Circle::get_area()` methods should be declared using `const`.

 Example 6.17

```cpp
// File circle.h

#ifndef CIRCLE_H
#define CIRCLE_H

#include "point.h"
class Circle
{
    public:
  int get_radius() const;
  double get_area() const;
  // Other declarations
    private:
  Point center;
  int radius;
};

#endif

// File circle.cpp

#include "circle.h"

int Circle::get_radius() const
{
  return radius;
}

double Circle::get_area() const
{
  return 3.1416 * radius * radius;
}
```

The reason it's important for you to write constant methods in a class is to allow those methods to *support constant objects*. Think about it: Does it make sense to send a mutator message to a constant object? After all, the whole idea behind a constant object is to create something that cannot be modified. Clearly, then, the answer is no, and the compiler will produce an error message if you attempt to do so.

In addition, a constant method of a class cannot invoke a mutator method (without the use of a cast). So a good rule to follow is simply this: if a nonstatic method is not a mutator, then *always* declare it const.

6.19   How to Instantiate a Class

After a class has been defined, you may then create *instances* or *objects* of the class in the normal fashion, i.e., just like you define the fundamental types. This process is called *instantiation*.

Classes may be instantiated on the stack, in which case their storage specification is auto. As with the fundamental types, they will exist until the scope in which they are defined terminates.

You may also instantiate a class object in the global space, so that it is created before the main() function gains control, and then is destroyed after the main() function terminates.

Finally, you may instantiate a class object on the heap via the keyword new, in which case it is your responsibility to destroy it with delete.

For example, here are several ways to create instances of the Circle class.

 Example 6.18

```
class Circle
{
   // class members
};

Circle global_obj;  // A Circle at global scope

void foo()
{
   Circle obj;                    // A Circle on the stack
   Circle array[5];               // An array of 5 Circle's
   Circle* ptr1 = new Circle;     // A Circle on the heap
   delete ptr1;                   // Release the heap space
   Circle* ptr2 = new Circle[3];  // An array of Circle's on
                                  // the heap
   delete [] ptr2;                // Release the heap space
}
```

6.20   How to Access Class Members via Instances

The way you access the members of a class is similar to the way you do it for structures in C. That is, you write the object's name followed by the dot (direct member) operator, followed by the member you want. But also recall that under the principle of data hiding, the only members of a class that you may legally call upon are those that have been declared public. This normally implies only the public *methods* of the class (called the *public interface*) since you will very rarely have any public data.

In object-oriented terminology, you are sending a message to some object, which is then carried out by the corresponding method. In this case, the object is called either the invoking object, the calling object, or the object to which the message is being sent.

So let's put it all together and write a complete program using the `Circle` class in which both the `store_radius()` and `get_area()` messages are sent to some instance.

 Example 6.19

```
// File circle.h

#ifndef CIRCLE_H
#define CIRCLE_H

#include "point.h"
class Circle
{
     public:
   void store_radius(int);
   double get_area() const;
   // Other declarations
     private:
   Point center;
   int radius;
};

#endif
```

(Continued)

```
// File circle.cpp

#include "circle.h"

void Circle::store_radius(int r)
{
    radius = r;
}

double Circle::get_area() const
{
    return 3.1416 * radius * radius;
}

// File main.cpp

#include <iostream.h>
#include "circle.h"

int main()
{
    // Create an instance of the Circle class
    Circle obj;

    // Store a radius
    obj.store_radius(2);       // Cannot say: obj.radius = 2;

    // Compute the area and display it
    cout << "area = " << obj.get_area() << '\n';

    return 0;
}

/* The output of this program is:

area = 12.5664

*/
```

6.21   Inline Functions

If you look at the preceding example very closely, you should be able to discern a problem with it in terms of efficiency. Whenever you invoke the methods `Circle::store_radius()` or `Circle::get_area()`, the compiler will generate an assembly language call instruction, and all of the overhead that goes along with it, such as pushing arguments onto the stack, and then eventually pop those arguments off the stack. For the simple tasks of storing a radius into `obj` via the method `Circle::store_radius()`, and then computing the area via the method `Circle::get_area()`, this is just too big a price to pay.

Now, of course, the C language does not have this problem because as the user of a structure, you can simply access its members directly with the dot operator, and not think twice about it. But in C++, under the principle of data hiding, this is not allowed, and instead you must always work through the public interface which, in this case, consists of the methods `Circle::store_radius()` and `Circle::get_area()`. (And please don't get any ideas about declaring the private data member `radius` public!)

Does this mean that the efficiency of the C language must be sacrificed to the principle of data hiding in C++? Fortunately, the answer is no, since the concept of an *inline function* neatly solves the preceding dilemma.

6.21.1   Definition

An inline function is, by definition, a function whose code gets substituted in lieu of the actual call to that function. That is, whenever the compiler encounters a call to that function, it merely replaces it with the code itself, thereby saving you all of that overhead. Such a function can be either a method of a class or a global function.

Inline functions work best when they are small, straightforward bodies of code that are not called from too many different places within your program (which could then significantly increase the size of your code).

Even if you request that the compiler make a function into an inline function, the compiler *may or may not* honor that request. It depends on the type of code the function contains. For example, Borland C++ will not inline any function that contains a loop, static data member, or aggregate initializer list. If this turns out to be the case, a warning message will be issued.

Obviously, in order for the compiler to make this code substitution, it must have access to the code itself. This simply means that the source code constituting the function body must be part of the project or program that you are compiling, and must appear prior to any call to it. Of course, the disadvantage with inline functions is that if the code itself ever needs to be modified, then all programs that use the function would then have to be recompiled. Furthermore, an inline function can be viewed as a violation of implementation hiding, but whoever said you get something for nothing?

6.21.2   Linkage of Inline Functions

You should also be aware that inline functions, by default, have static (internal) linkage, so even if the compiler does not honor the inline request, it will *not* cause the linker to generate a duplicate definition error. Instead, the code of the final executable file will be a little bigger because a copy of the function must be created in each of the object files.

6.21.3   How to Write a Global Inline Function

First, let's get away from class methods for a moment and consider a global inline function. To ask the compiler to inline this function, you must (1) precede the function's return type with the keyword `inline`, and (2) ensure that the function definition (not the declaration) appears before any calls to that function.

For example, in the following program, the global function `is_upper()` is not inlined, but `is_lower()` is.

 Example 6.20

```
bool is_upper(int ch)
{
    return ch >= 'A' && ch <= 'Z';
}

inline bool is_lower(int ch)
{
    return ch >= 'a' && ch <= 'z';
}

void foo(char ch)
{
    bool upper = is_upper(ch);   // generates a call
    bool lower = is_lower(ch);   // no call made
}
```

6.21.4   How to Write a Class Member Inline Function

As shown above, a member function that merely stores into a private data member, or returns the value of a private data member is an excellent candidate for inlining.

Before proceeding, there are two very important considerations to keep in mind: (1) A method of a class that is inlined should be included in the class's header file, and conversely (2) it should almost never appear in the class's definition file.

The justification for the first rule is quite simple. If the inline function is part of the public interface, then the code must be available at compilation time for the substitution to occur.

For the second rule, ask yourself what good it would do if the definition file were to be compiled into object format, thereby hiding the inline from the compiler when you compile your program. But more importantly, since inline functions have internal linkage, any calls to that function from within your program will generate a linker error because the linker is always totally ignorant of the existence of any inline functions. The only time you might want to put an inline function into a definition file is when it's private and for the exclusive use of other methods of the class.

6.21.4.1   Implicit Inlining

The inline request for class methods can be made in one of two ways. The first way is to define the member function completely within the class definition itself (called implicit inline). There is no need to write the word `inline` since it is implied by this scheme.

For example, here is the class `Circle` once again, but notice how the two methods are no longer defined outside the class definition.

 Example 6.21

```
// File circle.h

#ifndef CIRCLE_H
#define CIRCLE_H

#include "point.h"
class Circle
{
     public:
   void store_radius(int r) { radius = r; }
   double get_area() const { return 3.1416 * radius * radius; }
   // Other declarations
      private:
   Point center;
   int radius;
};

#endif
```

Ah, I know what you're thinking now. How can the methods `store_radius()` and `get_area()` access the private data member `radius` if the methods occur *before* the compiler has even seen `radius`? But this is not a problem because C++ guarantees that the inline functions are not evaluated until they are called, at which time the compiler substitutes the code. Then they are compiled to ensure that there are no syntax errors. By then, of course, `radius` is well known to the compiler. In other words, each inline function definition "knows" about all class members automatically, even members that appear later in the class definition.

6.21.4.2   Explicit Inlining

The second way to inline a class method is to *declare* the member function within the class definition, and then *define* it outside the class definition (but still as part of the class's header file!), preceding the return type with the word `inline`. This is called an explicit inline.

Also note that, to be on the safe side, the function declaration must also be preceded by the word `inline`. You may be able to "cheat" and not write it here, but to make your code as portable as possible, it's always a good idea to do so.

Here is the preceding example using explicit inlining.

 Example 6.22

```
// File circle.h

#ifndef CIRCLE_H
#define CIRCLE_H

#include "point.h"
class Circle
{
      public:
   inline void store_radius(int);
   inline double get_area() const;
   // Other declarations
      private:
   Point center;
   int radius;
};

inline void Circle::store_radius(int r)
{
   radius = r;
}

inline double Circle::get_area() const
{
   return 3.1416 * radius * radius;
}

#endif
```

So which of the two inlining methods is "better"? The unwritten rule is that you should keep the inline methods outside the class definition, on the theory that the smaller the class definition (public interface) is kept, the better off you are. But a lot of people say that there is nothing wrong with writing the methods inside the class definition either. I would only add that if you're going to do this, then restrict the method to no more than one line.

6.22   `mutable` **Keyword**

Recall that a member function declared with the keyword `const` as part of its signature promises to support constant objects and not modify any of the class's nonstatic data members.

The problem is that, on rare occasions, such a function really does need to modify a nonstatic data member, and still support constant objects. Maybe some piece of data needs to be cached, or a counter needs to be incremented.

The C++ keyword `mutable`, written as part of the declaration of a nonstatic data member, allows this member to be modified by a constant class method. This data member can either be part of the invoking object, or part of an explicit object of the same class type that gets passed in to the method.

Returning to the `Circle` class, let's assume that it's necessary to save the area whenever it is computed and returned. Then another method can retrieve this saved value. This is what the modified class would look like.

Example 6.23

```cpp
// File circle.h

#ifndef CIRCLE_H
#define CIRCLE_H

#include "point.h"
class Circle
{
     public:
  inline void store_radius(int);
  inline double get_area() const;
  inline double get_saved_area() const;
  // Other declarations
     private:
  Point center;
  int radius;
  mutable double save_area;
};

inline void Circle::store_radius(int r)
{
  radius = r;
}

inline double Circle::get_area() const
{
  return save_area = 3.1416 * radius * radius;
}

inline double Circle::get_saved_area() const
{
  return save_area;
}

#endif
```

6.23   Enumerated Types with Classes

As you know, writing an enumeration is a way to create a new type in order to make the code more readable and to restrict the possible values of any variables that are declared. The quintessential example is always that of a Boolean type. Because an enumeration can be promoted to an integral type, there is no problem displaying it, using a method that can be handled by the cout object.

Unfortunately, as you may recall from Chapter 1, the C language allows you to modify the content of a variable of some enumerated type with that of a non-enumerated type. But because enumerated types in C++ have stronger typing restrictions, it is no longer possible to assign or initialize an enumerated variable with anything but a legitimate value of the enumeration.

Another problem in C is that if an enumeration exists inside a class header file, and if two such header files both happen to use the same name for the enumerated type or have enumerated values with the same name, then the compiler will object.

The solution in C++, of course, is to encapsulate the enumeration within the class definition itself. In this manner, the possibility for conflict between different classes no longer exists. Note that when member functions are written outside the class definition, the enumerated type name does not have to be scoped with the class name *except when it is used in the return type of the function*. (The reason is that the compiler does not yet know that the function is logically part of the class, so it has no way of knowing that the return type is logically part of the class. Thus, the need for scoping.)

For nonmember functions to gain access to the actual values of the enumerated type, the type itself must be made public.

The following program shows how a class called Button uses an encapsulated enumerated type called Status whose values can only be out or in. The data member of the class called state is the instance of the type Status. The main() function instantiates the class, sets the object into its two possible states, and verifies these states.

Example 6.24

```cpp
// File button.h

#ifndef BUTTON_H
#define BUTTON_H

class Button
{
    public:
    void set_out() { state = out; }
    void set_in() { state = in; }
    bool is_out() const { return state == out; }
    bool is_in() const { return state == in; }
    private:
    enum Status { out, in };
    Status state;
};

#endif

// File main.cpp

#include <iostream.h>
#include "button.h"

int main()
{
    Button panic;
    panic.set_out();
    cout << "State is " << (panic.is_out() ? "out" : "in")
         << '\n';
    panic.set_in();
    cout << "State is " << (panic.is_out() ? "out" : "in")
         << '\n';
    return 0;
}

/* The output of this program is:

State is out
State is in

*/
```

If the number of enumerated values is fairly large, e.g., the number of days of the week, then providing 'set' and 'get' methods for each value could become rather burdensome. In this case you could provide just one 'set' method and one 'get' method for all of the values. The downside to this approach is that the enumeration itself must be made public so that its values are accessible outside the class.

Example 6.25

```cpp
// File button.h

#ifndef BUTTON_H
#define BUTTON_H

class Button
{
    public:
   enum Status { out, in };
   void set(Status s) { state = s; }
   Status get() const { return state; }
    private:
   Status state;
};

#endif

// File main.cpp

#include <iostream.h>
#include "button.h"

int main()
{
   const Button::Status out = Button::out;
   const Button::Status in = Button::in;
   Button panic;
   panic.set(out);
   cout << "State is "
        << (panic.get() == out ? "out" : "in")
        << '\n';
   panic.set(in);
   cout << "State is "
        << (panic.get() == out ? "out" : "in")
        << '\n';
   return 0;
}

/* The output of this program is:

State is out
State is in

*/
```

Review Questions

1. In what ways does a class differ from a structure? In what ways are they similar?

2. Why can't you initialize data members directly within a structure or a class?

3. What is the difference between private and public access rights?

4. What are the three types of member functions?

5. How does a class declaration differ from a class definition?

6. How does a function declaration differ from a function definition?

7. What is the scope resolution operator, and when do you need it?

8. When would you define a member function *inside* the class definition?

9. When would you define a member function *outside* the class definition?

10. What is an inline function?

11. What does it mean when a class member function terminates with the word `const`?

12. Why would you pass an instance of a class into a function by reference instead of by value?

13. How do you prevent a function from modifying an instance of a class passed in by reference?

 Exercise 6.1

Write a class called `Clock` that simulates the keeping of time. Use three private data members: `hours`, `minutes`, and `seconds`. Your class should be able to:

- `set()` the starting time. To do this, use three formal arguments representing the hours, minutes, and seconds.

- `increment()` the time by one second.

- `display()` the time. The function should take an argument with a default value of zero to imply military time. If this value is something other than zero, display the time in standard AM and PM notation. For example, 4 minutes and 31 seconds past 7 PM should be displayed as either 19:04:31 or 7:04:31 PM, and 5 minutes past midnight should be displayed as either 00:05:00 or 12:05:00 AM.

Declare all three functions within the class definition, and then define them as inline functions. To test your class, use the following `main()` function:

```
int main()
{
   Clock BigBen;
   BigBen.set(23, 59, 00);
   for(int i = 0; i < 100; ++i)
   {
      BigBen.increment();
      BigBen.display();
      BigBen.display(1);
   }
   return 0;
}
```

 Exercise 6.2

Write a class called `Date` that keeps track of the current date. Use three private data members: `month`, `day`, and `year`. Your class should be able to:

- `set()` the starting date. To do this, use three formal arguments representing the month, day, and year.

- `increment()` the day by 1. If the current month has overflowed, increment to the next month. If the current year has overflowed, increment to the next year. You may ignore leap year.

- `display()` the date in MM/DD/YYYY format. Print a blank line preceding each new month.

Define the following table in the global space to tell you the number of days in a month:

```
const int days_array[] =
{
   31, 28, 31, 30, 31, 30,
   31, 31, 30, 31, 30, 31
};
```

To test your class, use the following `main()` function:

```
int main()
{
    Date today;
    today.set(1, 1, 1996);
    for(int i = 0; i < 370; ++i)
    {
        today.increment();
        today.display();
    }
    return 0;
}
```

 Exercise 6.3

Given the following class definition that is designed to emulate an array of integers:

```
class Array
{
     public:
    // all function declarations
        private:
    int* ptr;
    unsigned length;
    void realloc(int);
};
```

and the `main()` function:

```
int main()
{
    const int dim = 5;
    Array A;
    A.initialize(dim);
    A.print();

    for(unsigned i = 0; i < A.get_length(); ++i)
        A.store(i, i);
    A.print();

    A.increment();
    A.append(6);
    A.print();

    A.reverse();
    A.print();

    A.trunc();
    A.print();

    A.del();

    return 0;
}
```

write the member function definitions for the `Array` class:

■ The private function `realloc()` gets heap space according to the value of its input argument. Of course, it must ensure that the existing heap space is copied into this new space, the old space is released, the `length` field is set accordingly, and `ptr` points to the new space;

■ The function `initialize()` stores the value of its input argument into `length` and allocates that many integers from the heap. It then sets each element to the value 0;

■ The accessor function `get_length()` returns the value of `length`;

■ The function `store()` stores its second argument into the array position indicated by the first argument;

■ The function `increment()` adds 1 to each element in the array;

■ The function `append()` calls upon the function `realloc()` to increase the size of the array by 1. It then appends its input argument to the end of the array;

■ The function `reverse()` reverses the order of elements in the array;

■ The function `trunc()` calls upon the function `realloc()` in order to truncate the last element in the array;

- The function `print()` outputs each array element with its index position;
- The function `del()` releases the heap space.

 Exercise 6.4

Write a class called `Parser` that can:

- Read in string input from the user;
- Parse the line one word at a time. That is, isolate and store the next word in the line;
- Return a pointer to the currently parsed word;
- Return the position in the line where the first character of the word is located relative to the start of the line.

A word is defined to consist of letters, numbers, and underscores. Letters are case sensitive. In lieu of a space, use a pseudo character, such as a backslash, to separate words.

To test the class, write a `main()` function that merely reads in strings and outputs the words one at a time, showing where the first character is in the line.

Chapter 7

Constructors and Destructors

7.1 Introduction

In Chapter 6 you had to write methods that initialized and destructed class instances, and the users of your classes then had to write explicit calls to these methods. You could rightly ask what would happen if the users failed to call these methods. The answer should be obvious—something very bad. Constructors and destructors solve this problem by providing the means by which your user-defined objects will be *automatically* initialized and destroyed.

7.2 Constructor Definition

A constructor (also known as a *ctor* by the language lawyers) is a special nonstatic member function whose name is the same as the class to which it belongs. This is how the compiler can identify it and differentiate it from all other named functions.

The execution of a constructor (assuming that it has been written properly) guarantees that the instance variables of the object will be initialized. Without a properly written constructor, the instance variables are left in an unstable condition, and this violates a fundamental rule in object-oriented programming that says that objects should always be well-defined and well-behaved. In addition, the constructor is responsible for the allocation of any private resources that the object may need, such as a disk file, an input/output device, or heap space.

7.2.1   When a Constructor is Invoked

A constructor *automatically* gets executed whenever an instance of the class to which it belongs comes into existence. It makes no difference where the instance lives: stack, data segment, or the heap. If the instance is contained within another instance, or is a subpart of some other instance (involving the process of derivation), it still implies the invocation of a constructor.

7.2.2   When a Constructor is *Not* Invoked

It is very important to understand that the creation of a pointer or reference to some class *never* invokes a constructor for the simple reason that pointers and references are *not* instances of any class. For example, when an instance of some class is passed as an argument into a function by pointer or by reference, no constructor is called. Similarly, if a non-`auto` instance of some class is returned from a function by pointer or by reference, no constructor is called.

Just remember: no instance, no constructor. It's that simple.

7.2.3   A Constructor is a UDC

The constructor represents what is called a *user-defined conversion* (UDC) function, because it literally converts from one type (usually fundamental) into a user-defined type. As you will see, this has important ramifications during the discussion on implicit type conversions.

 Tip

> *The operator conversion function, to be discussed later, is the other type of UDC.*

7.2.4   Syntax Rules

Here are the syntax rules for writing a constructor:

- Its name must be the *same* as that of the class to which it belongs;
- It is declared with *no return type* (not even `void`);
- It cannot be declared `static`, `const`, or `volatile`;
- It may have public, protected, or private access within the class, and it follows the same rules that exist for other class methods in this regard; (Protected access will be discussed in Chapter 10.)
- It can be overloaded. That is, the class can have more than one constructor.

7.2.5   The Default Constructor

If you fail to write a constructor in a class (as has been the case up to now), the compiler automatically supplies one for you. This function has public access within the class and does nothing more useful than to serve as a "place holder".

This default constructor supplied by the compiler, however, does not constitute the complete definition of the term itself. In point of fact, the term "default constructor" refers to *any* constructor that can be invoked with no arguments, whether it is supplied automatically by the compiler or is written by you. This implies that a constructor that takes all default arguments also serves as a default constructor. Of course, you cannot have more than one default constructor in a class because the compiler would get very confused as to which one it should invoke.

For example, here is the start of a typical `String` class with two constructors. The first can accommodate an argument of type `const char*` and serves as the default constructor. The second constructor overloads the first and accommodates an argument of type `char`.

  Example 7.1

```cpp
// File mystring.h

#ifndef MYSTRING_H
#define MYSTRING_H

#include <string.h>

class String
{
     public:
   inline String(const char* = "");    // Constructor
   inline String(char);                 // Constructor
     private:
   char* ptr;
};

inline String::String(const char* p)
{
   p = p ? p : "";    // Check for p == 0
   ptr = new char[strlen(p) + 1];
   strcpy(ptr, p);
}

inline String::String(char ch)
{
   ptr = new char[2];
   ptr[0] = ch;
   ptr[1] = '\0';
}

#endif
```

By the way, note how the default constructor guards against the possibility that some devious user will instantiate the class with a zero, thereby giving you all kinds of grief. (Remember: zero is always convertible to any pointer type.) Of course, if it's possible for a String object to legitimately exist at address 0 in your particular system, then this validity check should be removed.

7.2.6   A Constructor Cannot be Called Directly

Note that a constructor can *never* be called directly by the user of the class because it's simply invalid syntax to try to do so.

 Example 7.2

```
void foo(String& obj)
{
   obj.String();  // Error; won't compile
}
```

Instead, a constructor is always called *implicitly* by the compiler as a "hidden" function call whenever a temporary or permanent instance of the class is created.

7.3   Destructor Definition

A destructor (also known as a *dtor*) is a special member function that gets executed whenever an instance of the class to which it belongs goes out of existence. The primary purpose of a destructor is to release the private resources that the constructor may have allocated.

7.3.1   When a Destructor is Invoked

A destructor *automatically* gets executed whenever an instance of the class to which it belongs goes out of existence. As with the constructor, it makes no difference where the instance lives: stack, data segment, or the heap. However, if you terminate your program abnormally, for example, with an exit() call, then the destructor will be called *only* for global instances, and not for stack-based instances. If an object lives on the heap, then the only way the destructor will get called is if you issue a delete executed on a pointer to the object.

7.3.2   Syntax Rules

The rules for writing a destructor are:

■ Its name is the same as that of the class to which it belongs, except that the name is preceded by a tilde (~);

■ It is declared with *no return type* (not even `void`) since it cannot return a value;

■ It cannot be declared `const`, `static`, or `volatile`;

■ It may be declared `virtual` (discussed in Chapter 10);

■ It takes no input arguments, and therefore cannot be overloaded;

■ Access to it follows the same rules that exist for other class methods. It should probably have public access in the class definition, although there are some situations in which it should be declared private or protected.

 Tip

> *Note that unlike a constructor, a destructor may be called explicitly. However, you should not do so without a good reason. In addition, some compilers may insist that you explicitly scope the destructor name.*

In the case of the `String` class, the destructor is responsible for releasing the heap space that the constructor allocated, so here is the enhanced class definition with the destructor defined as an implicit inline function.

Example 7.3

```
// File mystring.h

#ifndef MYSTRING_H
#define MYSTRING_H

#include <string.h>

class String
{
     public:
   inline String(const char* = "");
   inline String(char);
   ~String() { delete [] ptr ; }  // Destructor
     private:
   char* ptr;
};

inline String::String(const char* p)
{
   p = p ? p : "";
   ptr = new char[strlen(p) + 1];
   strcpy(ptr, p);
}

inline String::String(char ch)
{
   ptr = new char[2];
   ptr[0] = ch;
   ptr[1] = '\0';
}

#endif
```

7.3.3   The Default Destructor

Like a constructor, if you fail to write a destructor, the compiler automatically supplies one for you. This function has public access within the class and essentially does nothing useful except to serve as a "place holder" for implicit calls that are made to it.

7.4   How to Instantiate a Class Invoking the Default Constructor

The process of creating objects (or instances) from a class or structure is called *instantiation*. Just as a cookie cutter instantiates (creates) cookies, a class instantiates objects, or instances. The C++ syntax to do so is really quite intuitive because it's the same syntax that the C language uses to create variables.

For example, to create a `String` object and invoke the default constructor, you would write this:

Example 7.4

```
String obj;  // Invoke the default constructor
```

7.5   How to Instantiate a Class and Pass Arguments to the Constructor

Most of the time you will want to instantiate a `String` object using a constructor that takes at least one argument. To do this, you write the object name followed by a parenthesized list of arguments, with each argument separated by a comma if there is more than one.

For example, this is how you would invoke the two constructors in the `String` class.

Example 7.5

```
// C++-style initialization
String obj1("C++");  // Call String::String(const char*)
String obj2('A');    // Call String::String(char)
```

This particular syntax is called "C++-style initialization", as opposed to "C-style initialization", which resembles the way you would write C code. In other words, using C-style initialization, the lines above would appear as:

Example 7.6

```
// C-style initialization
String obj1 = "C++"; // Call String::String(const char*)
String obj2 = 'A';   // Call String::String(char)
```

While technically correct, the C-style should not be used because (1) it does not extend itself easily when more than one argument is needed, (2) it may not be quite as efficient as C++-style initialization, and (3) it will fail to compile if the constructor has been qualified with the `explicit` keyword (discussed later in this chapter). So the moral of the story is this: use C++-style initialization, and you can't go wrong.

For the sake of consistency, a variable of some fundamental type may also be initialized by following it with the initializing value between parentheses.

 Example 7.7

```
int x(1);    // Same as: int x = 1
```

But you must be very careful that you don't do this:

 Example 7.8

```
String obj();    // Oops...a function declaration
```

While this is valid syntax, it declares a global function called `obj` that takes no arguments and returns a `String` object by value. Not good. Therefore, ensure that you do *not* write parentheses after the object's name when you wish to invoke the default constructor.

7.6   How to Avoid Instantiations With the Default Constructor

There are two ways to prevent users of your class from instantiating it with an implicit call to the default constructor. The first way is easy — just declare a default constructor in the *private* part of the class definition. Because it is private, the compiler will not be able to generate an implicit call to it.

You must also know that whenever you write *any* constructor for a class, the compiler-supplied default constructor is suppressed. This is as it should be, because now the compiler has no idea if you really want to have a default constructor in the first place. It just may be plausible, for example, that you do not want to give the users of your `String` class the capability to create an "empty" object. Therefore, the class definition would look like this.

Example 7.9

```cpp
// File mystring.h

#ifndef MYSTRING_H
#define MYSTRING_H

#include <string.h>

class String
{
     public:
   inline String(const char*);
   inline String(char);
   ~String() { delete [] ptr; }
     private:
   char* ptr;
};

#endif

// File foo.cpp

#include "mystring.h"

void foo()
{
   String obj1;            // Error; no default constructor
   String obj2("test");    // OK; invoke String(const char*)
   String obj3('A');       // OK; invoke String(char)
}
```

7.7   Implicit Type Conversion

Implicit type conversion is a wonderful feature in C++ that allows the users of your class to avoid doing a cast where one would appear to be mandatory. Instead, the compiler *implicitly* searches for a constructor with which it can convert the actual argument into a user-defined type that will match a function's formal argument.

For example, let's add a method to the `String` class called `search()` that will do a search of the invoking object to see if the explicit argument is contained anywhere within it. (Containment means that the characters pointed at by the explicit argument exactly match the same pattern of characters pointed at by the invoking object.)

 Example 7.10

```
// File mystring.h

#ifndef MYSTRING_H
#define MYSTRING_H

#include <string.h>

class String
{
     public:
    inline String(const char* = "");
    ~String() { delete [] ptr; }
    bool search(const String& obj) const;
     private:
    char* ptr;
};

inline String::String(const char* p)
{
  p = p ? p : "";
  ptr = new char[strlen(p) + 1];
  strcpy(ptr, p);
}

#endif
```

p = " c++ test string

(Continued)

```
// File mystring.cpp

#include <string.h>
#include "mystring.h"

bool String::search(const String& obj) const
{
  int length = strlen(obj.ptr);
  int loops = strlen(ptr) - length + 1;
  for(int i = 0;  i < loops;  ++i)
    if(!strncmp(ptr + i, obj.ptr, length))
      return true;
  return false;
}

// File main.cpp

#include <iostream.h>
#include "mystring.h"

int main()
{
   String obj("C++ test string");
   char buffer[128];
   cout << "Enter a search string: ";
   while(!(cin >> buffer).eof())
   {
      const char quote = '"';
      cout << quote << buffer << quote;
      if(obj.search(buffer) == true)
// if(obj.search(static_cast<String>(buffer)) == true)
        cout << " is present\n";
      else
        cout << " is not present\n";
      cout << "Next string: ";
   }
   cout << "End-of-file\n";
   return 0;
}

/* A typical run would yield:

Enter a search string: C++
"C++" is present
Next string: test
"test" is present
Next string: strong
"strong" is not present
Next string: ring
"ring" is present
Next string: ^Z
End-of-file
```

Note that when `main()` calls the `search()` method, it passes `buffer` as the actual argument. Yet, `buffer` is an array of characters, and its type will therefore be converted to `char*`. This certainly does *not* match the expected type of `String` that `search()` requires.

But using implicit type conversion, the compiler will automatically search for a user-defined conversion function (UDC) with which it can *implicitly* convert the pointer into a temporary `String` object. Such a UDC does indeed exist, and it's the constructor in the `String` class (called a *converting constructor*) that accommodates a `char*`. This constructor then creates an unnamed `String` object on the stack to which the formal argument `obj` is bound with a 'reference-to-`const`'. As a matter of fact, any constructor that can be invoked with one argument can serve as a converting constructor.

Of course, the call to `search()` could have been written using a cast as shown on the line that is commented out. But why bother? The generated code and end result will be the same.

7.8   Copy Constructor   — deep copy

The copy constructor is a special kind of constructor that is designed to make a copy of an existing class instance. This usually entails a member-by-member copy of each of the nonstatic data members. Its one mandatory (and usually only) explicit argument must be a *reference* to the class of which it is a member, and should be `const` qualified in order to support a constant object. (A disk file object from which you wish to copy would be a case where you might not be able to make a 'reference-to-`const`' to it.)

For example, in the `String` class, the copy constructor would be declared as:

Example 7.11

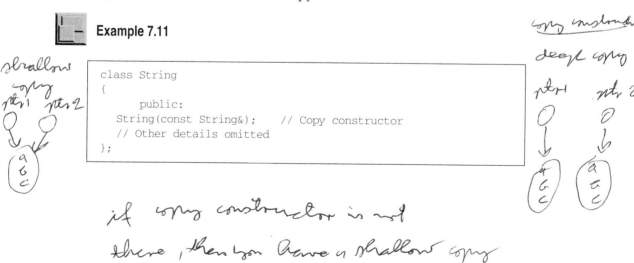

copy instanda
deep copy
ptr1   ptr 2
O   O
↓   ↓

shallow
copy
ptr1 ptr 2
O   O
↓   ↓
a
b
c

```
class String
{
    public:
    String(const String&);    // Copy constructor
    // Other details omitted
};
```

if copy constructor is not
there, then you have a shallow copy

To help you understand the basis of the copy constructor, consider this simple program written in C.

     Example 7.12

```
typedef struct
{
    int data1;
    double data2;
} T;

T foo(T arg)
{
    return arg;
}

void bar(void)
{
    T obj1 = {1, 2.34};
    T obj2 = obj1;
    T obj3 = foo(obj2);
}
```

After the object `obj1` has been initialized, it should be apparent that (1) the object `obj2` is made from a *copy* of `obj1`, (2) the formal argument `arg` in the function `foo()` is made from a *copy* of `obj2`, and (3) the variable `obj3` is made from a *copy* of `arg` when the function `foo()` terminates.

Since the creation of any user-defined type in C++ (including a structure) *always* invokes a constructor, a constructor that can accommodate copying must exist in the class or structure. This is called the *copy constructor*.

Based upon the example above, you can see that the copy constructor will be invoked automatically by the compiler under these three conditions:

■ An instance of a class is made directly from some existing instance of that same class;   T obj 2 = obj 1

■ An instance of a class is passed into a function *by value*;   foo (string s)

■ An instance of a class is returned from a function *by value*.

As a general rule, you should almost *never* pass an instance of a class into a function by value. Instead, pass it in by reference-to-`const` to avoid the wasteful call to the copy constructor and destructor. Of course, as mentioned in Chapter 1, you must *never* return an `auto` (stack-based) object or pointer type from a function by reference, because the resultant pointer or reference would then be pointing or referring to space you no longer own. So sometimes you've got to "pay the penalty" of returning an object by value from a function.

to suppress suppress copying objects, make it private

7.8.1   Default Copy Constructor

If you fail to write an explicit copy constructor, then the compiler will supply one for you that does a *memberwise copy* of the instance variables. The reason is that any C language program compiled using C++ must exhibit the same behavior (since such a memberwise copy is done for you in C whenever you initialize one structure object with another structure object). Unlike the default constructor, the copy constructor is guaranteed to exist regardless of whether you write no other constructors or a hundred of them. So your class will always have exactly one copy constructor.

This copy of the members that the default copy constructor performs is "recursive" in the sense that if a data member itself is a user-defined instance, its sub-object members will also be recursively copied, etc., (using either the instance's own copy constructor or the default copy constructor) until it's determined that a member is just a fundamental type.

As a general rule, except for the most trivial classes, you should plan on writing your own copy constructor. This is especially important when the class contains a pointer that manages the heap space, as is the case for the String class.

7.8.2   Writing Your Own Copy Constructor

Once again let's return to the String class, and now include a copy constructor. Since each String object must hold its own internal representation of a string literal, the copy constructor is responsible for doing what's called a "deep copy" involving the allocation of new heap space each time a String object is instantiated. Using the default copy constructor, both the new object and the existing object will have their respective ptr data members pointing to the same space on the heap, and when the destructor for each one runs, one of them will try to release heap space it doesn't own!

Example 7.13

```cpp
// File mystring.h

#ifndef MYSTRING_H
#define MYSTRING_H

#include <string.h>

class String
{
    public:
    inline String(const char* = "");
    inline String(char);
    inline String(const String&);    // Copy constructor
    ~String() { delete [] ptr; }
    private:
    char* ptr;
};

inline String::String(const char* p)
{
    p = p ? p : "";
    ptr = new char[strlen(p) + 1];
    strcpy(ptr, p);
}

inline String::String(char ch)
{
    ptr = new char[2];
    ptr[0] = ch;
    ptr[1] = '\0';
}

inline String::String(const String& obj)// Copy constructor
{
    // ptr = obj.ptr; // What the default copy ctor would do
    ptr = new char[strlen(obj.ptr) + 1];
    strcpy(ptr, obj.ptr);
}

#endif

// File foo.cpp

#include "mystring.h"

void foo(const String& obj1)
{
    String obj2(obj1) ;   // Invoke copy constructor
}
```

Tip

> *As noted in Chapter 6, even with the principle of data hiding, the copy constructor has unrestricted access not only to the private parts of the invoking instance, but also to the private parts of an explicit instance of the same class.*

7.9   Write *All* of the Manager Functions

The general rule regarding pointers within a class is that if a pointer data member must point to dynamically allocated heap space, then *all* of the manager functions must be written. In other words, ensure that you have written a default constructor, a destructor, and a copy constructor. (The overloaded assignment operator, discussed in Chapter 9, is the fourth manager function that you must write.)

 On the other hand, if the class does not contain a pointer that points to the heap, then you very well may be able to get away with using the compiler-supplied default copy constructor. However, some C++ gurus believe that for all but the most trivial classes, it's just not a good idea to accept the "free" manager functions.

7.9.1   How to Suppress Copying Objects

Suppose you decide to create a class whose instances should not be copied. For example, a `Card` class representing the abstraction of a playing card is a good example. After all, once a card has been instantiated, e.g., the ace of spades, do you *really* think it's a wise idea to let the user make any number of copies of it?

The answer to how this can be done is very simple: just make the copy constructor private.

Example 7.14

```
// File card.h

#ifndef CARD_H
#define CARD_H

class Card
{
     public:
  enum Suit { Clubs, Diamonds, Hearts, Spades };
  enum Rank { Ace, Deuce, Trey, Four, Five, Six, Seven,
              Eight, Nine, Ten, Jack, Queen, King };
  Card(Suit, Rank);
     private:
  const Suit suit;
  const Rank rank;
  Card(const Card&);   // Private copy constructor
};

#endif

// File foo.cpp

#include "card.h"

void foo()
{
  Card c1(Card::Spades, Card::Ace);   // OK
  Card c2(c1);   // Error
}
```

In addition, the `Card` class is an excellent example of a situation where you should *not* have a default constructor, thereby forcing the user to provide a suit and rank whenever a playing card gets created. (And please, no talk about creating jokers.)

 Caution

It is still possible for class methods to invoke a privately declared copy constructor, but if you do not define it, then the linker will fail.

7.10   Function-style Cast

Very frequently the compiler needs to create a stack-based unnamed temporary instance of a class. The simplest (and most efficient) way to allow the compiler to create this instance is to write *the class name followed by a parenthesized list of arguments, if any.* This particular syntax is called a *function-style* (or C++-style) cast. Note that it is the "opposite" of a C-style cast in the sense that the parentheses surround the expression instead of the type.

This kind of cast is most frequently done when a function needs to return a brand new class object by value. Now, if a named object must be created, then manipulated, and finally returned, then go ahead and do so. But if at all possible, you should try to avoid the creation of a named object and instead opt for a function-style cast. By doing this, you give the compiler a much better chance of optimizing by avoiding the call to the copy constructor (called *return value optimization*). On the other hand, the return of a named object will almost surely invoke the overhead of a call to the copy constructor. (Would this be called *return value pessimization?*)

For example, consider a `Complex` number class that has the capability to add two `Complex` numbers together with a *non-member* function called `add()`.

Example 7.15

```cpp
// File complex.h

#ifndef COMPLEX_H
#define COMPLEX_H

class Complex
{
     public:
   inline Complex(int r = 0, int i = 0);
   int get_real() const { return real; }
   int get_imag() const { return imag; }
     private:
   int real;
   int imag;
};

inline Complex::Complex(int r, int i)
{
   real = r;
   imag = i;
}

// add() is not a member of the Complex class
inline Complex add(const Complex& c1, const Complex& c2)
{
   // Efficient way using a function-style cast
   return Complex(c1.get_real() + c2.get_real(),
                  c1.get_imag() + c2.get_imag());

   // Inefficient way using a named object
   Complex obj(c1.get_real() + c2.get_real(),
               c1.get_imag() + c2.get_imag());
   return obj;
}

#endif

// File foo.cpp

#include "complex.h"

void foo(const Complex& obj1, const Complex& obj2)
{
   Complex obj3(add(obj1, obj2));
}
```

Note how the efficient way employs a function-style cast to create a temporary Complex object on the stack that is being returned from the function by value.

In addition, an unnamed temporary instance can be created if it's only needed to invoke some member function, after which it is immediately discarded. This is not that useful, but you have to admit, it *does* save a line of code.

  Example 7.16

```
#include "complex.h"

void foo()
{
   // Using a named object...
   Complex obj(3, 5);
   obj.display();

   // Using a function-style cast...
   Complex(3, 5).display();
}
```

7.11   How to Suppress Implicit Type Conversion

If you like, you may suppress implicit type conversion for a class. This is done by writing the keyword `explicit` ("not implicit") in front of a constructor declaration. It may appear before or after the keyword `inline`, if present.

Here is an example showing what does and does not work for the `String` class when dealing with the constructor taking type `char`.

Example 7.17

```
class String
{
     public:
   inline explicit String(char);    // Suppress implicit conv.
   // Other details omitted
};

void foo(char ch)
{
   // These instantiations are OK
   String obj1(ch);
   String obj2 = String(ch);
   String obj3 = (String)ch;
   String obj4 = static_cast<String>(ch);
   String* ptr = new String(ch);
   String obj5[] = { String(ch) };
   String obj6[] = { (String)ch };

   // These assignments are OK
   obj1 = String(ch);
   obj1 = (String)ch;
   obj1 = static_cast<String>(ch);

   // These instantiations are erroneous
   String obj7 = ch;
   String obj8[] = { ch };

   // This assignment is erroneous
   obj1 = ch;
}
```

Note that in all of the erroneous cases, the class name does not appear to the right of the '=' sign. In all of the good cases, the class name does indeed appear to the right of the '=' sign. Of course, the one case that instantiates obj1 using a C++-style cast is always valid.

The real purpose of explicit is to inform the compiler to suppress the implicit construction of an object that would normally take a single argument, but where an object of the class is not naturally seen as simply a different representation of the value used to initialize the object.

For example, take the case of a Vector class that is created by supplying its constructor with the number of elements.

Example 7.18

```
class Vector
{
      public:
    explicit Vector(int length);
    // Other details omitted
};

void foo(Vector& obj)
{
    obj = 10;    // Error; no conversion
}
```

The use of the `explicit` keyword implies that the constructor *cannot* be used implicitly to create a temporary `Vector` object. Therefore, if you were to attempt to assign an `int` value to a `Vector` object, the compiler would complain. This is as it should be because it just doesn't make sense, and the `explicit` keyword ensures this. Without the `explicit` keyword, a temporary `Vector` object would be created, and the compiler-supplied assignment operator would then be called, which is probably not what you want to happen.

7.12   Initialization vs. Assignment

As noted in Chapter 1, you must never, never, never confuse the processes of initialization and assignment. (Was that enough never's for you?) *Initialization* occurs when an object (fundamental or user-defined) is instantiated and gets a value. Essentially, it is a one-step process. When space is first allocated for the object, its contents are unknown, but initialization turns it into a valid object. On the other hand, *assignment* occurs when an *existing* object is overwritten with the content of another object, again, either fundamental or user-defined.

So how does the compiler know the difference between the two? Recall from Chapter 1 that it simply asks the question, "Does the statement begin with a type name (ignoring qualifiers)? If the answer is yes, it's initialization. If the answer is no, it's assignment. For user-defined objects, initialization is done with constructors, and assignment is done with the assignment operator. But note that sometimes the '=' means initialization, and sometimes it means assignment, so be careful!

 Tip

> *As you will soon see, one of the most fundamental rules in writing good C++ code is to prefer initialization to assignment whenever possible, particularly when it involves nonstatic data members of a class.*

7.13   Base/Member Initialization List

The base/member initialization list (also known as a constructor initialization list) is used to initialize the nonstatic data members of a class. Any action that occurs within the body of the constructor can only assign to, not initialize, the members.

7.13.1   Syntax

The base/member initialization list is valid *only* in the context of a constructor definition. It appears immediately after the closing parenthesis of the formal argument list, and has the following syntax:

- A single colon;

- The name of a nonstatic data member to be initialized;

- A parenthesized list of initializing values for the nonstatic data member. For a fundamental type, only one such value may appear. For a user-defined type, any number of values may appear, assuming that a suitable constructor exists and is callable. Each initializing value may be any valid C++ expression, including a function call;

- A comma after the closing parenthesis, and a repeat the previous two steps, if more than one nonstatic data member is to be initialized.

Here is a simple example in which a `Person` class contains both a `String` object (for the name) and a `long` (for the Social Security number).

 Example 7.19

```
// File person.h

#ifndef PERSON_H
#define PERSON_H

#include "mystring.h"
class Person
{
    public:
  inline Person(const String&, long);
    private:
  String name;
  long ssn;
};

inline Person::Person(const String& name_, long ssn_)
              : name(name_), ssn(ssn_) {}

#endif
```

Admittedly, you could have *assigned* the formal arguments name_ and ssn_ into the class members name and ssn, respectively, but as noted earlier, it's still better style to prefer initialization to assignment. But for the name field, it now becomes a matter of efficiency, as you will soon see.

7.13.2   Default Initialization

Obviously, if you fail to initialize a data member of a class, then its value is unknown after the instantiation is done. In the case of a fundamental type, however, if the variable name is followed by *empty parentheses*, then it will be initialized with the variable's default static value, i.e., zero.

In the case of a user-defined type, empty parentheses implies that the default constructor will be called (if it's defined and accessible). But unlike a fundamental type, if you fail to say anything one way or the other about the object, then the default constructor will still be invoked because the compiler guarantees that a constructor *must* be called whenever an object comes into scope.

Thus, in the following example, class Person again contains both a user-defined object (name) and a fundamental type (ssn). The base/member initialization list specifies that the default constructor for name will be invoked, and that ssn will be initialized to zero. If the specification for name had been omitted, as shown in the commented line, then the identical result would have been obtained.

 Example 7.20

```
// File person.h

#ifndef PERSON_H
#define PERSON_H

#include "mystring.h"
class Person
{
    public:
  inline Person();
    private:
  String name;
  long ssn;
};

inline Person::Person() : name(), ssn() {}
// inline Person::Person() : ssn() {}

#endif
```

7.13.3 When It's Mandatory

Do you remember from Chapter 1 that *all* constants and *all* reference variables in C++ *must* be initialized? Well, the rule also holds true for nonstatic data members of a class. In this case, the base/member initialization list *must* be used to perform the initialization.

In addition, it should be used to initialize any nonstatic data member that itself is a user-defined instance and needs to be constructed with something other than the default constructor.

 Tip

> *In Chapter 10 you will see a fourth situation in which the base/member initialization list must be used.*

7.13.4 Initializing a Constant Data Member

Let's revisit the `Card` class from earlier in this chapter, in which the `suit` and `rank` data members were declared to be constant, and provide an implicit inline constructor that initializes them. Obviously, assignment within the body of the constructor will not work because, as you know, it's impossible to assign into a constant.

 Example 7.21

```
// File card.h

#ifndef CARD_H
#define CARD_H

class Card
{
     public:
   enum Suit { Clubs, Diamonds, Hearts, Spades };
   enum Rank { Ace, Deuce, Trey, Four, Five, Six, Seven,
               Eight, Nine, Ten, Jack, Queen, King };
   Card(Suit s, Rank r) : suit(s), rank(r) {}  // Initialize
       private:
   const Suit suit;
   const Rank rank;
   Card(const Card&);   // Private copy constructor
};

#endif
```

7.13.5   Initializing a Reference Data Member

As mentioned above, *all* reference variables *must* be initialized. This simply means that if your class contains one or more reference variables, and no constructor exists, the compiler will complain. In addition, the compiler will examine all of the constructors that you do write, and ensure that each and every one of them initializes any and all reference variables.

When a class data member is a reference to a user-defined object, it creates what is called a using relationship. This allows instances of the class to share just one "real" object to which the reference is bound. Note the difference between this situation and a containing relationship in which each class instance has its own copy of the contained object.

For example, a deck of cards certainly contains cards (usually 52, but not necessarily), and in many games more than one player needs to share this one deck. If each player class contains a reference to the deck object, then this can be done quite easily.

Example 7.22

```cpp
// File deck.h

#ifndef DECK_H
#define DECK_H

class Card;
class Deck
{
    public:
  Deck(int number_of_cards = 52);
  // Remainder of the public interface
    private:
  Card** cards;
  // Other private data
};

#endif

// File player.h

#ifndef PLAYER_H
#define PLAYER_H

class Deck;
class Player
{
    public:
  Player(Deck& ref) : bicycle(ref) {}
  // Remainder of public interface
    private:
  Deck& bicycle;
  // Other private data
};

#endif

// File foo.cpp

#include "deck.h"
#include "player.h"

void foo()
{
   Deck deck;
   Player player1(deck);
   Player player2(deck);
}
```

7.13.6   Initializing a Contained Object

Once again here is the `Person` class containing an instance of the `String` class in order to represent the `name` object. As shown earlier, the `name` is being initialized with the string literal that the user has specified. It is very important to see what would happen if the formal argument had instead been *assigned* to the class member, as shown in the code that is commented out. In this case, because no assignment can occur until an object is first created, the compiler will instantiate the `name` object using the `String` class's default constructor. Next, it will assign the formal argument into `name` using the `String` class's overloaded assignment operator (discussed in Chapter 9). Now, that's a lot of heap management occurring needlessly, and why would you want to invoke two methods in `String` as opposed to one? The answer, of course, is that you wouldn't, which is why you should always prefer initialization of the nonstatic data to assignment, especially for contained objects.

 Example 7.23

```
// File person.h

#ifndef PERSON_H
#define PERSON_H

#include "mystring.h"
class Person
{
      public:
   Person(const String& name_) : name(name_) {} // Initialize
   /*
   Person(const String& name_)
   {
      name = name_;    // Assign
   }
   */
      private:
   String name;
};

#endif

// File foo.cpp

#include "person.h"

void foo()
{
   Person student("Your name");
}
```

By the way, note the implicit type conversion that is occurring as the compiler tries to find a constructor in the `String` class that can be used to convert the string literal into a temporary `String` object to which the formal argument in the `Person` constructor can be bound. After this succeeds (because the `String` class does indeed contain a constructor that can accept a `char*` type), the `String` copy constructor is called to initialize `name`.

7.14   The Importance of Initializing Pointers

In order to properly accommodate exception handling (discussed in detail in Chapter 12), all pointer data members that will eventually point to heap space locations must be (1) initialized to zero in the base/member initialization list, and then (2) assigned the heap space address within the body of the constructor. Thus, if `operator new()` should ever fail, then at the very minimum a stable object will have been created, and whatever heap space has already been reserved can safely be released via `delete` before rethrowing the exception.

Here is the previous example, but now class `Person` contains, in its data space, a pointer to an `String` object called `ptr_name` that will point to the name.

Example 7.24

```
// File person.h

#ifndef PERSON_H
#define PERSON_H

#include "mystring.h"
class Person
{
        public:
    inline Person(const String&);
    ~Person() { delete ptr_name; }
        private:
    String* ptr_name;
};

inline Person::Person(const String& name_) : ptr_name(0)
{
    ptr_name = new String(name_);
}

#endif

// File foo.cpp

#include "person.h"

void foo()
{
    Person student("Your name");
}
```

 Caution

> *If a class contains either a constant or reference data member, and no con-*
> *structor, then the compiler will* not *generate a default constructor because*
> *it would then be creating an instance in which the constant and/or refer-*
> *ence would be uninitialized.*

7.14.1   Constant Pointers

Of course, there is no C++ law that says that just because you have a pointer as a class member that it must point to a heap space address. Instead, you have the option to simply bind the pointer to whatever object the formal argument is pointing at. Just be careful that the object will hang around and not get destroyed at some point during the execution of the program.

For example, in the `String` class, in order to support a constant argument, the class pointer must be declared as `const char*`, and to ensure that it never points to anything else and is initialized, the pointer itself should be declared `const`.

 Example 7.25

```
class String
{
     public:
  String(const char* p = "") : ptr(p) {}
     private:
  const char* const ptr;
};

void foo()
{
  const char* data = "test string";
  String obj1(data);
  String obj2(data);
  String obj3;
}
```

Now the instances `obj1` and `obj2` will both be pointing to the same string literal in the data segment. `obj3` will point to an empty string literal.

7.14.2   Formal argument names vs. class member names

C++ allows a formal argument name to be identical to that of a class nonstatic data member. There is no ambiguity in the base/member initialization list because the member to be initialized will always be resolved at class scope, so it's not as though the formal argument is being "initialized" with itself. Of course, within the body of the constructor, it's a different story.

In the following example, the `name` object in the `Person` class is being initialized with a formal argument also called `name`.

Example 7.26

```
// File person.h

#ifndef PERSON_H
#define PERSON_H

#include "mystring.h"
class Person
{
        public:
    Person(const String& name) : name(name) {}   // OK
        private:
    String name;
};

#endif
```

7.14.3   Order of Initialization

The order of initialization of the data members is completely dependent upon the order of declaration of the nonstatic data members, and has absolutely nothing to do with the order of items in the base/member initialization list itself. See if you can figure out why this is so.

Consequently, you should never create an ordering type of dependency between two or more data members. For example, do you see the bug in the following class?

 Example 7.27

```
class String
{
        public:
    String(int len = 1) : length(len <= 0 ? 1 : len),
                          ptr(new char[length + 1]) {}
        private:
    char* ptr;
    int length;
};
```

The problem is that `ptr` is being initialized first, and at this time the value of `length` is completely unknown because it has not yet been initialized.

The corrected class definition is:

Example 7.28

```
class String
{
     public:
   String(int len = 1)   : ptr(0), length(len <= 0 ? 1 : len)
   {
     ptr = new char[length + 1];
   }
     private:
   char* ptr;
   int length;
};
```

Now the order of the data members is irrelevant because the dependency of ptr upon length has been broken.

Tip

> *As a general rule, it's a good idea to specify the nonstatic data members in the base/member initialization list in the same order in which they are declared.*

7.15   An Array as a Data Member

The C++ language does not provide any syntax to use the base/member initialization list to initialize the individual elements of an array declared as part of a class. The best you can do is *assign* to each element of the array within the body of the constructor.

For example, here is a class called DayTable that will be used to hold an array containing the number of days in each month of the year (and please, no comments about leap year). The constructor contains an array of numbers that is used in an assignment statement for each month.

Example 7.29

```
class DayTable
{
        public:
    DayTable();
    // Other details...
        private:
    int array[12];
};

DayTable::DayTable()
{
    static const int max_days[] = { 31, 28, 31, 30, 31, 30,
                                    31, 31, 30, 31, 30, 31 };

    for(int i = 0; i < 12; ++i)
        array[i] = max_days[i];
}
```

 Caution

One important ramification of this syntax rule is that if you declare an array of user-defined instances within a class, then the compiler has no choice but to generate a call to the default constructor for each and every element. This is probably not what you want to happen.

7.16   How to Initialize an Array of User-Defined Instances

As with an array of fundamental types, you may specify initializers when declaring an array of class instances (outside a class definition).

As a quick review, let's see how it's done with a fundamental type. The actual values are listed between braces and separated by commas. Remember that the dimension of the array does not need to be written if you let the compiler do the counting for you. In addition, if you specify the dimension, and the number of initializing values is less than this dimension, then all remaining elements are automatically set to binary zero. That is, under ANSI C it is *not* possible to partially initialize an array; it's an all-or-nothing situation.

 Example 7.30

```
int array1[3] = {1, 2, 3};      // 3 elements of 1, 2, 3
int array2[3] = {1, 2};         // 3 elements of 1, 2, 0
int array3[];// Error; no dimension
int array4[3] = {1, 2, 3, 4}; // Error; too many initializers
```

When the array consists of instances of some class, it should be obvious that if you provide initial values, then a constructor that accepts these values as formal arguments must be written. In addition, for any uninitialized array element, the compiler will attempt to invoke the default constructor, so this particular constructor must also be written.

Note that when you write the values that each array element will take on, you must use a function style cast unless the constructor expects only one value, in which case the cast is optional (do you remember implicit type conversion?). To invoke the default constructor, write a function style cast with empty parentheses.

In the following example, a 10-element array of type Complex is created and initialized three different ways:

- Element 0 is initialized using the default constructor, accepting both default arguments of zero;

- Element 1 is initialized by overriding the default value of zero for the real part with the value 1 (using implicit type conversion) and accepting the default value of zero for the imaginary part;

- Element 2 is initialized by overriding both default values with the new values of 2 and 3 for the real and imaginary parts, respectively.

The remaining 7 elements are initialized by using the default constructor. It should be apparent that a function-style cast is needed in all cases *except* the one in which only one argument is specified, because now implicit type conversion can be used. Of course, you may certainly use a function-style cast, but it buys you nothing.

 Example 7.31

```
class Complex
{
     public:
   inline Complex(int r = 0, int i = 0);
   // Other details omitted
};

Complex array[10] =
{
   Complex(),     // Element 0; function-style cast mandatory
   1,             // Element 1; same as Complex(1)
   Complex(2, 3)  // Element 2; function-style cast mandatory
};
```

7.17   An Array of Constant Data Members

If you ever need to declare an array of constant data members in some class, you come face to face with a real dilemma. On the one hand, C++ insists that all constants be initialized. On the other hand, it will not let you initialize the individual elements of an array. So what's a poor C++ programmer to do?

This conundrum can be illustrated as follows:

 Example 7.32

```
class DayTable
{
   // public interface
      private:
   const int array[12];
};
```

Different compilers are likely to yield different results. Just thought you'd like to know.

7.18   How to Initialize a User-Defined Type on the Heap

Like a fundamental type, a single instance of a user-defined type created on the heap can also be initialized by specifying some value or values between parentheses.

 Example 7.33

```
String* ptr = new String("test string");
// Process...
delete ptr;
```

Of course, in this case the `String` constructor that accepts a `char*` type will be invoked.

If you wish to invoke the default constructor, you may write empty parentheses after the class name, or eliminate the parentheses entirely. However, this is probably not a good idea for the simple reason that it's guaranteed to invoke the default constructor. Afterward, you will find yourself in the position of having to send mutator messages to the instance in order to provide meaningful data. Of course, this violates the guideline that says you should prefer initialization to assignment.

But if you're determined, the following example shows how it can be done.

 Example 7.34

```
String* ptr = new String;      // or...
String* ptr = new String();
// Process...
delete ptr;
```

Similarly, you can allocate an array of some user-defined type on the heap. But for the same reasons noted above, this is usually a poor idea. Nevertheless, the solution is to create an *array of pointers* to the objects, and then iterate across this array and get the data for each object before allocating the object and invoking the proper constructor.

Here is an example of this technique using the `string` class (defined in the header file `cstring.h`) that is part of the standard C++ library.

Example 7.35

```cpp
#include <iostream.h>
#include <cstring.h>

int main()
{
    cout << "How many strings? ";
    int dim;
    cin >> dim;
    if(dim <= 0)
        return 1;
    // Allocate an array of pointers
    string** ptr = new string*[dim];
    // Iterate across the array
    for(int i = 0; i < dim; ++i)
    {
        cout << "Enter string number " << i + 1 << ": ";
        char buffer[256];
        cin >> buffer;
        ptr[i] = new string(buffer);
    }
    // Process and release each string
    for(int j = 0; j < dim; ++j)
    {
        const char quote = '"';
        cout << quote << *ptr[j] << quote << '\n';
        delete ptr[j];
    }
    // Release the array of pointers
    delete [] ptr;
    return 0;
}

/* A typical run of this program is:

How many strings? 3
Enter string number 1: How
Enter string number 2: are
Enter string number 3: you?
"How"
"are"
"you?"

*/
```

7.19   Aggregate Style Initialization

It is still possible in C++ to initialize a user-defined object using C's aggregate style initialization. This entails writing an '=' followed by a list of constant initializing values between braces. However, C++ restricts you to classes that have no constructors, no private or protected members, no base classes (involving derivation), and no virtual functions (also involving derivation).

As an illustration of this, here is a repeat of Example 7.29.

 Example 7.36

```
struct DayTable
{
    int array[12];
};

DayTable table =
{
    {
        31, 28, 31, 30, 31, 30, 31, 31, 30, 31, 30, 31
    }
};
```

Review Questions

1.   What is the purpose of the constructor and destructor?

2.   Why don't the constructor and destructor have return types?

3.   What is the default constructor?

4.   Why would you overload a constructor?

5.   What is the copy constructor and when is it used?

6.   In what order are class data members initialized?

7.   What is the difference between initialization and assignment?

8.   When do you need to initialize (not assign) class data members?

9.   How are constructor arguments passed to a contained instance?

10. In a copy constructor, is it really necessary for the existing instance to be passed into the function by reference? Wouldn't a pass by value still work, even though it may not be as efficient?

11. How do you allocate a single instance of a class on the heap? How do you initialize this instance?

12. How do you allocate an array of instances of a class on the heap? Why can't you initialize these instances at the same time?

 Exercise 7.1

Write a program that proves that the order in which the data members of a class are declared governs the order in which they are initialized.

 Exercise 7.2

Given the class declaration for a `Complex` number:

```
#include <iostream.h>
class Complex
{
    public:
  inline Complex(double = 0.0, double = 0.0);
  inline Complex(const Complex&);
  inline double get_real() const;
  inline double get_imag() const;
  void increment();
  void accumulate(const Complex&);
  ostream& print(ostream& = cout) const;
    private:
  double real;
  double imag;
};
```

and the `main()` function:

```
int main()
{
    Complex c1;
    Complex c2(1.1);
    Complex c3(2.2, 3.3);
    c1 = add(c2, c3);
    c1.increment();
    Complex c4(c1);
    Complex c5 = add(c4, 6.2);
    c5.accumulate(c1);
    Complex c6 = multiply(c4, c5);

    c1.print();
    c2.print();
    c3.print();
    c4.print();
    c5.print();
    c6.print();
    return 0;
}
```

write:

■ A default and a copy constructor.

■ The two accessor functions.

■ The function `Complex::increment()` that adds 1 to the real portion of the invoking instance.

■ The function `Complex::accumulate()` that adds the real and imaginary portions of the explicit argument into the real and imaginary portions of the invoking instance, respectively.

■ The function `Complex::print()` that displays a complex number to the output device for which its formal argument is an alias.

■ The global function `add()` that adds two complex numbers together and returns the sum as a new complex number.

■ The global function `multiply()` that multiplies two complex numbers together and returns the product as a new complex number.

 Exercise 7.3

Rewrite Chapter 3, Exercise #3 so that the `Coin` structure is now a class. Eliminate the `initialize()` function and replace it with a constructor. In addition, make `change()` and `print()` member functions. The `main()` function instantiates an array of type `Coin` with each element specifying the appropriate data to be passed to the constructor.

 Exercise 7.4

Write a C++ program that simulates the movement of an elevator, as follows.

Start by creating a class called `Button` that abstracts a push button located inside the elevator. Use an enumerated type to represent its state—either pressed or not pressed. (See the example from Chapter 6.) Write implementor functions to change the state, and constant functions to retrieve the state. If a button is pressed that is already in the pressed state, or is invalid for the number of floors in the building, then display an error message.

Next, write a class called `Panel` that is abstracted as follows:

```
// File panel.h

#ifndef PANEL_H
#define PANEL_H

#include "button.h"
class Panel
{
     public:
  // public interface
     private:
  Button** ptr;
};

#endif
```

Next, write a class called `Elevator` that is abstracted as follows:

```
// File elevator.h

#ifndef ELEVATOR_H
#define ELEVATOR_H

#include "panel.h"
class Elevator
{
      public:
  // public interface
  void prompt();
      private:
  int current_floor;
  const int top_floor;
  Panel panel;
  // Other private data
};

#endif
```

The top floor will be passed in to the elevator's constructor, but you may assume that the bottom floor is always number 1. You may not assume that the Elevator knows anything whatsoever about the number of floors that it must accommodate.

Write member functions for the elevator class that allow the user to press any number of valid buttons. Assume that button number 0 means that it is time to close the elevator doors. When this happens, the elevator must move to a floor for which the corresponding button is pressed. When this floor is reached, stop and prompt for more buttons. When determining which floor to go to next, use any algorithm that you find convenient.

If the user enters end-of-file from the keyboard, terminate the program.

Be sure to output messages so that the movement and direction of the elevator can easily be traced. Finally, if you are superstitious, you may want to totally avoid floor number 13.

A typical main() function to set the elevator in motion would appear as follows:

```
int main()
{
   const int top = 15;    // Top floor
   Elevator Otis(top);
   Otis.prompt();
   return 0;
}
```

Exercise 7.5

Write a C++ program that allows the user to create a data base of people, list the items in the data base, and perform a simple search routine.

Start by ensuring that you have a working `String` class. Next, create a class called `Person` whose interface is as follows:

```
// File person.h

#ifndef PERSON_H
#define PERSON_H

#include "mystring.h"
class Person
{
    public:
  Person(const String&);
  ~Person();
  bool search(const String&) const;
  void display() const;
    private:
  String name;
};

#endif
```

■ The function `Person::search()` returns `true` if the input search string is contained anywhere within the `name` field; otherwise, it returns `false`.

■ The function `Person::display()` displays the name.

Next, create a class called `People` whose abstraction is as follows:

```
// File people.h

#ifndef PEOPLE_H
#define PEOPLE_H

class Person;
class People
{
    public:
  People();
  ~People();
  void menu();
  void add();
  void list();
  void search() const;
    private:
  Person** array;
  int length;
  void prompt();
};

#endif
```

■ The function `People::prompt()` displays the choices to the user, as follows:

A — Add a person
L — List all persons
S — Search
EOF — Quit

■ The function `People::menu()` prompts the user to enter the menu choice, checks the answer's validity, and calls the proper member function. Exit the function if end-of-file is entered.

■ The function `People::add()` prompts the user for a name and allocates a new person object from the heap space to hold this name. The address for this person is then appended to the end of the existing array, the space for which must be dynamically allocated.

■ The function `People::list()` calls upon the function `Person::display()` for each person in the data base.

■ The function `People::search()` prompts the user to enter a string value. It then calls upon the function `Person::search()` for each person in the data base. If the search string matches any part of a name, then display that name.

A suggested `main()` function would be:

```
// File main.cpp

#include "people.h"

int main()
{
   People all;
   all.menu();
   return 0;
}
```

Chapter 8

More Class Features

8.1   Introduction

In Chapters 6 and 7 you learned how to write a class definition, encapsulate member data and functions, specify access categories, create instances of the class, and write constructors and destructors. However, there are many more features of C++ classes with which you must be familiar, such as the `this` pointer, friends, static members, operator conversion functions, and pointers to class members.

8.2   The `this` Pointer

OK, I lied to you. (Well, it wasn't a big lie.) In Chapter 6 I said that member functions and member data are encapsulated within the class definition, thereby giving the functions direct access to the data without the need to have a pointer to some instance explicitly passed in to the function. This is true, but only in a logical sense. Physically speaking, encapsulation does not exist, which means that the member functions and member data are not literally kept together in the computer's memory.

Think about it. Does it make sense to really duplicate the class methods for all of the instances that you might want to create (and this doesn't even take into consideration the fact that hardware architecture would prohibit it anyway)? In point of fact, there is only *one* copy of each class method kept by the compiler, and each copy is therefore shared by *all* of the instances of the class.

To solve the problem of *which* instance a given method is operating on, the compiler generates code that looks very much like a C language program. That is, the compiler automatically generates the address of the invoking instance, and passes this address to each nonstatic method as a *hidden* first argument. Now the method can add the offset address of each nonstatic data member to the address of the invoking instance and obtain the true memory address to be used.

The pointer variable that is used to hold the address of the invoking instance has been given a special name by the compiler, called `this` (which is a reserved word in C++). The `this` pointer *always* exists as a hidden first argument in *every* nonstatic member function.

 Tip

> *The word "nonstatic" must be used when referring to the `this` pointer, because static member functions, discussed later in this chapter, do not have a `this` pointer.*

Even though the `this` pointer is implicitly declared, you always have access to it and may use the variable name anywhere you deem appropriate. Remember: like any other formal argument, the `this` pointer has absolutely no meaning outside the scope of a nonstatic member function.

The implicit declaration of the `this` pointer varies slightly, depending upon whether the method has been declared `const`. For a class called `Circle`, it's declared as:

 Example 8.1

```
Circle* const this        // mutator method
const Circle* const this  // constant method
```

The `const` that appears immediately to the left of `this` means that the pointer itself cannot be modified (and why would you ever *want* to modify it?). The first `const` in the second declaration says that the object to which `this` points cannot be modified, and isn't that the meaning of a constant method in the first place?

 Tip

> *It's perfectly legal to write the `this` pointer, followed by the indirect member operator, in front of any nonstatic member of the class. But with the exception of a few rare cases, it really buys you nothing.*

So what happens when you invoke a nonstatic member function? Given this typical code that sends a `store_radius()` message to some `Circle` object called `obj`:

Example 8.2

```
class Circle
{
        public:
    void store_radius(int r);
    // Other declarations
};

void foo(Circle& obj)
{
    obj.store_radius(3);
}
```

the compiler generates the address of the invoking object `obj` and calls `Circle::store_radius()`. This process is somewhat akin to calling a global function.

 Example 8.3

```
void store_radius(Circle* const this, int r);
// ...
store_radius(&obj, 3);
```

Thus, it's clear that the address of `obj` is passed as the first argument and gets stored into the `this` pointer.

 Tip

In order to differentiate the method `Circle::store_radius()` *from a global function called* `store_radius()`, *the compiler goes through a process called "name mangling". This is discussed further in the next chapter.*

Remember: In a C++ program, since the pointer variable `this` contains the address of the invoking instance, when you refer to some nonstatic member of the class within a nonstatic member function, the compiler will *automatically* precede the member name with `this` and the indirect member operator (->).

Example 8.4

```
class Circle
{
    public:
  void store_radius(int);
  // Other declarations
    private:
  int radius;
};

void Circle::store_radius(int r)
{
  radius = r;     // Same as: this->radius = r;
}

void foo(Circle& obj)
{
  obj.store_radius(3);     // 'this' contains address of obj
}
```

8.2.1   Dereferencing the `this` Pointer

Since the `this` pointer always points to the invoking instance of a nonstatic member function call, if you were to write the expression `*this`, you would be obtaining the invoking object itself. What good does this (!) do you? For one thing, sometimes a nonstatic member function needs to make a *copy* of the invoking instance so that it can modify this copy without affecting the original instance.

For example, suppose that the `String` class has a method called `upper()` that returns a new copy of the invoking object with all letters in upper case. This is how such a function could be written, with a program to test the `upper()` method.

Example 8.5

```
// File mystring.h

#ifndef MYSTRING_H
#define MYSTRING_H

#include <iostream.h>
#include <string.h>

class String
{
    public:
  inline String(const char* = "");
  inline String(const String&);
  ~String() { delete [] ptr; }
  String upper() const;
  void display(ostream& = cout) const;
    private:
  char* ptr;
};

inline String::String(const char* p) : ptr(0)
{
  p = p ? p : "";
  ptr = new char[strlen(p) + 1];
  strcpy(ptr, p);
}

inline String::String(const String& obj) : ptr(0)
{
  ptr = new char[strlen(obj.ptr) + 1];
  strcpy(ptr, obj.ptr);
}

#endif
```

(Continued)

```
// File mystring.cpp

#include <iostream.h>
#include <string.h>
#include "mystring.h"

String String::upper() const
{
   String new_instance(*this);
   strupr(new_instance.ptr);
   return new_instance;
}

void String::display(ostream& str) const
{
   const char quote = '"';
   str << quote << ptr << quote << '\n';
}

// File main.cpp

#include "mystring.h"

int main()
{
   const String obj1("This is a test");
   String obj2(obj1.upper());
   obj2.display();
   return 0;
}

/* The output of this program is:

"THIS IS A TEST"

*/
```

 Tip

> *Note how the* `display()` *method receives the* `cout` *object as an argument in order to allow the data to appear on literally any output device.*

In Chapter 9 you will see other reasons to use `*this` in a nonstatic member function.

8.3   Function Chaining

Suppose that you have an unruly child named Johnny who has not been particularly good lately. You might say to him, "Johnny, I want you to go to your room, pick up your clothes, make your bed, and wash your hands". In this sentence note that Johnny was mentioned by name only *once*, and yet four different concatenated "messages" were sent to him. Contrast this with saying, "Johnny, I want you to go to your room. Johnny, pick up your clothes. Johnny, make your bed. Johnny, wash your hands". Certainly the latter style of talking is more "choppy" and just doesn't sound as smooth as the former.

Since user-defined instances in C++ are just emulations of real world objects, it naturally follows that messages sent to them should be able to be concatenated in much the same fashion as were the messages sent to Johnny. That is, it should be possible to write an instance name just *once* followed by a series of messages.

In point of fact, the syntax in C++ allows this to happen. The technique is called *function chaining* or *function concatenation*. All you have to do is write the method with these two restrictions:

- The return type is the class name followed by an ampersand, which will create an unnamed reference variable on the stack;

- The actual value to be returned must be the invoking object itself, or `*this`. The reference is then bound to the invoking object, and becomes the value of the function. In other words, the value of the function *is* the invoking object.

As noted in Chapter 2, you've probably been using function chaining all along to do input and output. That is, when you write a simple program such as:

exi x 192 (*)

Example 8.6

```
#include <iostream.h>

int main()
{
   cout << "Enter 2 integer values: ";
   int data1, data2;
   cin >> data1 >> data2;
   cout << "You entered " << data1 << " and " << data2 << '\n';
   return 0;
}

/* A typical run of this program would be:

Enter 2 integer values: 4 6
You entered 4 and 6

*/
```

you are chaining the two extraction messages to the `cin` object, and chaining the five insertion messages to the `cout` object. In the case of the extraction messages, each method within class `istream` has a return type of `istream&`, and returns `*this`. In the case of the insertion messages, each method within class `ostream` has a return type of `ostream&`, and returns `*this`. Later in this chapter you will see more examples of function chaining.

8.4   Static Class Data Members

Static class data members were mentioned back at the start of Chapter 6. They were also called class variables. What purpose do they serve, and how do you create them?

Let's create a `Circle` class and include a constant variable that contains the value of the constant pi (3.1416).

const pi ; is constant for only one instance ; like one circle object

static const pi ; is constant for all instance of object (circle)

Example 8.7

```
// File circle.h

#ifndef CIRCLE_H
#define CIRCLE_H

class Circle
{
    public:
  inline Circle(int r = 0);
  inline Circle& store_radius(int r);
  inline double get_area() const;
    private:
  int radius;
  const double pi;     // Very inefficient
};

inline Circle::Circle(int r) : radius(r), pi(3.1416)   {}

inline Circle& Circle::store_radius(int r)
{
  radius = r;
  return *this;
}

inline double Circle::get_area() const
{
  return pi * radius * radius;
}

#endif
```

Do you see the problem with the design of this class? Since pi is a nonstatic data member, it will literally be encapsulated within each and every Circle object. Obviously, this is very inefficient because there is absolutely no reason for each Circle object to have its own private copy of pi. Instead, doesn't it make more sense for *all* Circle objects to share just *one* copy of pi? This is the basis of a static data member.

In C++, the magic words that should come to mind when talking about static data members are *instance independent*. That is, each static member is independent of any instantiations that may or may not be done with the class of which it is a member. Simply put, there will be just one definition of the static data member whether the user performs zero or 1,000 instantiations.

8.4.1   Declaring Static Class Data Members

Specifying a static data member constitutes a *declaration*, and where it is declared in the class follows the normal rules of data member access (`private` or `protected` or `public`). Like all statics in a C program, it lives in the global space and is created and initialized before the `main()` function gains control. It may also be declared `const` to ensure that it is never changed.

In the case of the `Circle` class, this is how `pi` should now be declared.

 Example 8.8

```
// File circle.h

#ifndef CIRCLE_H
#define CIRCLE_H

class Circle
{
  // Other details omitted
  static const double pi;   // declaration; pi is private
};

#endif
```

8.4.2   Defining Static Class Data Members

You are now responsible for providing the *definition* for all static data members. This is done by providing a definition in a definition file, *never* in a header file. By default, the value for this definition is zero (as it is in C) for fundamental and pointer types. For user-defined types, if no initializing value or values are provided, then the default constructor is called. Otherwise, the appropriate constructor is called that can unambiguously accept the arguments that are provided.

When writing the definition, you must *not* repeat the word `static`. You repeat the type of the variable, followed by the class name, scope resolution operator, and variable name. This process is very similar to how you define a method outside its class.

Here is the definition for the static member `pi`.

 Example 8.9

```
// File circle.h

#ifndef CIRCLE_H
#define CIRCLE_H

class Circle
{
   // Other details omitted
   static const double pi;   // declaration
};

#endif

// File circle.cpp

#include "circle.h"

const double Circle::pi = 3.1416;   // definition
```

8.4.2.1   Initializing Static Class Data Members Within the Class Definition

The C++ Draft (and Borland 5.0) also supports a new way of initializing a static class data member within the class definition itself if (1) it is declared `const`, and (2) it is an integral (not floating point) type. To do this, simply write an equal sign ('=') followed by the initial value. These values are known to the compiler, and therefore may be used, for example, to dimension an array. Note that you are still responsible for providing a definition, but in this case you can *not* specify any initial value whatsoever.

 Tip

The Borland linker may forgive you if you fail to provide a definition for the static data member in this situation.

Here is some class `Alphabet` that wishes to dimension an array called `letters` that will eventually hold all of the letters of the alphabet. Of course, if you stop to think about it, the same result can be obtained by using an enumeration.

Example 8.10

```
// File alphabet.h

#ifndef ALPHABET_H
#define ALPHABET_H

class Alphabet
{
   static const char start = 'A';
   static const char end = 'Z';
   static const int dim = end - start + 1;
   char letters[dim];   // OK; dim is known to the compiler
   // Other details omitted
};

#endif

// File alphabet.cpp

#include "alphabet.h"

const char Alphabet::start;
const char Alphabet::end;
const int Alphabet::dim;
```

8.4.3   Using a Static Data Member to Keep a Count

Perhaps the most common use of a static data member is to keep a count of the number of instantiations of a particular class. In the following example, the `Complex` class adds 1 to the counter each time it gets instantiated, and decrements the counter each time an instance goes out of scope.

Example 8.11

```cpp
// File complex.h

#ifndef COMPLEX_H
#define COMPLEX_H

class Complex
{
    public:
  inline Complex(double r = 0.0, double i = 0.0);
  inline Complex(const Complex&);
  inline ~Complex();
    private:
  double real;
  double imag;
  static int counter;      // declaration
};

inline Complex::Complex(double r, double i) : real(r), imag(i)
{
  ++counter;
}

inline Complex::Complex(const Complex& obj)
        : real(obj.real), imag(obj.imag)
{
  ++counter;
}

inline Complex::~Complex()
{
  --counter;
}

#endif

// File complex.cpp

#include "complex.h"

int Complex::counter = 0;      // definition
```

8.4.4   Static Member Functions

The problem with the preceding example is that if you want to write a non-static member function that displays (or returns) the value of the static data member counter to prove that it is initially equal to zero, it can't be done. (Well, it *could* be done using an uninitialized pointer, but you know that's not a good idea.) The reason is that you must perform an instantiation of the class Complex in order to call this particular method, but by then the counter will have been incremented to 1. Since counter is *instance independent*, it makes sense that it should be accessed via a function that itself is *instance independent*. This is called a *static member function*.

A static member function:

■ Is called by using the class name and scope resolution operator. In other words, instead of sending a message to an object, you are sending a message to the class itself;

■ Does *not* have a this pointer (because it is instance independent). This simply means that it can do anything a non-static member function can do *except* access any non-static member (data or function) of the class of which it is a member;

■ May *not* be declared const (because const only applies to the this pointer);

■ May be inlined.

  Tip

> *A static member function can also be invoked by using an instance or properly initialized pointer of the class, but I do not recommend it.*

In the following example, the Complex class has now added the static member function total(). Now it's easy to display the value of counter before any instantiations are done. Of course, after the main() function has terminated, all local Complex objects go out of scope, and the value of counter reverts to zero. As an interesting exercise, you might want to prove this *without* modifying either the Complex class, any of its methods, or the main() function.

Example 8.12

```
// File complex.h

#ifndef COMPLEX_H
#define COMPLEX_H

#include <iostream.h>
class Complex
{
      public:
   inline Complex(double r = 0.0,double i = 0.0);
   inline Complex(const Complex&);
   inline ~Complex();
   static void total(ostream& = cout);   // static declaration
      private:
   double real;
   double imag;
   static int counter;
};

inline Complex::Complex(double r, double i)
                        : real(r), imag(i)
{
   ++counter;
}

inline Complex::Complex(const Complex& obj)
                        : real(obj.real), imag(obj.imag)
{
   ++counter;
}

inline Complex::~Complex()
{
   --counter;
}

#endif
```

(Continued)

```
// File complex.cpp

#include <iostream.h>
#include "complex.h"

int Complex::counter = 0;

void Complex::total(ostream& str)   // static definition
{
   str << "counter = " << counter << '\n';
}

// File main.cpp

#include <iostream.h>
#include "complex.h"

int main()
{
   Complex::total();
   Complex* obj1 = new Complex;
   Complex obj2(*obj1);
   Complex::total();
   delete obj1;
   Complex::total();
   return 0;
}

/* The output of this program is:

counter = 0
counter = 2
counter = 1

*/
```

8.4.5   A Random Number Generator Class

Another use of a class that needs a static data member occurs when this member must be an instance of some other class that should be instantiated *only once* regardless of the number of instantiations of the containing class.

For example, here is a class called Random whose job is to seed the random number generator and return a random number in some range specified by the user. Note that there are no data members in this class, so that instantiations have no state.

Example 8.13

```
// File random.h

#ifndef RANDOM_H
#define RANDOM_H

#include <stdlib.h>
#include <time.h>

class Random
{
    public:
    Random() { srand(static_cast<unsigned>(time(0))); }
    unsigned get_random(int n) const { return rand() % n; }
};

#endif
```

Such a class would be very useful in gambling situations when the seeding of the random number generator should be transparent to the user.

8.4.6   A Die Class

Speaking of gambling situations, here is a class called Die that emulates a die that you would use in games of chance, such as Monopoly, or Parcheesi, or Yatzhee, or even Dungeons and Dragons, if that's your preference. It is also used in one of the exercises at the end of this chapter in which you are asked to write a program to play the game C Raps++. (Think about it.)

For complete flexibility, neither the actual nor minimum number of sides on a Die object has been "hard-coded". Instead, default values for both have been declared as static const types within the class definition, and then defined in the Die definition file (6 for the actual number of sides, and 4 for the minimum number of sides). Of course, the user is given the opportunity to override the default number of sides by passing an argument to the constructor, but cannot override the minimum number of sides. Note that if either of these two default values should ever need to be changed in the future, the public interface to the Die class will not have been affected.

Note also that an instance of the Random class called rand has been declared static in the Die class so that only *one* such instance will ever exist, even though the class Die itself will get instantiated more than once. The constructor for the rand instance will be called even before the main() function is entered. Finally, the method toss() has been declared to return a Die by reference so that function chaining can occur.

Example 8.14

```cpp
// File die.h

#ifndef DIE_H
#define DIE_H

#include "random.h"

class Die
{
   static const int def_num_sides;
      public:
   inline Die(int = def_num_sides);
   inline Die& toss();      // allows chaining
   inline int get_value() const;
      private:
   const int sides;
   int value;
   static const int def_min_sides;
   static Random rand;    // only 1 instance of Random class
   Die(const Die&);         // private copy constructor
};

inline Die::Die(int s)
                 : sides(s < def_min_sides ? def_num_sides : s)
{
   toss();
}

inline Die& Die::toss()
{
   value = rand.get_random(sides) + 1;
   return *this;
}

inline int Die::get_value() const
{
   return value;
}

#endif

// File "die.cpp"

#include "die.h"

// static definitions
const int Die::def_num_sides = 6;
const int Die::def_min_sides = 4;
Random Die::rand;
```

Notice how the `Die` constructor validity checks the number of sides requested, and guarantees that if it's less than `def_min_sides`, then the default value is used.

 Tip

The `static` *variable* `def_num_sides` *was declared before its usage in the constructor declaration even though some compilers may not deem this necessary.*

8.4.7 A `Dice` Class

From here it's easy to create a class called `Dice` that contains a variable number of `Die` objects, the default value of which is 2. There are three ways to instantiate the `dice` class:

- Use the default constructor and supply no arguments. In this case the number of dice will be 2, and each die will contain 6 sides;

- Use the default constructor and supplying one argument. In this case the number of dice will be set to the value of the argument, and each die will contain 6 sides;

- Use the constructor that takes two arguments. The first argument is the number of dice, and the second argument is the number of sides for each die.

 Tip

The constructor for dice has been overloaded to avoid repeating the default value that was specified in the `Die` *class.*

Example 8.15

```cpp
// File dice.h

#ifndef DICE_H
#define DICE_H

#include <iostream.h>
class Die;
class Dice
{
   static const int def_number;
       public:
   Dice(int num_dice = def_number);
   Dice(int num_dice, int num_sides);
   ~Dice();
   Dice& roll();
   int get_total() const;
   const Dice& display(ostream& = cout) const;
       private:
   Die** ptr;
   const int number_of_dice;
   Dice(const Dice&);   // private copy constructor
};

#endif

// File dice.cpp

#include <iostream.h>
#include "die.h"
#include "dice.h"

const int Dice::def_number = 2;

Dice::Dice(int num_dice)
     : number_of_dice(num_dice < 1 ? def_number : num_dice)
{
   ptr = new Die*[number_of_dice];
   for(int i = 0; i < number_of_dice; ++i)
     ptr[i] = new Die;
}

Dice::Dice(int num_dice, int num_sides)
     : number_of_dice(num_dice < 1 ? def_number : num_dice)
{
   ptr = new Die*[number_of_dice];
   for(int i = 0; i < number_of_dice; ++i)
     ptr[i] = new Die(num_sides);
}
```

(Continued)

```
Dice::~Dice()
{
   for(int i = number_of_dice - 1; i >= 0; --i)
     delete ptr[i] ;
   delete [] ptr;
}

Dice& Dice::roll()
{
   for(int i = 0; i < number_of_dice; ++i)
     ptr[i]->toss();
   return *this;
}

int Dice::get_total() const
{
   int total = 0;
   for(int i = 0; i < number_of_dice; ++i)
     total += ptr[i]->get_value();
   return total;
}

const Dice& Dice::display(ostream& str) const
{
   for(int i = 0; i < number_of_dice; ++i)
   {
     str << ptr[i]->get_value();
     if(i < number_of_dice -1)
        str << " + ";
   }
   str << " = " << get_total() << '\n';
   return *this;
}
```

(Continued)

```
// File main.cpp

#include <iostream.h>
#include "dice.h"

int main()
{
   const int loops = 2;
   Dice obj1;
   for(int i = 0; i < loops; ++i)
      obj1.roll().display();
   cout << "====================\n";
   Dice obj2(3);
   for(int j = 0; j < loops; ++j)
      obj2.roll().display();
   cout << "====================\n";
   Dice obj3(5 , 12);
   for(int k = 0; k < loops; ++k)
      obj3.roll().display();
   return 0;
}

/* A typical run of the program would yield:

3 + 6 = 9
2 + 5 = 7
====================
4 + 3 + 6 = 13
2 + 1 + 4 = 7
====================
12 + 2 + 1 + 10 + 8 = 33
5 + 11 + 5 + 9 + 1 = 31

*/
```

8.5   The Size of a Class

If you ever need to compute the size of a class, you may use the `sizeof` operator.
This will tell you how much space any instance of the class is occupying in the global space, on the stack, or on the heap. Just be aware that the only members that are
considered are *nonstatic data* members. In other words, functions and static data
members are *not* counted for the simple reason that they are *not* replicated for each
instantiation.

In addition, the size of a class is guaranteed to be greater than zero. In other words, all instantiated objects will have a size of at least one byte.

 Example 8.16

```
class Point
{
   int x;
   int y;
};

class Circle
{
   Point center;
   int radius;
   static const double pi;
};

#include <stdlib.h>
#include <time.h>
class Random
{
     public:
   Random() { srand((unsigned)time(0)); }
   unsigned get_random(int n) const { return rand() % n; }
};

#include <iostream.h>

int main()
{
   cout << "size of class Circle = " << sizeof(Circle) << '\n';
   cout << "size of class Random = " << sizeof(Random) << '\n';
   return 0;
}

/* The output of this program is:

size of class Circle = 6
size of class Random = 1

*/
```

 Tip

This definition of the size of a class will be modified slightly in Chapter 10 when virtual functions are introduced.

8.6   Friend Functions /* not recommended by teacher to be used */

provide access to private variables

As you know, because of encapsulation and the principle of data hiding, the only functions that have unrestricted access to a class's private members are the member functions of that particular class. Any attempt by a non-member function to directly access these data members (read or write) will result in a compilation error.

However, there are several circumstances in which a *non-member* function must have access to these private members. The easy way to do this would be to change the access category from `private` to `public`, but then this completely violates the whole concept of encapsulation and data hiding. So what can you do?

This dilemma can be solved by declaring the function in question to be a *friend* of the class in which the private data members are located. That is, *the class in which the private members are located bestows friendship upon the function*, not the other way around. In this fashion, the friend function then has access to *all* of the class's members, including the private and protected ones. Remember, the function itself *cannot* choose to become a friend of a class ("I choose to be your friend; therefore, I now have complete and unlimited access to your private members"), because this would make no sense and violate the principle of data hiding.

While a class also may grant friendship to a member function of another class, this situation is very rarely done, and is more easily handled by friend classes, as shown in the next section.

8.6.1   How a Class Grants Friendship to a Function

A class grants friendship to a global function by specifying the function's declaration inside the class's definition, preceding the declaration with the keyword `friend`. This keyword cannot ever be written outside a class definition.

For example, here the class `Complex` is granting friendship to the global function called `add()`.

    Example 8.17

```
class Complex
{
    inline friend Complex add(const Complex&, const Complex&);
    // Other details omitted
};
```

It only makes sense that the global function receives at least one argument of the class type. Otherwise, how could it possibly gain access to the private or protected non-static parts of the class (since there is no `this` pointer)? Also, it should be obvious that access specifiers in the class (`public`, `protected`, `private`) have *no bearing whatsoever* on a friend declaration because they only pertain to *members* of the class. The convention used in the book will be to declare all friends first.

Note that a friend function may also be an inline function. That is, if the friend function is defined completely within the scope of the class definition, then the inline request to the compiler is automatically made. If the friend function is defined outside the class definition and within the header file, then you must precede the return type with the keyword `inline` in order to make the request. The keyword `friend` is *never* allowed to appear outside a class definition.

Perhaps you're wondering why the `add()` function wasn't declared to be a member of the `Complex` class in the first place, thereby negating the need to make it a nonmember function, let alone a friend function. Since `add()` is just an emulation of the '+' operator, the answer gets into issues involving the commutative rule of arithmetic and implicit type conversion. This is discussed in detail in the next Chapter when you will learn how to overload operators.

Having said that, let's continue by writing the complete definition of the `Complex` class.

 Example 8.18

```
// File complex.h

#ifndef COMPLEX_H
#define COMPLEX_H

#include <iostream.h>

class Complex
{
   inline friend Complex add(const Complex& obj1,
                             const Complex& obj2);
      public:
   Complex(int r = 0, int i = 0) : real(r), imag(i) {}
   inline void display(ostream& = cout) const;
      private:
   int real;
   int imag;
};

inline Complex add(const Complex& obj1, const Complex& obj2)
{
   return
   Complex(obj1.real + obj2.real, obj1.imag + obj2.imag);
}

inline void Complex::display(ostream& str) const
{
   str << real << " + " << imag << "i\n";
}

#endif
```

(Continued)

```
// File main.cpp

#include "complex.h"

int main()
{
   Complex obj1(1, 2);
   Complex obj2(3, 4);
   Complex obj3(add(obj1, obj2));
   obj3.display();
   Complex obj4(2, -7);
   obj3 = add(6, obj4);
   obj3.display();
   return 0;
}

/* The output of this program is:

4 + 6i
8 + -7i

*/
```

Now, you could certainly make the argument that while the add() function should be a nonmember, it doesn't necessarily have to be a friend if a suitable public interface had been provided. Well, is this correct for the Complex class? Maybe, and maybe not. It all depends on whether you deem it appropriate to give your users access to the private members real and imag via constant methods. Think about it. What should the users be doing with Complex numbers? Perhaps adding them, subtracting them, displaying them, etc. Is it really necessary to let them get at the data members? But if you're not convinced, then I'll concede the point and rewrite the class with this public interface included. Now the add() function no longer needs the friendship.

Example 8.19

```cpp
// File complex.h

#ifndef COMPLEX_H
#define COMPLEX_H

#include <iostream.h>

class Complex
{
     public:
  Complex(int r = 0, int i = 0) : real(r), imag(i) {}
  int get_real() const { return real; }
  int get_imag() const { return imag; }
  void display(ostream& = cout) const;
     private:
  int real;
  int imag;
};

inline Complex add(const Complex& obj1, const Complex& obj2)
{
  return Complex(obj1.get_real() + obj2.get_real(),
                 obj1.get_imag() + obj2.get_imag());
}

inline void Complex::display(ostream& str) const
{
  str << real << " + " << imag << "i\n";
}

#endif

// File main.cpp

#include "complex.h"

int main()
{
  Complex obj1(1, 2);
  Complex obj2(3, 4);
  Complex obj3(add(obj1, obj2));
  obj3.display();
  Complex obj4(2, -7);
  obj3 = add(6, obj4);
  obj3.display();
  return 0;
}

/* The output of this program is:

4 + 6i
8 + -7i

*/
```

8.7   Friend Classes

Sometimes it's necessary for a class to grant friendship to another class. This means that each member function of the class receiving the friendship is inherently a friend function of the first class.

Now, why would you want to do this? The situation occurs when there is naturally a tight relationship between the two classes. That is, the class receiving the friendship needs the services of the class granting the friendship, and it is the only class that needs these services.

For example, consider a linked list class. Typically such a class contains objects called nodes that are chained together via a pointer, and the class has only to keep track of and manage these nodes. Since the nodes in and of themselves constitute a class that exists expressly for the use of the linked list class and no one else, it makes sense to grant friendship.

To have the `Node` class grant friendship to the `List` class, the C++ code would be something like this:

 Example 8.20

```
class Node
{
   friend class List;
   // Other details omitted
};
```

Here are both classes. Even though there is a close relationship between the two, the `Node` class has provided `set_next()` and `get_next()` methods that set and return the private data member `next`. Thus, the methods in the `List` class do not ever need to directly access any of the private data members of `Node`.

 Caution

A friend of a friend is not a friend. Say what? This means that in the next example, if the `List` class grants friendship to another function or to another class, then this new friend would not be a friend of the `Node` class. After all, isn't this the way it is in real life?

Example 8.21

```cpp
// File node.h

#ifndef NODE_H
#define NODE_H

#include <iostream.h>

class Node
{
   friend class List;
   friend inline bool equal(const Node&, const Node&);
      public:
   void set_next(Node* n) { next = n; }
   Node* get_next() const { return next; }
      private:
   int data;
   Node* next;
   Node(int n = 0) : data(n), next(0) {}
   void display(ostream& str) const { str << data << '\n'; }
};

inline bool equal(const Node& n1, const Node& n2)
{
   return n1.data == n2.data;
}

#endif

// File list.h

#ifndef LIST_H
#define LIST_H

class Node;
class List
{
      public:
   List();
   List(int);
   ~List();
   void add(int);
   bool remove(int);
   void display(ostream& = cout) const;
      private:
   Node* head;
   Node* tail;
};

#endif
```

(Continued)

```cpp
// File list.cpp

#include "list.h"
#include "node.h"

// Construct an empty List object
List::List() : head(0), tail(0) {}

// Construct one Node object from an int
List::List(int n) : head(0), tail(0)
{
   add(n);
}

// Delete all Nodes from the List object
List::~List()
{
   Node* p = head;
   while(p != 0)
   {
      Node* temp = p->get_next();
      delete p;
      p = temp;
   }
}

// Add a new Node to the List
void List::add(int value)
{
   // Make the int into a Node object
   Node* n = new Node(value);

   // If this is the first node to be created, its
   // address becomes the head
   if(!head)
      head = n;
   // Otherwise, it's not the first node and the tail
   // must point to the node being added
   else
      tail->set_next(n);

   // The new node is now the tail
   tail = n;
}
```

(Continued)

```
// Delete a Node from the List. Return true if successful
bool List::remove(int value)
{
   // Make the int into a Node object
   Node* temp = new Node(value);
   // Start searching at the head
   Node* current = head;
   // Pointer to the previous Node
   Node* prev = 0;
   // Search as long as the current pointer points to a
   // Node and no match has yet been found
   bool flag = false;
   while(current && !flag)
   {
      if(equal(*current, *temp))
      {
         // For a match, if it's the head, then the second Node
         // becomes the new head
         if(current == head)
            head = head->get_next();
         else
         {
            // If it's not the head, then link the previous and
            // next Nodes
            Node* n = current->get_next();
            prev->set_next(n);
         }
         // If a match was found on the tail, the previous
         // Node becomes the new tail
         if(current == tail)
            tail = prev;
         // Release the space for the Node
         delete current;
         flag = true;
      }
      // Since no match was found, remember the current
      // position, and go to the next Node
      else
      {
         prev = current;
         current = current->get_next();
      }
   }
   delete temp;
   return flag;
}
```

(Continued)

```cpp
// Print the data from all of the nodes in the list
void List::display(ostream& str) const
{
   str << "The list:\n";
   Node* p = head;
   while(p != 0)
   {
      p->display(str);
      p = p->get_next();
   }
   str << "==========\n";
}

// File main.cpp

#include <iostream.h>
#include "list.h"

int main()
{
   List my_list;
   for(int i = 0; i < 4; ++i)
      my_list.add(i);
   my_list.display();
   for(int j = 0; j < 4; j += 2)
      if(my_list.remove(j))
         cout << j << " removed\n";
   my_list.display();
   return 0;
}

/* The output of this program is:

The list:
0
1
2
3
==========
0 removed
2 removed
The list:
1
3
==========

*/
```

8.8   Nesting of Class Definitions

One class definition may be literally nested within the definition of another class as a way to avoid having inner class grant friendship to the outer class. In the linked list example above, this means that the definition of the Node class is contained within the definition of the List class. In order to emulate the friendship, the Node class is really a structure so that all of its members are available to the List class. But at the same time, the Node class resides within the private part of the List class so that only members of the List class have access to it.

This is how the class definitions would appear.

 Example 8.22

```cpp
// File list.h

#ifndef LIST_H
#define LIST_H

#include <iostream.h>

class List
{
    public:
  List();
  List(int);
  ~List();
  void add(int);
  bool remove(int);
  void display(ostream& = cout) const;
    private:
  struct Node
  {
    friend bool equal(const Node& n1, const Node& n2)
      { return n1.data == n2.data; }
    void set_next(Node* n) { next = n; }
    Node* get_next() const { return next; }
    int data;
    Node* next;
    Node(int n = 0) : data(n), next(0) {}
    void display(ostream& str) const {str << data << '\n';}
  };
  Node* head;
  Node* tail;
};

#endif
```

8.9   Operator Conversion Functions

An operator conversion function is the second example of a User-Defined Conversion function (UDC). Recall that the first UDC was the constructor whose purpose is to convert *from* some fundamental or user-defined type *into* a user-defined type. An operator conversion function is just the opposite of a constructor in the sense that its purpose is to convert *from* some user-defined type *into* some fundamental or other user-defined type.

8.9.1   Syntax

■ Its name is the keyword `operator` followed by the type to which the conversion is to be made;

■ No formal arguments are allowed;

■ It should be declared `const` to support constant invoking objects;

■ No return type can be written. The reason is that the name of the function itself implies the return type.

Of course, the type cannot be identical to the class of which it is a member, nor can it be type `void` (but `void*` is allowed).

8.9.2   Purpose

One purpose of an operator conversion function is to provide a friendly interface to the user of a class by allowing the user to write an instance name where the compiler would normally expect to find the name of a fundamental type.

For example, the `String` class might provide an operator conversion function to allow the user to use an instance in conjunction with the insertion operator. Of course, there is no insertion operator in the iostream library that can accommodate a `String` object, but in this case the compiler is smart enough to implicitly convert the object into whatever value is stored in the variable `ptr`, which is a `char*` type, and this certainly can be handled by an iostream method. While it doesn't buy you much, you may explicitly invoke the operator conversion function just like any other method of a class.

Example 8.23

```
#include <iostream.h>

class String
{
     public:
   operator const char*() const { return ptr; }
   // Other details omitted
     private:
   char* ptr;
};

void foo(const String& obj)
{
   cout << obj << '\n'; // Invoke operator conversion function
   cout << obj.operator const char*() << '\n';  // Ditto
}
```

Another purpose of an operator conversion function is to provide the user with an easy way to check the status of an object. That is, the user can write the name of an instance any place where the compiler would normally expect to find a bool expression. In this case, the compiler will automatically search for an operator conversion function that returns a bool type, or a type that can be converted into type bool. Typically, if the condition evaluates to 'true', it would imply that a stable object exists, whereas a zero result would represent an unstable object.

For example, the cin object (the keyboard) will put itself into a "fail state" if an unexpected bit pattern is encountered, such as non-numeric input when numeric is required. By testing the cin object itself, you can determine whether it has entered this fail state.

Example 8.24

```
// File main.cpp

#include <iostream.h>

int main()
{
   cout << "Enter an integer: ";
   int data ;
   while(!(cin >> data).eof())
   {
      if(cin)  // Invoke operator conversion function
         // Good data was entered
      else
         // Handle the error
      cout << "Next integer: ";
   }
   return 0;
}
```

When the compiler detects the use of `cin` in the `if` statement above, it will automatically invoke the operator conversion function in class `istream` (inherited from class `ios`). This is how it is written.

 Example 8.25

```
ios::operator void*()
{
   return fail() ? 0 : this;
}
```

The call to `fail()` will return `true` if `cin` is in a fail state, thereby making the function return the value zero (`false`). If `cin` is not in a fail state, the function will return the value of the `this` pointer, which is certainly the equivalent of `true`. In addition, note that this function returns type `void*` instead of type `bool` in order to prevent the user from writing meaningless arithmetic statements involving `cin`, which would then compile successfully. Nevertheless, type `void*` is still convertible to type `bool`, so the `if` statement compiles successfully.

 Caution

If you provide more than one operator conversion function, each of which returns a `bool` type, then the compiler will not know which one to choose, and the call will be ambiguous.

8.10 Introduction to Pointers to Class Members

Suppose you have a class that contains various public functions to do a variety of tasks. Instead of executing these tasks as they are encountered, you need to queue them up in an array or linked list for execution at a later time. One way to "remember" which member function is to be called would be to store the address of that function in an array or linked list. Then, later on in the program, the array or linked list would be traversed and the appropriate function executed.

Obviously, what is needed in this scenario is the ability to create a pointer to a class method. Just as you can declare pointers to non-class variables and functions, you can declare pointers to the individual function members of a class. The syntax, however, is a little different than what you are accustomed to using. The main difference is that such a pointer must always be qualified with the name of the class to which it pertains. This implies that a pointer-to-function of some class A can never be the same type as a pointer-to-function of some class B, even if the functions themselves take the same argument list and have the same return type.

8.10.1 Pointers to Global Functions

Ignoring classes for the moment, let's do a quick review of pointers to global functions. A pointer to a function called `ptr_function` that takes a `float` as its one argument and returns an `int` would be declared as:

 Example 8.26

```
int (*ptr_function)(float);
```

If you wish, you may use a `typedef` to simplify the code.

 Example 8.27

```
typedef int (*Ptr)(float);    // Ptr is a type
Ptr ptr_function;
```

If you have a function `f()` that does indeed take a `float` and return an `int`, you may store its address into the pointer variable. Since the name of a function without parentheses always yields the address of that function, the address-of ('&') operator is optional. When it's time to invoke the function, you may use the pre-ANSI-style of enclosing the pointer variable within parentheses, preceded by the dereferencing operator, or you may use the ANSI-style of just writing the pointer variable. Of course, both styles then specify the actual arguments, if any.

Example 8.28

```
typedef int (*Ptr)(float);      // Ptr is a type
int f(float);

void g()
{
   Ptr ptr_function = f;
   int x = (*ptr_function)(2.345);   // pre-ANSI-style
   int y = ptr_function(2.345);      // ANSI-style
}
```

8.10.2   Pointers to Class Member Functions

Now let's do the same thing for a class member function. First, in order to create a pointer-to-member-function variable of some class X, you must qualify the pointer name with the class name and scope resolution operator.

Example 8.29

```
int (X::*ptr_function)(float);
```

Once again, you may use a `typedef`.

Example 8.30

```
typedef int (X::*Ptr)(float);      // Ptr is a type
Ptr ptr_function;
```

To take the address of a class member function called X::f(), you must qualify the function name with the class name and scope resolution operator. And unlike a global function, the use of the '&' is *mandatory*. In addition, the member must have public access if its address is being taken by a function other than a member function.

Example 8.31

```
ptr_function = &X::f;   // & is mandatory
```

8.10.3   Invoking Functions Using Pointers to Class Members

Creating a pointer-to-member-function is only half the story. In order to provide a `this` pointer, all nonstatic member functions of a class still need to be invoked by an instance or pointer of the class to which they belong. However, in this case a new C++ operator is needed.

■   If you want to use an instance of the class to call the member function through the pointer, then the instance must be followed with the operator '.*' (dot-star).

■   If you want to use a pointer of the class to call the member function through the pointer, then the pointer must be followed with the operator '->*' (arrow-star).

■   Be sure to enclose the instance or pointer name, the operator itself, and the function name in one set of parentheses. This is then followed by the actual argument list.

Note the similarity to calling non-member functions using the dot or arrow operators, only now you add an asterisk.

Here is a simple program that uses pointers to class members.

    Example 8.32

```
// File x.h

#ifndef X_H
#define X_H

#include <iostream.h>

class X
{
    public:
    inline int f(float n);
};

inline int X::f(float n)
{
    cout << "number = " << n << '\n';
    return n;
}

#endif
```

(Continued)

```
// File main.cpp

#include "x.h"
int main()
{
   // Create pointer to function
   int (X::*ptr_function)(float);

   // Use a typedef
   typedef int (X::*Ptr)(float);
   Ptr ptr_func;

   // Store address of function f() into both pointers
   ptr_function = ptr_func = &X::f;

   // Create an instance
   X x;
   // Call function f() directly
   int n1 = x.f(1.1);
   cout << "n1 = " << n1 << '\n';

   // Call the function f() with an instance of the class
   int n2 = (x.*ptr_function)(2.2);
   cout << "n2 = " << n2 << '\n';
   int n3 = (x.*ptr_func)(3.3);
   cout << "n3 = " << n3 << '\n';

   // Store the address of the instance into a pointer
   // to the instance
   X* ptr_X = &x;

   // Call function f() with a pointer to the class
   int n4 = (ptr_X->*ptr_function)(4.4);
   cout << "n4 = " << n4 << '\n';
   int n5 = (ptr_X->*ptr_func)(5.5);
   cout << "n5 = " << n5 << '\n';
   return 0;
}

/* The output of this program is:

number = 1.1
n1 = 1
number = 2.2
n2 = 2
number = 3.3
n3 = 3
number = 4.4
n4 = 4
number = 5.5
n5 = 5

*/
```

Here is another example, but now a member function takes as an argument a pointer to another member function. In order to call the function that the pointer points at, the invoking instance, as specified by the `this` pointer, must be used.

 Example 8.33

```
// File x.h

#ifndef X_H
#define X_H

#include <iostream.h>

class X
{
   typedef void (X::*Ptr)(int);
      public:
   // f1 is a function that takes 2 arguments:
   // 1) A pointer to a member function that takes an
   //    int as its one argument, and returns void
   // 2) An int

   void f1(Ptr ptr, int n)
   {
      // Call the function pointed at by ptr, using 'n'
      // as the one argument
      (this ->* ptr)(n);
   }

   // f2 is a function that takes an int as its one
   // argument, and returns void

   void f2(int n)
   {
      cout << "X::f2 called with " << n << '\n';
   }
};

#endif
```

(Continued)

```
// File main.cpp

#include "x.h"

int main()
{
   X x;

   // Call f1() passing it 2 arguments:
   //    1) The address of f2
   //    2) The constant 1

   x.f1(&X::f2, 1);
   return 0;
}

/* The output of this program is:

X::f2 called with 1

*/
```

If the member function is declared `static`, then for purposes of declaring a pointer to it, you must treat it as a non-member function. For instance, in this example the member function `X::f()` is `static`.

 Example 8.34

```
// File x.h

#ifndef X_H
#define X_H

#include <iostream.h>

class X
{
     public:
   inline static int f(float n);
};

inline int X::f(float n)
{
   cout << "number = " << n << '\n';
   return n;
}

#endif
```

(Continued)

```
// File main.cpp

#include <iostream.h>
#include "x.h"

int main()
{
    // Create pointer to function and initialize
    int (*ptr_function)(float) = &X::f;

    // Call the function directly
    int n1 = X::f(1.2);
    cout << "n1 = " << n1 << '\n';

    // Call the function using a pointer
    // to function
    int n2 = (*ptr_function)(3.4);
    cout << "n2 = " << n2 << '\n';

    return 0;
}

/* The output of this program is:

number = 1.2
n1 = 1
number = 3.4
n2 = 3

*/
```

8.10.4   How to Write a Callback Using Pointers-to-Class-Members

A *callback* is a programming idiom in which a client registers itself with a server so that when some future event occurs, and the server gains control, it can then call back the client. In the C language, without the use of objects, this can be achieved by having the address of a function passed as an argument to another function, so that when the latter function gains control, it can call back the first function via the pointer it received.

In C++, the same effect can be gotten by having both an object and the address of some method in the object passed as arguments to a completely different object.

To illustrate a generic case of this, in the following example, when the Server class is instantiated in main(), its constructor receives a Client object and the address of the methods Client::callback(). Then, when the Server class receives the start() message, it's easy to call back the Client::callback() method.

Example 8.35

```
// File client.h

#ifndef CLIENT_H
#define CLIENT_H

#include <iostream.h>
class Client
{
        public:
   void callback() { cout << "Called back\n"; }
};

#endif

// File server.h

#ifndef SERVER_H
#define SERVER_H

#include "client.h"

class Server
{
   typedef void (Client::*Ptr)();
        public:
   Server(Client& ref, Ptr ptr)
                       : ref_obj(ref), ptr_mem(ptr) {}

   void start() { (ref_obj.*ptr_mem)(); }
        private:
   Client& ref_obj;
   Ptr ptr_mem;
};

#endif
```

(Continued)

```
// File main.cpp

#include "client.h"
#include "server.h"

int main()
{
   Client client;
   Server server(client, &Client::callback);
   server.start();
   return 0;
}

/* The output of this program is:

Called back

*/
```

In Chapter 11 you will see another example of a callback, but this time the server class will be much more generic so that it can accommodate any type of client.

8.11   Unions

Recall from C that a union is a kind of structure whose members all begin at offset zero and whose size is sufficient to hold the largest member. In other words, all members of a union occupy the same memory location once the union is instantiated.

In C++ a union may have member functions, including constructors and a destructor (but no virtual functions are allowed). It is illegal to have as a member of a union an instance of another class that contains either a constructor, destructor, or user-defined assignment operator. In addition, a member of a union cannot be declared static.

A union may be anonymous. This means that it declares an unnamed object within the scope of a class. The members of this union must have names distinct from the other names within the class and may be referenced directly. The access specifier of the members of an anonymous union may not be private or protected. Also, unlike a "normal" union, an anonymous union may not have member functions.

Consider the following situation. You wish to examine the bits of a floating point number (stored in IEEE format) in order to display them in some meaningful representation. The problem here is that the bitwise operators cannot be used on floating point data types. Therefore, by using an anonymous union containing both a float and a long, you can "trick" the compiler into thinking that it is operating upon a long data type, whereas in fact it is really operating upon the float.

The following example shows how this can be done.

 Example 8.36

```
// File ieee.h

#ifndef IEEE_H
#define IEEE_H

#include <iostream.h>
#include <math.h>

const int bits = 8;
const int size = bits * sizeof(float);

class IEEE
{
     public:
  IEEE(float = 0.0);
  int input();
  void print();
     private:
  int sign_bit, exp, digit;
  double man;
  unsigned long mask;
  const int sign_start;
  const int exp_start, exp_end;
  const int man_start;
  void sign();
  void exponent(int);
  void mantissa(int);
  void results();
  // Anonymous union
  union
  {
    float fl;
    long number;
  };
};

#endif
```

(Continued)

```cpp
// File ieee.cpp

#include "ieee.h"

IEEE::IEEE(float n)
      : fl(n), exp(0), man(0.0), mask(1L << size - 1),
        sign_start(0), exp_start(1), exp_end(8),
        man_start(9) {}

int IEEE::input()
{
   cout << "Enter the float value: ";
   return (cin >> fl).eof();
}

void IEEE::print()
{
   for(int i = 0; i < size; ++i)
   {
      digit = (number & mask) ? 1 : 0;
      if(i == sign_start)
         sign();
      else if(i >= exp_start && i <= exp_end)
         exponent(i);
      else
         mantissa(i);
      number <<= 1;
   }
   results();
}
void IEEE::sign()
{
   cout << digit;
   sign_bit = digit;
}

void IEEE::exponent(int i)
{
   if(i == exp_start)
   {
      cout << '-';
      exp = 0;
   }
   cout << digit;
   exp = (exp * 2) + digit;
}
```

(Continued)

```cpp
void IEEE::mantissa(int i)
{
   if(i == man_start)
   {
      cout << '-';
      man = 0.0;
   }
   cout << digit;
   man += digit / pow(2, i - 8);
}

void IEEE::results()
{
   double result;
   cout << "\n\nExponent: " << exp << '\n';
   cout << "Mantissa: " << man << '\n';
   result = (1 + man) * (pow(2, exp - 127));
   if(sign_bit == 1)
      result = -result;
   cout << "Original value: " << result << '\n';
}

// File main.cpp

#include "ieee.h"

int main()
{
   IEEE number;
   while(number.input() == false)
      number.print();
   return 0;
}

/* A typical run would be:

Enter the float value: -1.2
1-01111111-00110011001100110011010

Exponent: 127
Mantissa: 0.2000000477
Original value: -1.200000047683716

Enter the float value: 8.0
0-10000010-00000000000000000000000

Exponent: 130
Mantissa: 0.0000000000
Original value: 8.000000000000000

Enter the float value: ^Z

*/
```

Review Questions

1. Explain how the pointer `this` works.

2. What is `*this`?

3. Explain how nonstatic member function calls can be concatenated together.

4. What is a static data member of a class? Why would you use one?

5. What is a static member function?

6. Why can't a static member function access a nonstatic member of a class?

7. What is a friend function, and why is it needed?

8. How is friendship granted by a class?

9. Why does a friend function need to take as an input argument at least one instance of the class bestowing the friendship?

10. Explain how a pointer to a member function works.

11. Explain how a union works.

 Exercise 8.1

Given the following class definition that emulates a fractional number:

```
class Fraction
{
  // All friend functions
      public:
  // All member functions
      private:
  long num;     // numerator
  long den;     // denominator
};
```

declare within the function definition and define outside the definition:

- An inline constructor that accepts zero, one or two arguments. The numerator defaults to zero, while the denominator defaults to 1. If one argument is specified, assume that it represents the numerator. Use only the member initialization list to construct the instance. If the denominator is equal to zero, change it to a 1. Be sure to maintain the fraction in its reduced form by factoring out the greatest common denominator, which can be obtained by calling the following global function.

```
long gcd(long x, long y)
{
   return (x == 0L) ? y : gcd(y % x, x);
}
```

- An inline copy constructor. Use only the member initialization list to construct the instance.

- A method called `print()` that displays the fraction.

- A friend function called `add()` that returns the sum of two fractions.

- A friend function called `subtract()` that returns the difference of two fractions.

- A friend function called `multiply()` that returns the product of two fractions.

- A friend function called `divide()` that returns the quotient of the first fraction divided by the second fraction.

- An inline function called `inc()` that adds 1 to the invoking instance. Be sure to use the `add()` function and to allow for function chaining.

Use the following `main()` function:

```
int main()
{
    Fraction f1;
    Fraction f2(2L, 0L);
    Fraction f3(f2);
    f1.print();
    f2.print();
    f3.print();
    f3 = add(f3, Fraction(-5, 4));
    f1 = add(f2, f3);
    f1.print();
    f1 = sub(f2, f3);
    f1.print();
    f1 = mult(f2, f3);
    f1.print();
    f1.inc().inc().print();
    f1 = div(f2, f3);
    f1.print();
    return 0;
}

/* The output of this program is:

0/1
2/1
2/1
11/4
5/4
3/2
7/2
8/3

*/
```

 Exercise 8.2

Write a class called `Date` whose purpose is to convert a month and day into the absolute day of the year, ranging from 1 to 365. An operator conversion function within the class must perform the actual conversion. As part of the class, include a static table that contains the number of days in each of the 12 months. Then write the `main()` function that loops and prompts the user for a month and a day. If the constructor detects that an invalid date is entered, exit from the program.

Ignore leap year, but be sure to have the constructor check the month and day for valid data. If invalid data is found, then exit the program.

Write a `main()` function to test your class by having the terminal operator interactively enter various months and days until end-of-file is encountered.

Exercise 8.3

Write a program that plays a dice game called C Raps++. (Note: Any resemblance to the dice game craps is purely coincidental.) This game consists of 3 sub-games, any one of which you may choose to play.

■ Pass Line—In this game you roll the dice (called the come-out roll) and look at the total. If this total is equal to 7 or 11, then you win the amount of the bet. If the total is equal to 2, 3 or 12, then you lose the bet. Any other total of the dice becomes the "point", and you continue to roll the dice until you either (a) roll the point total again, in which case you win the amount of the bet, or (b) roll a total of 7, in which case you lose the amount of the bet. If the total of the dice is not 7 and not equal to the point, then you roll again, and continue to roll, until either condition (a) or (b) is met. Note that once the point has been determined, it does not change for subsequent rolls of the dice.

■ Field Bet—In this game you roll the dice just once. If this total is 3, 4, 9, 10 or 11, then you win the amount of the bet. If the total is 2, then you win double the bet. If this total is 12, then you win triple the bet. For any other total of the dice (5, 6, 7, or 8), you lose the amount of the bet.

■ Any 7—In this game you roll the dice just once. If this total is equal to 7, then you win quadruple the bet. For any other total of the dice, you lose the amount of the bet.

At the minimum, include classes for the following objects:
■ Pass Line sub-game
■ Field Bet sub-game
■ Any 7 sub-game
■ Random number generator
■ Die
■ Dice
■ Bankroll
■ Player
■ C Raps++ game

The Player class contains an instance of the Bankroll class, and the C Raps++ class contains instances of the Pass Line, Field Bet, Any 7, Player and Dice classes. The C Raps++ constructor must initialize each sub-game object (Pass Line, Field Bet, and Any 7) with the Player and Dice objects.

To determine which sub-game the player wishes to play, the C Raps++ class must display a menu of choices, as follows:

(P)ass Line
(F)ield bet
(A)ny 7
(E)xit

Before the start of each sub-game, display the amount of money in the player's bankroll. Then display a prompt to enter an (integer) bet. If this bet amount is greater than what is currently in the player's bankroll, or is less than or equal to zero, display an error message and re-prompt.

At the end of each sub-game, display what the outcome is, and update the player's bankroll accordingly.

Play continues until you choose Exit, or run out of money. At this time have the player display either his or her net gain, net loss, or a break-even message for this session at the C Raps++ table.

The `main()` function should appear as follows:

```
int main()
{
    const int start = 100;    // Starting bankroll amount
    C_raps game(start);
    game.prompt();
    return 0;
}
```

 Exercise 8.4

Using the `Card` class from Chapter 7, write three member functions: `get_suit()` that returns the value of `suit`, `get_rank()` that returns the value of `rank`, and `display()` that translates `suit` and `rank` into meaningful verbiage, e.g., "The Four of Hearts". Also write a friend function called `equal()` that returns `true` if its two input card instances are equal.

Next, write a class called `Deck_of_cards` whose private data members consist of a 52-position array of pointers to card and an integer called `cards_in_use` that reflects the number of cards that have been dealt. Also include an instance of the random number generator class. The constructor must allocate space for the cards themselves from the heap, and provide the proper initialization for a standard deck. Write a mutator function that shuffles the deck and optionally displays a message, an accessor function that obtains a pointer to the next card in the deck, and an accessor function that returns the number of cards that have been dealt.

To test all classes, write a program that instantiates the deck of cards, shuffles it, and deals out all 52 cards. Also, prove that all 52 cards have been dealt.

Exercise 8.5

Using the classes `Card` and `Deck_of_cards` that were developed in Exercise #4, write a program that empirically determines the chances of obtaining at least one exact match if the top cards of two decks are turned over one at a time until both decks are completely dealt. Be sure to use a friend function called `equal()` to do the comparison of the cards. Run 10,000 tests to obtain a good statistical average.

 Exercise 8.6

Using the classes `Card` and `Deck_of_cards` that were developed in Exercise #4, write a program that plays a game called Simple Bridge. In this game four players, North, South, East and West, each receive 13 cards. Each hand is valued according to the following scheme:

Ace:	4 points
King:	3 points
Queen:	2 points
Jack:	1 point
Anything else:	0 points

You must create a new class called `Hand` that contains an array of 13 cards, and a count of the number of cards currently in use. You should have member functions to initialize the hand, store a card into the next available array element, display the entire hand, and get the point total of the hand.

The `main()` function should contain an instance of the `Deck_of_cards` class and a 4-element array consisting of the `Hand` class. Elements 0 and 2 of this array comprise the North-South team, and elements 1 and 3 comprise the East-West team. After dealing out the four hands, show each hand followed by the total points in that hand. Then add the North-South points together, and the East-West points together, and show these totals. Whichever team has the higher total should be declared the winner of the hand.

 Exercise 8.7

Using the classes `Card` and `Deck_of_cards` that were developed in Exercise #4, write a program that plays the card game Blackjack (also known as "21"). You, as the player, will be competing against the computer (the dealer). The player starts with some initial amount of money as the bankroll.

In this game you are dealt 2 cards, and the dealer 2 cards, but you are only able to see one of the dealer's cards. The object of the game is to draw cards from the deck so that the total of the cards comes as close to 21 as possible without going over 21. Each card counts at its own face value, except that picture cards count as 10 and aces count as either 1 or 11. To determine what value to give to an ace, use this rule: if the total of all cards is less than 12, then add 10 to the total.

If your or the dealer's original 2 cards total 21, then that hand ends immediately with a winner (called Blackjack), unless both of you have 21, in which case it is a draw and no money is exchanged. Any other time a total of 21 is reached, it is *not* considered to be a Blackjack.

You have the first choice to receive additional cards ("hits"). If you go over 21, then you lose your bet and that hand is over. If you choose to receive no more cards ("stand"), then the dealer *must* draw cards until the total reaches 17 or higher. If the dealer goes over 21, then you win the hand. Otherwise, the dealer's total is compared against your total, and whoever has the higher total wins. If the totals are equal, then it is a draw.

If your first 2 cards total either 10 or 11, then you have the option to "double down", which means that the amount of the bet is automatically doubled (assuming that the money is in the bank account), and you will receive *exactly one more card*, after which it becomes the dealer's turn. (In this case it is impossible for you to go "bust".) Of course, you may choose *not* to double down, in which case you have the normal option to hit or stand.

At the minimum, include classes for the following objects:

- Bankroll
- Random number generator
- Card
- Deck of cards
- Hand
- Player
- Dealer
- Blackjack

Both the `Player` and `Dealer` classes contain instances of the `Hand` class. The `Player` has an instance of the `Bankroll` class. (Assume that the dealer has unlimited funds.) The `Blackjack` class contains instances of the `Deck`, `Dealer` and `Player` classes.

The `main()` function should appear as follows:

```cpp
int main()
{
   const int start = 100;// Starting bankroll amount
   Blackjack game(start);
   game.prompt();
   return 0;
}
```

Chapter 9

Function Overloading

9.1 Introduction

Because the concept of function overloading is so fundamental to the C++ language, it has been impossible to ignore up to now. The first real use of it came in Chapter 7 when you saw how it was possible to write more than one constructor in a class. With the power of function overloading you can write more than one function having the same name. This frees the user of your program from having to remember many different function names that essentially do the same task.

The term "function overloading" itself means the ability to declare more than one function with the same name at the same scope. The compiler distinguishes one function from another by examining the formal argument lists, and noting differences in the number of arguments and their types.

9.1.1 Some Examples of Overloading

For example, all of the functions at the global scope, and all of the functions at the two different class scopes have been overloaded and are distinct from each other.

Example 9.1

```
int f();
int f(int);
int f(char);
int f(int, int);

class X
{
   int f();
   int f(int);
   int f(char);
   int f(int, int);
};

class Y
{
   int f();
   int f(int);
   int f(char);
   int f(int, int);
};
```

 Tip

Shortly you will see how you can overload two member functions that differ only in the sense that one is a mutator and the other is constant. A good use of this feature will be shown later in this chapter.

9.2   Return Type is Ignored

The return type of the function is always ignored when the compiler does overloading resolution. The reason for this is quite simple. In the following example the compiler has no idea which f() to choose. In point of fact, just the mere declaration of any function called f() after the first declaration has been seen causes a compilation error.

Example 9.2

```
int f();
char f();    // Redeclaration error
void f();    // Redeclaration error

void g()
{
    f();     // Which f() to call?
}
```

9.3   Avoid Ambiguity

As mentioned above, the determination as to which overloaded function is selected at compile-time depends primarily on the number and type(s) of the argument(s) that are supplied in the actual call of the function. Your first job is to ensure that the overloaded functions you write are sufficiently distinct from each other, according to the rules set forth below.

9.3.1   Pass-by-Value vs. Pass-by-Reference

The first step in writing an overloaded function is to ensure that no other function exists in that scope with an argument list that is identical or simply too similar to the argument list of some other function. A pass-by-value can be differentiated from a pass-by-reference, but a call may or may not be ambiguous because both functions can receive a modifiable argument, but only the pass-by-value can receive a non-modifiable argument, such as a constant.

 Example 9.3

```
void f(int);
void f(int&);    // OK; overloading

void g(int x)
{
    f(x);    // Ambiguous
    f(0);    // OK; calls f(int)
}
```

9.3.2   Qualifying a Pass-by-Value

Also, a pass-by-value cannot be differentiated if a `const`/`volatile` modifier is added to the argument. However, in this case the second declaration is simply considered to be a redeclaration of the first, and no error is generated.

 Example 9.4

```
void f(int);
void f(const int);    // Redeclaration; no overloading

void g(int);
void g(volatile int);    // Redeclaration; no overloading
```

It's different, though, if the functions are actually *defined*, because now you're asking the compiler to create two functions whose names are identical.

 Example 9.5

```
void f(int) {}
void f(const int) {}   // Error; duplicate definition

void g(int) {}
void g(volatile int) {} // Error; duplicate definition
```

9.3.3   Qualifying a Pass-by-Reference or Pass-by-Address

On the other hand, a pass-by-reference is distinct if a `const`/`volatile` modifier is added. Assuming it's `const`, a constant object will invoke the function with the constant argument, while a non-constant object will invoke the function with the non-constant argument.

 Example 9.6

```
void f(int&);
void f(const int&);     // OK; now overloading

void g(int a, const int b)
{
   f(a);      // OK; calls f(int&)
   f(b);      // OK; calls f(const int&)
}
```

The same is true for pass-by-address.

Example 9.7

```
void f(int*);
void f(const int*);      // OK; now overloading

void g(int* a, const int* b)
{
   f(a);    // OK; calls f(int*)
   f(b);    // OK; calls f(const int*)
}
```

9.3.4   Nonstatic vs. Static Methods

Methods of a class or structure cannot be differentiated on the basis of static vs. nonstatic.

 Example 9.8

```
class X
{
   void f();
   static void f();      // Error; multiple declaration
};
```

9.3.5   Mutator vs. Constant Methods

A mutator method of a class or structure can be differentiated from a constant method with the same name and same formal argument list. A constant object will invoke the constant method, while a non-constant object will invoke the mutator method.

Example 9.9

```
class X
{
    public:
   void f();           // mutator method
   void f() const;     // OK; constant method overloads
};

void foo(X& a, const X& b)
{
   a.f();       // Calls f()
   b.f();       // Calls f() const
}
```

 Tip

This feature will prove to be very useful later in this chapter in the discussion of overloading the bracket operator.

9.4   Rules of Overloading Resolution

In order to unambiguously determine which overloaded function to call, the compiler goes through a process known as *overloading resolution*, which involves an algorithm that matches the actual arguments in the function call against the argument list of all the functions with that same name. The compiler then chooses the function that best matches the actual argument(s) from among all of the functions with that name and for which a set of conversions exists so that the function could possibly be called. The order of the declarations of all functions participating in this process is completely irrelevant.

Stated differently, the compiler will, for each actual argument, look for all functions that could possibly be called for that argument, according to the rules listed below, and select those function(s) that constitute the "best match". As soon as at least one function has been found for a particular argument, the searching stops.

9.4.1   Implicit Conversion Sequence

In order to determine which of (possibly) many functions with the same name to call, the compiler will attempt to perform an *implicit conversion sequence* on each actual argument in the function call. This means that it will try to convert each argument to the type of the corresponding parameter of the function being called. An implicit conversion sequence consists of these three parts, and it is done in this order:

- A standard conversion sequence;

- A user-defined conversion sequence;

- An ellipsis conversion sequence.

9.4.2 Standard Conversion Sequence

A standard conversion sequence consists of:

- An exact match, which entails any of the following:

    ❑ Identity (No conversions required)

    ❑ Lvalue transformation

        - Lvalue-to-rvalue conversion
        - Array-to-pointer conversion
        - Function-to-pointer conversion

    ❑ Qualification adjustment

        - Qualification conversions

- Promotion

    ❑ Integral and floating point promotions

        - `char` to `int`
        - `unsigned char` to `int`
        - `signed char` to `int`
        - `enum` to `int`
        - `short` to `int`
        - `unsigned short` to `int`
        - `int` bit field to `int`
        - `wchar_t` to `int`
        - `bool` to `int`
        - `float` to `double`

- Conversion

    ❑ Integral conversions

    ❑ Floating point conversions

    ❑ Floating-integral conversions

    ❑ Pointer conversions

    ❑ Pointer to member conversions

    ❑ Base class conversion (discussed in Chapter 10)

9.4.3   User-Defined Conversion Sequence

A user-defined conversion sequence consists of the following:

■   Constructor;

■   Operator conversion function.

9.4.4   Ellipsis Conversion Sequence

An ellipsis conversion sequence consists of any function whose formal argument list is ellipsis (3 dots). This will constitute an acceptable match for any actual argument.

9.4.5   How the Function is Selected

After these rules have been examined for the first actual argument, the compiler puts the selected functions into set #1, and repeats the process for the second argument to create set #2. The process is repeated for all subsequent arguments.

Next, from all of the sets that have been created, the compiler takes the intersection, and if there is exactly one function in the intersection, then that is the one that is chosen to be called. If no such function exists, or if there is more than one function, then the compiler yields a fatal error message.

9.4.6   Examples of the Rules

Here is an example using standard conversion sequences.

 Example 9.10

```
void f(int);
void f(char, int = 0);
void f(float, int);
void f(int, double);

void g()
{
    f('A');          // #1; Call is valid
    f(1, 'A');       // #2; Call is invalid
    f(1, 3.4);       // #3; Call is valid
    f(3.4);          // #4; Call is invalid
    f('A', 3.4);     // #5; Call is invalid
    f(3.4, 1);       // #6; Call is invalid
}
```

- For call #1, only f(int) and f(char, int) are callable. Since f(char, int) is a better match (exact), it is chosen.

- For call #2, only the last three functions are callable. Since f(int, double) matches the first argument exactly, this is one chosen for the first set. For the second argument, f(char, int) and f(float, int) are chosen because of the promotion, which is better than a conversion. Since the intersection of the two sets is empty, the call is invalid.

- For call #3, only the last three functions are callable, and f(int, double) is chosen for the first argument because of the exact match. For the second argument, f(int, double) is again chosen because of the exact match. So the call is valid.

- For call #4, only the first two functions are callable. Since a double to int and a double to char are both conversions, the call is invalid.

- For call #5, only the last three functions are callable. The first argument will prefer f(char, int), while the second argument will choose f(int, double). So the call is invalid.

- For call #6, only the last three functions are callable. A double to char, double to float, and double to int are all conversions, so all three functions are chosen for the first set. The second argument of type int will choose f(char, int) and f(float, int) for the second set. Since both f(char, int) and f(float, int) are common in both sets, the call is ambiguous and invalid.

For user-defined conversion sequences, consider the following program.

Example 9.11

```
// File mystring.h

#ifndef MYSTRING_H
#define MYSTRING_H

class String
{
    friend String add(const String&, const String&);
        public:
    inline String(const char* = "");
    inline operator const char*() const;
    // Other details omitted
        private:
    char* ptr;
};

#endif

// File foo.cpp

#include <iostream.h>
#include "mystring.h"

void foo()
{
    String s1("Test");
    String s2(add(s1, "ing"));
    cout << s2 << '\n';
}
```

In attempting to resolve the call to the global function `add()`, the first argument of type `String` constitutes an exact match under a standard conversion sequence. For the second argument of type `char[]`, there is no standard conversion sequence, so the compiler looks for a user-defined conversion sequence, and discovers that a constructor can be used to convert the string literal into a temporary object of type `String`. Since the `add()` function is the one and only function that satisfies both explicit arguments, it will be called. This whole process, of course, is what was called implicit type conversion in Chapter 7.

In attempting to resolve the call to the insertion operator, which expects its second argument, `s2`, to be of type `String`, there is no standard conversion sequence to apply to the actual argument. But applying a user-defined conversion sequence, the compiler discovers that an operator conversion function exists that can convert `s2` into type `char*`. Since an insertion operator that accommodates type `char*` does, in fact, already exist, it gets invoked automatically with the `char*` that is created.

For an example of an ellipsis conversion sequence, all of the following calls to f () are valid.

 Example 9.12

```
void f(...);

void g()
{
    f(1, 2, 3);     // OK
    f(5.23);        // OK
    f('A');         // OK
}
```

9.5   Overloading on a Pointer Type

Note that the following code is OK because zero is type int, so that an exact match occurs under rule 1, while the conversion to a pointer occurs under rule 3.

 Example 9.13

```
void f(int);
void f(char*);

void g()
{
    f(0);  // OK; calls f(int)
}
```

On the other hand, the following code doesn't work because an int to a long and an int to a char* are both standard conversions, so the compiler will not choose one function over the other.

 Example 9.14

```
void f(long);
void f(char*);

void g()
{
    f(0);  // Ambiguous
}
```

Therefore, you must be very careful when overloading a pointer type with an integral type.

9.6   Taking the address of an Overloaded Function

If you ever need to take the address of an overloaded function, you may do so only if you give the compiler enough information to determine exactly which function you're talking about. The compiler infers the proper function from the kind of pointer that will be used to hold the address.

 Example 9.15

```
void f();
double f(int);
char f(const char*);

void (*ptr1)() = f;              // OK
double (*ptr2)(int) = f;         // OK
char (*ptr3)(const char*) = f;   // OK
f;                               // Error
```

9.7   Name Mangling

The concept of function overloading presents a potential problem to the linker because it must be able to associate any particular function call with its corresponding library code. In other words, since there could be many functions in the library having the same name, it is not enough for the linker to identify a function simply by using only its name. Instead, the number and types of function arguments must also be factored in.

The compiler solves this problem by a process known as "name mangling" in which the unique identity of each function is, in fact, some combination of the function name and its arguments.

Thus, given:

 Example 9.16

```
void foo(char, int, const char*);
```

a call to this function using Borland C++ will yield the following assembly language code:

Example 9.17

```
call @foo$qcipxc
```

Now that's a mangled name! The `@foo` means a global function, and `$q` separates the function name from the start of the formal argument list. `c` means `char`, `i` means `int`, `p` means `pointer`, and `x` means `const`.

9.7.1 How to Avoid Name Mangling

The only problem now is that this mangled name no longer matches any C-style library functions, since they have nothing to do with C++, and therefore do *not* have their names mangled. Nevertheless, they must still be available for use in any C++ program.

To resolve this dilemma, you may tell the compiler to "escape" from using the C++ name mangling scheme by using a special form of the `extern` keyword. This declaration tells the compiler *not* to perform name mangling on the specified functions. You may declare more than one function by writing a scope, or declare just one function without the braces.

For example, the header file `stdio.h` contains code similar to this.

 Example 9.18

```
extern "C"     // Escape name mangling
{
    int printf(const char*, ...);
    int puts(const char*);
    // more declarations
}
```

Typically such declarations are found in the C library header files already provided for you. But because a C program cannot recognize such a declaration, a test for the macro `__cplusplus` (two leading underscores) must be made. (Do you remember this from Chapter 1?) Therefore, the code in the `stdio.h` header file must be:

Example 9.19

```
#ifdef __cplusplus
extern "C" {
#endif

int printf(const char*, ...);
int puts(const char*);
// more declarations

#ifdef __cplusplus
}
#endif
```

You should inspect the header file `stdio.h` or any other C header file to see this technique for yourself.

9.7.2   Type-Safe Linkage

As a benefit from name mangling, all C++ compilers will perform type-safe linkage. To understand what this is all about, consider this code:

Example 9.20

```
// File #1

void f(double);
void g()
{
    f(1.234);
}

// File #2
void f(int n)
{
    // Body of function
}
```

In the C language the call to `f()` compiles successfully, and the linker is very happy to use the definition of `f()` that accepts an argument of type `int` to satisfy the assembly language call that was generated. (After all, function names in any C library know nothing about formal arguments.) But since the definition converts the actual argument from `double` to `int`, an incorrect result is quite likely to be the outcome.

C++ does not have this problem since the assembly language call to `f()` will incorporate the type `double`, and the linker will fail because it only finds a function called `f()` that accepts an `int`.

9.8   Operator Function Overloading

Operator function overloading allows the designer of a class to provide a more intuitive interface to the user by allowing the user to write classes that make use of the native operators that C++ always provides for fundamental types.

For example, a `String` class would be easier to use if the `string.h` library functions such as `strcpy()`, `strcmp()` and `strcat()` were replaced by C++ operators such as '=', '==', and '+=', respectively. In general, any mathematical-type class can benefit from operator function overloading. Of course, whatever operators you overload should have inherent meaning within the class so that they can be easily understood. For example, you should not overload the '+' operator to mean any kind of subtraction (that is, not if you value your job).

9.8.1   Start with the Precedence Chart

The only operators that you may overload are the ones from the C++ precedence chart shown below (and not all of those are available). You cannot arbitrarily choose a new symbol (such as '@' or '**') and attempt to give it meaning by "overloading" it.

Table 9-1   C++ Precedence Chart

Symbol	Name	Associativity
::	scope resolution	Left to right
.	direct member access	
->	indirect member access	
[]	subscripting	
()	function call	
()	function-style cast	
++	postfix increment	
--	postfix decrement	
sizeof	size of	Right to left
++	prefix increment	
--	prefix decrement	
~	one's complement	
!	not	
-	unary minus	
+	unary plus	
&	address of	
*	dereference	
new	allocate single instance	
new []	allocate array of instances	
delete	delete single instance	

Table 9-1   C++ Precedence Chart (Continued)

Symbol	Name	Associativity
delete []	delete array of instances	
()	C-style cast	Right to left
.*	pointer-to-member selection	Left to right
->*	pointer-to-member selection	
*	multiply	Left to right
/	divide	
%	modulus	
+	add	Left to right
-	subtract	
<<	shift left	Left to right
>>	shift right	
<	less than	Left to right
<=	less than or equal to	
>	greater than	
>=	greater than or equal to	
==	equal	Left to right
!=	not equal	
&	bitwise AND	Left to right
^	bitwise exclusive OR	Left to right
|	bitwise inclusive OR	Left to right
&&	logical AND	Left to right
||	logical OR	Left to right
? :	conditional expression	N/A
=	assignment	Right to left
*=	multiply and assign	
/=	divide and assign	
%=	modulus and assign	
+=	add and assign	
-=	subtract and assign	
<<=	shift left and assign	
>>=	shift right and assign	
&=	bitwise AND and assign	
|=	inclusive OR and assign	
^=	exclusive OR and assign	
,	comma	Left to right

9.8.2 Overloadable Unary Operators

The unary operators that you may overload are:

Table 9-2   Unary Operators

->	indirect member operator
!	not
&	address
*	dereference
+	plus
-	minus
++	prefix increment
++	postfix increment
--	prefix decrement
--	postfix decrement
~	one's complement
->*	indirect pointer-to-member

9.8.3 Overloadable Binary Operators

The binary operators that you may overload are:

Table 9-3   Binary Operators

()	function call
[]	subscript
operator new	create space (single object)
operator new[]	create space (array of objects)
operator delete	destroy space (single object)
operator delete[]	destroy space (array of objects)
*	multiply
/	divide
%	modulus
+	add
-	subtract
<<	left shift
>>	right shift
<	less than
<=	less than or equal to
>	greater than

(Continued)

Table 9-3   Binary Operators (Continued)

>=	greater than or equal to
==	equal to
!=	not equal to
&	bitwise AND
^	bitwise exclusive OR
		bitwise OR
&&	logical AND
||	logical OR
=	assignment
*=	multiply and assign
/=	divide and assign
%=	modulus and assign
+=	add and assign
-=	subtract and assign
<<=	shift left and assign
>>=	shift right and assign
&=	bitwise AND and assign
|=	bitwise OR and assign
^=	bitwise excl. OR and assign
,	comma

9.8.4   Operators that Cannot be Overloaded

These operators *cannot* be overloaded:

Table 9-4   Operators that Cannot be Overloaded

.	direct member
.*	direct pointer-to-member
::	scope resolution
? :	conditional
sizeof	size of
new	allocate
delete	delete

9.8.5   Creating a Function Name

You start the process of operator overloading by declaring a function in the normal fashion, but its name must be the expression `operator@` where the symbol '@' generically represents the operator itself that is to be overloaded. You may leave one or more spaces before the '@'.

9.8.6   Default Arguments

No default arguments are allowed in overloaded operator functions. The one exception to this rule will be shown later in regard to the function call operator.

9.8.7   Inherently Supplied Operators

Who says there's no such thing as a free lunch? In C++ there is, because every class has operators that the compiler will define and make available automatically.

The following `String` class exhibits these operators explicitly. They are the assignment operator (`=`) and address-of operators (`&`) for both constant and non-constant instances. The assignment operator performs a memberwise copy of the nonstatic data members, and is provided so that C programs compiled using C++ can be backward-compatible.

Example 9.21

```
// File mystring.h

#ifndef MYSTRING_H
#define MYSTRING_H

class String
{
    public:
  String& operator=(const String& s)
                { ptr = s.ptr; return *this; }
  String* operator&() { return this; }
  const String* operator&() const { return this; }
    private:
  char* ptr;
};

#endif

// File foo.cpp

#include "mystring.h"

void foo(const String& s1, String& s2)
{
  s2 = s1;                    // Assignment
  String* ptr1 = &s2;         // Address-of (non-const)
  const String* ptr2 = &s1;   // Address-of (const)
}
```

 Tip

Strictly speaking, the comma operator can also be considered to be supplied inherently by the compiler, but if it's not overloaded, then it serves only as a statement separator.

9.8.8   Built-In Rules Cannot be Changed

The pre-defined operator precedence rules cannot be changed. That is, you cannot, for example, make binary '+' have a higher precedence than binary '*'.

Also, you must adhere to the unary/binary characteristics of the operator in the sense that if it's unary, you may overload it as a unary operator, if it's binary, you may overload it as a binary operator, and if it's both unary and binary, then you may overload it either way or both ways. (The operators '+', '-', '*' and '&' are both unary and binary.)

Associativity is retained in the sense that if an operator normally binds right-to-left, such as an assignment operator, then an overloaded assignment operator for a class will also bind right-to-left.

9.8.9   Sequence Points are Not Retained

A sequence point is a place in a statement that physically separates one expression from another, and guarantees that order of evaluation.

 Example 9.22

```
int f(), g();

void foo()
{
   f() + g();      // No sequence point
   f() && g();     // Sequence point defined
   f() || g();     // Sequence point defined
   f(), g();       // Sequence point defined
}
```

In the first statement the binary addition operator does *not* define a sequence point, so the compiler is free to call function g() before it calls function f(). But in the last three statements, the operators Boolean 'and' (&&), Boolean 'or' (||) and comma (,) define sequence points, so the call to function f() is now guaranteed to occur before the call to function g().

But if, for example, '&&' were overloaded for the `String` class:

 Example 9.23

```
class String
{
    friend String operator&&(const String&, const String&);
        public:
    String f();
    String g();
};

void foo(String& a, String& b)
{
    a.f() && b.g();   // Caution; no sequence point defined
}
```

then there is no guarantee whatsoever that the call to `String::f()` will occur before the call to `String::g()`.

9.8.10   Member vs. Nonmember

An operator function for a class may be either (1) a nonstatic member function or (2) a nonmember function. A nonstatic member function automatically has one argument implicitly defined, namely the address of the invoking instance (as specified by the pointer variable `this`). Since a nonmember function has no `this` pointer, it needs to have all of its arguments explicitly declared.

There is no one "catch-all" rule that dictates whether an operator should be overloaded as a member or as a nonmember. Sometimes the decision is a toss-up. However, you won't go wrong if you remember to *always* use a *member* function unless you either (1) need to do implicit type conversion on the left-hand argument, or (2) the operator needs to be invoked by some instance that is not of the class type in which the operator is located. In this latter case, use a nonmember function and grant it friendship only if necessary.

Nevertheless, the following operators *must* be overloaded as *member* (not nonmember) functions:

Table 9-5   Operators that Must be Members

=	assignment
()	function call
[]	subscript
->	indirect member operator

9.8.11 Supply at Least One Class Instance

At least one of the arguments (implicit or explicit) to an overloaded function *must* be an instance of the class to which the operator belongs. This is done automatically for a non-static member function via the `this` pointer. You must do it explicitly for a non-member function.

 Example 9.24

```
class String
{
     public:
   // Other details omitted
   String operator+() const; // OK; Member function has 'this'
};

String operator*(int, int);     // Error; no class arguments
String operator-(int, const String&);   // OK; one class arg.
```

9.8.12 Which is the Invoking Object?

In the case of a binary member operator in which only one explicit argument is written, the invoking instance is *always* assumed to be the one on the *left-hand side* of the operator.

 Example 9.25

```
class String
{
     public:
   // Other details omitted
   String& operator=(const String&);
};

void foo(String& s1, String& s2)
{
   s1 = s2;     // s1.operator=(s2);
}
```

9.8.13 Binary Members and Implicit Type Conversion

In the case of a binary member operator, *no implicit type conversion is ever done on the left-hand value*. This means that it *must* be an instance of the class of which the overloaded operator is a member.

Example 9.26

```
class String
{
      public:
    String(const char* = "");
    String operator+(const String&) const;
    // Other details omitted
        private:
    char* ptr;
};

void foo(const String& s1, const String& s2)
{
    String s3(s1 + s2);     // OK
    String s4(s1 + "A");    // OK
    String s5("A" + s1);    // Error; no conversion of "A"
}
```

The solution is to make operator+() a nonmember function (with or without friendship).

 Example 9.27

```
class String
{
    friend String operator+(const String&, const String&);
      public:
    String(const char* = "");
    // Other details omitted
        private:
    char* ptr;
};

void foo(const String& s1, const String& s2)
{
    String s3(s1 + s2);     // OK
    String s4(s1 + "A");    // OK
    String s5("A" + s1);    // OK
}
```

9.8.14   Don't Forget to Support Constant Objects

In the case of a non-static member function, don't forget to declare it const if it must support constant objects. For example, here the unary 'not' operator is over-loaded as a constant method to return true if the invoking object is empty, false otherwise.

Example 9.28

```
class String
{
      public:
    String(const char* = "");
    bool operator!() const { return *ptr == '\0'; }
    // Other details omitted
      private:
    char* ptr;
};

void foo(const String& s)
{
    if(!s)
        // s is null
    else
        // s is not null
}
```

9.8.15   Overload the Whole Family

If you decide to overload the binary '+' operator, then the users of your class may reasonably assume that the operators unary '+', '++' and '+=' are also available. So it's probably a good idea to overload these operators as well for the sake of completeness.

9.8.16   Assignment Operator

As noted above, if you fail to write an assignment operator, then the compiler supplies one for you that automatically does a member-by-member assignment of the instance variables. For very simple classes, this should suffice.

However, you *must* overload it whenever the class contains a pointer that points to heap space and you want the user to have the capability to assign one instance to another instance. The reason is that the assignment operator is the last of the manager functions, and you saw in Chapter 7 the problem that arose when you accepted the compiler-supplied copy constructor. The same problem exists here, so you had better write your own. And in the same vein, if you do not want the user of your class to be able to assign one object to another, then simply declare it to be private.

In the case of the `String` class, the assignment operator encompasses these features:

■ It first checks for self-assignment for sake of efficiency;

■ It checks to see if the existing heap space can be re-used;

■ It returns `*this` to allow function chaining to occur.

Example 9.29

```cpp
// File mystring.h

#ifndef MYSTRING_H
#define MYSTRING_H

#include <string.h>

class String
{
    public:
  String& operator=(const String&);   // Allow chaining
  // Other details omitted
    private:
  char* ptr;
};

#endif

// File mystring.cpp

#include "mystring.h"

String& String::operator=(const String& s)
{
  // Check for self-assignment
  if(&s != this)
  {
    // Why get new heap space if the length hasn't changed?
    int len = strlen(s.ptr);
    if(strlen(ptr) != len)
    {
      delete [] ptr;
      ptr = new char[len + 1];
    }
    strcpy(ptr, s.ptr);
  }
  return *this;
}

// File foo.cpp

#include "mystring.h"
void foo(String& s1, String& s2, String& s3)
{
  s1 = s1;         // OK; self-assignment
  s1 = s2 = s3;
```

Tip

You might want to have the assignment operator return *this *by refer-ence-to-*const *to ensure that a non-modifiable object is always being returned.*

9.8.17 Function Call Operator

The overloaded function call operator operator()() is unique because it may take any number of explicit arguments and may even take a default argument. In this sense, when it is applied to an instance of a class, it appears as though the instance itself is the name of a function.

For example, the String class has been overloaded to accept one argument of type const char* and return the number of times the string literal occurs within the invoking object. If it is called with no argument, then the default search string is "C++".

Example 9.30

```cpp
// File mystring.h

#ifndef MYSTRING_H
#define MYSTRING_H

class String
{
     public:
  unsigned operator()(const char* = "C++") const;
  // Other details omitted
     private:
  char* ptr;
};

#endif

// File mystring.cpp

#include <string.h>
#include "mystring.h"

unsigned String::operator()(const char* s) const
{
  unsigned counter = 0;
  unsigned size = strlen(s);
  int loops = strlen(ptr) - size + 1;
  for(int i = 0; i < loops; ++i)
    if(!strncmp(ptr + i, s, size))
      ++counter;
  return counter;
}

// File foo.cpp

#include "mystring.h"

void foo(const String& s)
{
  unsigned answer1 = s("test");
  unsigned answer2 = s();
}
```

9.8.18   Subscript Operator

The subscript operator is useful whenever the class contains an array (e.g., the String class that contains an array of characters) and you want to give the user the capability to access and/or modify an individual character. For modification, you must return a 'reference-to-non-const' to the character in order to create an 'lvalue'.

You may also overload the subscript operator as a constant function in order to accommodate constant instances *and* preserve the integrity of the heap space. In this case you must return an element *by value* or by 'reference-to-const'.

The determination as to which subscript operator gets invoked is quite simple. If the class instance is not constant, then the non-constant function will be invoked. If the class instance is constant, then the constant function will be invoked.

Here the String class has been overloaded to exhibit both overloaded subscript operators.

 Example 9.31

```
// File mystring.h

#ifndef MYSTRING_H
#define MYSTRING_H

class String
{
     public:
   inline char operator[](int) const; // for constant objects
   inline char& operator[](int);  // for non-constant objects
   // Other details omitted
     private:
   char* ptr;
};

inline char String::operator[](int index) const
{
   return ptr[index];
}

inline char& String::operator[](int index)
{
   return ptr[index];
}

#endif

// File foo.cpp

#include "mystring.h"

void foo(String& s1, const String& s2)
{
   s1[0] = 'A';        // OK
   s1[0] = s2[0];      // OK
   s2[0] = 'A';        // Error
}
```

Caution

> *What guarantee is there that the subscript value is always in range of the array? In case it is out of range, you should throw an exception. The topic of exception handling is discussed in Chapter 12.*

9.8.19 Indirect Member Operator

The indirect member operator is useful for implementing what is known as a "smart pointer". Consider the following example that uses the string class from the standard C++ library (in the header file cstring.h).

Example 9.32

```
// File main.cpp

#include <iostream.h>
#include <cstring.h>

int main()
{
   string* ptr;          // Uninitialized pointer!
   ptr->to_upper();      // Convert to upper case letters
   // more code...
   return 0;
}
```

This, of course, will not work because an uninitialized pointer is being dereferenced, and the program is likely to either crash or produce unexpected output.

The solution is to create a smart pointer class called, for example, Autoptr, that contains a pointer, or handle, to some underlying class that represents the true abstraction. The constructor of Autoptr must initialize the handle either to zero by default, or to the address of some instance of the underlying class. It must also overload operator->() (as a unary member) so that it can examine the handle to see whether it has been properly initialized. If so, then the function returns the handle itself which is then automatically used to invoke the proper member function of the underlying class. If not, an exception can be thrown.

The overloaded operator->() for the pointer ptr in the example above is equivalent to writing:

Example 9.33

```
ptr.operator->()->to_upper();
```

In addition, since `operator->()` is just an abbreviation for the dereferencing operator, it's probably a good idea to overload `operator*()` for the sake of consistency.

Now let's write an `Autoptr` class that is hard-coded to refer to an instance of the
C++ library's `string` class. Typically, the objects to which an `Autoptr` object
points are allocated from the heap, and the `Autoptr` class then takes ownership of
them.

 Example 9.34

```cpp
// File autoptr.h

#ifndef AUTOPTR_H
#define AUTOPTR_H

#include <iostream.h>
#include <cstring.h>

class Autoptr
{
    public:
   Autoptr(string* p = 0) : ptr(p) {}
   ~Autoptr() { delete ptr; }
   string* operator->() const;
   string& operator*() const;
       private:
   string* ptr;
   Autoptr(const Autoptr&);   // Disallow copying
   void operator=(const Autoptr&);   // Disallow assignment
};

#endif

// File autoptr.cpp

#include <iostream.h>
#include "autoptr.h"

string* Autoptr::operator->() const
{
   if(ptr)
      return ptr;
   cout << "Uninitialized pointer!\n";
   // Throw an exception
}

string& Autoptr::operator*() const
{
   return *operator->(); // Call operator->() for consistency
}
```

(Continued)

```
// File main.cpp

#include <iostream.h>
#include <cstring.h>
#include "autoptr.h"

int main()
{
   Autoptr p1(new string("Test string"));  // Initialized OK
   p1->to_upper();
   cout << *p1 << '\n';
   Autoptr p2;          // p2 is uninitialized
   p2->to_upper();      // Error generated
   return 0;
}


/* The output of this program is:

TEST STRING
Uninitialized pointer!

*/
```

 Tip

The "real" auto_ptr *class has been implemented in its entirety in the standard C++ library.*

9.8.20   Compound Assignment Operators

While not strictly mandatory, you should overload all compound assignment operators ('+=', '-=', '*=', etc.) as member functions. One easy way to overload these operators is to implement them in terms of their C definitions. For example, '+=' adds the left-hand argument to the right-hand argument, and stores the sum back into the left-hand argument.

In the following example, the String class has overloaded the binary '+' operator to concatenate two String objects. This allows the overloaded '+=' operator to be written in just one line of code.

Example 9.35

```
// File mystring.h

#ifndef MYSTRING_H
#define MYSTRING_H

#include <string.h>

class String
{
   friend String operator+(const String&, const String&);
     public:
   // Manager functions, other details
   String& operator+=(const String&);
      private:
   char* ptr;
};

#endif

// File mystring.cpp

#include "mystring.h"

String operator+(const String& s1, const String& s2)
{
   char* buff = new char[strlen(s1.ptr) + strlen(s2.ptr) + 1];
   strcpy(buff, s1.ptr);
   strcat(buff, s2.ptr);
   String temp(buff);
   delete [] buff;
   return temp;
}

String& String::operator+=(const String& s)
{
   return *this = *this + s;
}

// File foo.cpp

#include "mystring.h"

void foo()
{
   String s1("This is a test");
   String s2(s1 + " of ");
   s2 += "concatenation";
}
```

On the other hand, some people like to take the opposite approach and write the overloaded `operator+()` in terms of `operator+=()`. By doing this the `operator+()` never has to be a friend function.

Example 9.36

```
// File mystring.h

#ifndef MYSTRING_H
#define MYSTRING_H

#include <string.h>

class String
{
    public:
  // Manager functions, other details
  String& operator+=(const String&);
    private:
  char* ptr;
} ;
String operator+(const String&, const String&);

#endif

// File mystring.cpp

#include "mystring.h"

String operator+(const String& s1, const String& s2)
{
  return String(s1) += s2;
}

String& String::operator+=(const String& s)
{
  char* buff = new char[strlen(ptr) + strlen(s.ptr) + 1];
  strcpy(buff, ptr);
  strcat(buff, s.ptr);
  delete [] ptr;
  ptr = buff;
  return *this;
}

// File foo.cpp

#include "mystring.h"

void foo()
{
  String s1("This is a test");
  String s2(s1 + " of ");
  s2 += "concatenation";
}
```

9.8.21   Increment and Decrement Operators

You may choose to overload the operators '++' and '--' as either prefix, postfix, or both. If you overload both as unary member functions, then in theory both of them receive no explicit arguments, so it's an ambiguous situation for the compiler when it tries to decide which one to invoke.

In order to distinguish the prefix operator from the postfix operator, the compiler will automatically generate an extra argument of type int when the postfix operator is called. The actual value of this int, of course, is meaningless, so that a formal argument name should not be written when the function is defined. Nevertheless, this extra argument allows both prefix and postfix versions of the operator to be present with no ambiguity. It's also an excellent idea to write the postfix form so that it calls upon the prefix form in order to save on redundant coding and to ensure consistency between the two functions.

For example, here is the String class again in which the operator '++' has been overloaded in both prefix and postfix forms to convert the characters into upper case.

Example 9.37

```
// File mystring.h

#ifndef MYSTRING_H
#define MYSTRING_H

#include <string.h>

class String
{
    public:
  String& operator++();           // prefix
  const String operator++(int);   // postfix
  // Other details omitted
    private:
  char* ptr;
} ;

#endif

// File mystring.cpp

String& String::operator++()
{
  strupr(ptr);
  return *this ;
}

const String String::operator++(int)
{
  String temp(*this);
  ++(*this);    // call prefix ++
  return temp;
}

// File foo.cpp

#include "mystring.h"

void foo(String& s1, String& s2)
{
  String s3(++s1);   // Initialize s3 with uppercase of s1
  String s4(s2++);   // Initialize s4 with lowercase of s2
}
```

Note the postfix operator in which a temporary instance is created and subsequently returned to become the value of the function. However, it's the invoking instance that actually gets modified, not the temporary instance.

Tip

> *It is possible to chain calls to the prefix operator, but not to the postfix operator. This is consistent with the way the fundamental types behave.*

9.8.22   Overloading the Comma Operator

Don't get fancy and attempt to overload the comma operator unless you're looking to make yourself an enemy of the users of your class. For example, suppose class X overloads the comma operator to do something useful.

 Example 9.38

```
class String
{
    friend String operator,(const String&, const String&);
    // Other details omitted
};

void foo(const String& s1, const String& s2)
{
    String s3;
    // ...
    s3 = s1, s2;    // Oops... (s3 = s1), s2;
}
```

Since comma is the lowest operator on the precedence chart, *everything else*, including assignment, will occur before the operator executes.

9.8.23   Overloading the Insertion Operator

You may overload the insertion operator as a nonmember function, with or without friendship. By doing this you give the user the ability to output an instance of your class in a manner identical to that of a fundamental type. The first argument is always an alias to the output stream device to which the data should be sent (usually cout), and the second is an instance of the class to be displayed.

Example 9.39

```
// File mystring.h

#ifndef MYSTRING_H
#define MYSTRING_H

#include <iostream.h>
#include <string.h>

class String
{
   friend
   inline ostream& operator<<(ostream& str, const String& s);
      public:
   // public interface
      private:
   char* ptr;
};

inline ostream& operator<<(ostream& str, const String& s)
{
   return str << s.ptr;
}

#endif

// File foo.cpp

#include "mystring.h"

void foo(const String& s)
{
   cout << "s = " << s << '\n';
}
```

What's also interesting about this example are the machinations that the compiler has to go through to translate the infix notation in `foo()` into functional notation.

Example 9.40

```
void foo(const String& s)
{
   operator<<(cout.operator<<("s = "), s).operator<<('\n');
}
```

As a test of your understanding of how member and nonmember functions are called, you should be able to follow this code and convince yourself that it produces the same answer that the infix notation produces.

9.8.24 Overloading the Extraction Operator

You may also overload the extraction operator as a nonmember function, with or without friendship. By doing this you give the user the ability to input an instance of your class in a manner identical to that of a fundamental type. The first argument is always an alias to the input stream device from which the data should be read (usually `cin`), and the second is an instance of the class that is to receive the data.

 Example 9.41

```cpp
// File mystring.h

#ifndef MYSTRING_H
#define MYSTRING_H

#include <iostream.h>
#include <string.h>

class String
{
   friend inline istream& operator>>(istream& str, String& s);
      public:
   // public interface
      private:
   char* ptr;
};

inline istream& operator>>(istream& str, String& s)
{
   return str >> s.ptr;
}

#endif

// File foo.cpp

#include "mystring.h"

void foo(String& s)
{
   cin >> s;
}
```

 Tip

From a design standpoint, it's probably not a good idea to overload the extraction operator for the simple reason that an instance of the class first has to be defined (invoking the default constructor) and then "filled with data" via input from some device. This violates the programming guideline that says to prefer initialization to assignment.

9.8.25   Enumerated Types

If desired, you may write overload operators for any enumerated type. If you recall from Chapter 1, it is no longer legal to increment or decrement a variable of some enumerated type using the increment and decrement operators:

 Example 9.42

```
enum days
{
    Sunday, Monday, Tuesday, Wednesday, Thursday, Friday,
    Saturday
};

void foo(days& d)
{
    ++d;   // Error; invalid operation
}
```

Yet, this seems like a perfectly reasonable thing to do in order to advance to the next day. Fortunately, it's quite easy to overload the increment operator in order to make such code valid.

Example 9.43

```cpp
#include <iostream.h>

enum days
{
   Sunday, Monday, Tuesday, Wednesday, Thursday, Friday,
   Saturday
};

days& operator++(days& d)   // prefix
{
   switch(d)
   {
      case Sunday : d = Monday; break;
      case Monday : d = Tuesday; break;
      case Tuesday : d = Wednesday; break;
      case Wednesday : d = Thursday; break;
      case Thursday : d = Friday; break;
      case Friday : d = Saturday; break;
      case Saturday : d = Sunday; break;
   }
   return d;
}

days operator++(days& d, int)   // postfix
{
   days temp(d);
   ++d;
   return temp;
}

int main()
{
   const char* message[] =
   {
      "Sunday", "Monday", "Tuesday", "Wednesday",
      "Thursday", "Friday ", "Saturday"
   };
   days today = Sunday;
   for(int i = 0; i < 10; ++i)
      cout << "Today is " << message[today++] << '\n';
   return 0;
}
```

(Continued)

```
/* The output of this program is:

Today is Sunday
Today is Monday
Today is Tuesday
Today is Wednesday
Today is Thursday
Today is Friday
Today is Saturday
Today is Sunday
Today is Monday
Today is Tuesday


*/
```

The `days` enumerated type can also be encapsulated within a class, but the `operator++()` must still be overloaded as a non-member function.

9.8.26   Overloading `operator new()` and `operator delete()`

Both `operator new()` and `operator delete()` may be written (not over-loaded) as static member functions of a class, effectively replacing the ones supplied by the compiler. (But note that the word `static` is optional in the function declaration.) `operator new()` must take an argument of type `size_t` and return `void*`, while `operator delete()` must take an argument of type `void*` and return `void`. (`size_t` is usually `typedef`'ed as an `unsigned int`.)

In addition, you may write `operator new[]()` and `operator delete[]()` so that they will be invoked when an array of class objects gets created and destroyed.

The `operator new()` function is responsible for allocating its own heap space and then returning a pointer to this space. Then the constructor will be executed. `operator delete()` will run after the destructor has been called, and will receive a pointer to the heap space, which then must be released.

The following program shows how to do this overloading, and traces the calls as they are made.

Example 9.44

```cpp
// File mystring.h

#ifndef MYSTRING_H
#define MYSTRING_H

#include <iostream.h>
class String
{
     public:
  String() { cout << "ctor" << '\n'; }
  ~String() { cout << "dtor" << '\n'; }
  inline void* operator new(size_t s);
  inline void operator delete(void* ptr);
  inline void* operator new[](size_t s);
  inline void operator delete[](void* ptr);
     private:
  char* ptr;
};

inline void* String::operator new(size_t s)
{
  cout << "operator new(): size = " << s << '\n';
  return new char[s];
}

inline void String::operator delete(void* p)
{
  cout << "operator delete()\n";
  delete p;
}

inline void* String::operator new[](size_t s)
{
  cout << "operator new[](): size = " << s << '\n';
  return new char[s];
}

inline void String::operator delete[](void* p)
{
  cout << "operator delete[]()\n";
  delete [] p;
}

#endif
```

(Continued)

```
// File main.cpp

#include <iostream.h>
#include "mystring.h"

int main()
{
    cout << ">>> Single instance\n";
    String* ptr1 = new String;
    delete ptr1;

    cout << ">>> Array of instances\n";
    String* ptr2 = new String[2];
    delete [] ptr2;
    return 0;
}

/* The output of this program is:

>>> Single instance
operator new(): size = 2
ctor
dtor
operator delete()
>>> Array of instances
operator new[](): size = 8
ctor
ctor
dtor
dtor
operator delete[]()

*/
```

Note the output of 8 for the size of the array of 2 instances. Assuming that type `char*` occupies 2 bytes, two such instances would then occupy 4 bytes. The extra 4 bytes are needed for the overhead involved in keeping track of the size of the array.

 Tip

It is probably a good idea to avoid overloading the global `operator new()`.

9.8.27   **Overloading** `operator new()` **with the Placement Syntax**

`operator new()` may also be written using the placement syntax if you want the allocated space to reside in a place other than the heap. If this is the case, then the location is specified in parentheses between the keyword `new` and the type. The `operator new()` is written as a global function with two parameters: (1) `size_t`, which may be ignored, and (2) a `void*` pointer which must merely be returned. Note that if a user-defined type is being allocated, then an explicit call to the destructor must be made, since no `delete` can be written.

For example, if space for some I/O port is to be allocated in the data segment, then the code might be:

 Example 9.45

```
#include <stdlib.h>

const void* operator new(size_t, const void* p)
{
   return p;
}

class IOport
{
      public:
   IOport(int t)  : data(t) {}
   ~IOport() {}
      private:
   int data;
};

char port[sizeof(IOport)];

void foo()
{
   IOport* ptr_port = new(port) IOport(1);
   // process
   ptr_port->~IOport();   // Explicit call to destructor
}
```

Another reason to overload `operator new()` using the placement syntax is to allow an object to be "re-initialized". In other words, suppose that you have the following class:

Example 9.46

```
class String
{
     public:
   String(const char* p = "") : ptr(p) {}
   operator const char*() const { return ptr; }
     private:
   const char* const ptr;
};

int main()
{
   const String array[] = { "Hello", "there" };
   array[0] = "No";      // Error; can't assign to a constant
   array[1] = " way";    // Error; can't assign to a constant
   cout << array[0] << array[1] << '\n';
   return 0;
}
```

This does not work because each element in the array of type String is constant, and the compiler refuses to generate a default assignment operator that will assign into a constant object. Also, even if the array were not declared constant, the assignment operator still could not be generated because the class itself contains a data member that is constant.

However, this problem can be solved by overloading operator new() using the placement syntax, and then calling it with the address of each existing object while at the same time supplying the new value to which the private data member ptr can be bound.

Example 9.47

```
#include <iostream.h>

class String
{
      public:
   String(const char* p = "") : ptr(p) {}
   operator const char*() const { return ptr; }
      private:
   const char* const ptr;
};

const void* operator new(size_t, const void* p)
{
   return p;
}

int main()
{
   const String array[] = { "Hello", "there" };
   new(array) String("This");
   new(array + 1) String(" works!");
   cout << array[0] << array[1] << '\n';
   return 0;
}

/* The output of this program is:

This works!

*/
```

9.8.28   Infix vs. Function Call Notation

One last item to keep in mind: When the infix version of an operator is used, the corresponding operators supplied inherently to work with the fundamental types are honored during overloading resolution, and always take priority over a user-defined overloaded operator. If no user-defined object exists as an actual argument, then even if the call cannot be satisfied by a built-in operator, an overloaded operator will never be called.

If, on the other hand, you write the call using function notation, then the operators for the fundamental types are never considered, and instead the compiler will look only for overloaded operators.

 Example 9.48

```
class String
{
    public:
   String(const char* = "");
   // Other details omitted
};

void operator+(const String&, const char*);

void foo()
{
   "A" + "B";              // Error; invalid pointer arithmetic
   operator+("A", "B");   // OK; calls overloaded operator+()
}
```

Review Questions

1. Why would you want to overload a function?

2. What are the five steps that the compiler goes through in order to determine which of several overloaded functions it should call?

3. In what cases would you overload a class function as a member, and in what cases would you overload it as a nonmember?

4. Why would a member function return *this?

5. What is type-safe linkage, and why is it needed?

6. When and why should the overloaded assignment operator check for self-assignment?

7. What are the advantages and disadvantages of overloading an operator more than once so that it can accommodate all possible input argument types?

8. Why does an overloaded operator [] () sometimes return by reference and other times return by value?

9. How does the compiler distinguish an overloaded prefix operator from a postfix operator (increment or decrement)?

10. Why would you ever use the placement syntax of operator new()?

 Exercise 9.1

Enhance the String class to accommodate the following main() function. You will need to add:

■ an overloaded binary '+' operator that concatenates two String objects and creates a brand new String;

■ an overloaded binary '+=' operator that emulates the function strcat();

■ an overloaded unary '-' operator that returns true if the String object is empty; false otherwise;

■ an overloaded binary '<<' operator that displays a String object.

```
int main()
{
   String s1("Test"), s2(s1 + "ing");
   String s3(s2);
   s3 += " the String class";
   cout << s3 << '\n';
   if(!s3)
      cout << "s3 is null\n";
   s1 = "";
   if(!s1)
      cout << "s1 is null\n";
   return 0;
}
```

 Exercise 9.2

Modify the `Fraction` class from Chapter 8, Exercise #1 so that the named arithmetic functions are replaced by the corresponding operators. Also, replace the `print()` method with an overloaded insertion operator. Finally, modify the `main()` function so that it uses the overloaded operators.

 Exercise 9.3

Revise the `Array` class in Exercise #3 in Chapter 6 to take advantage of operator overloading.

 Exercise 9.4

Given the following outline for the class `Complex`:

```
class Complex
{
     public:
   // All member and nonmember functions
     private:
   float real;
   float imag;
};
```

and the `main()` function:

```
int main()
{
   Complex c1(2.0);
   Complex c2(1.2, 3.4);
   Complex c3(c1 + 1.0 + c2);
   Complex c4;
   c4 = c3;
   cout << "c1 = " << c1 << '\n';
   cout << "c2 = " << c2 << '\n';
   cout << "c3 = " << c3 << '\n';
   cout << "c4 = " << c4 << '\n';
   return 0;
}

/* The output of this program is:

c1 = 2 + 0i
c2 = 1.2 + 3.4i
c3 = 4.2 + 3.4i
c4 = 4.2 + 3.4i

*/
```

write the methods and nonmember functions needed to produce the expected output.

 Exercise 9.5

Recall that you cannot allocate a 2-dimensional array from the heap at execution time because the compiler needs to know the number of columns. You can solve this dilemma by creating a class called `TwoDimensionalArray`. This class contains an array of pointers to integers (the length of which is equal to the number of rows), each element of which will point to an array of integers (the length of which is equal to the number of columns).

The outline for the class is:

```
class TwoDimensionalArray
{
     public:
   TwoDimensionalArray(int, int);
   ~TwoDimensionalArray();
   // This overloaded operator[]() function will return
   // the address contained in element 'i' of the array
   // of pointers
   int* operator[](int i) const;
   // A pointer to an array of pointers to ints
     private:
   int** ptr;
   // Number of rows and columns
   int rows, cols;
};
```

Write the member functions for this class and a `main()` function to test the class.

 Exercise 9.6

Write a class called `Long` that models an integral number of virtually unlimited magnitude. Perhaps the easiest way is to have the class encapsulate a pointer to an unknown number of characters, each of which is a digit in the range from '0' to '9'.

```
class Long
{
   // public interface
     private:
   char* ptr;
};
```

Write all of the requisite methods and friend functions to accommodate the following `main()` function, but at the very minimum you must overload `operator+()`, `operator*()`, `operator+=()`, `operator*=()`, and *all* of the manager functions.

```
int main()
{
   const Long limit(100);
   Long Long_sum(0);
   Long Long_fact(1);
   for(Long i(1); i <= limit; ++i)
   {
      Long_sum += i;
      Long_fact *= i;
   }
   cout << "Sum from 1 to " << limit << " = " << Long_sum
        << '\n';
   cout << "Factorial of " << limit << " = " << Long_fact
        << '\n';
   return 0;
}
```

Note: The factorial of 100 starts with 933262154439..., and the sum of the numbers from 0 to 100 is 5050.

 Exercise 9.7

Given the following abstraction for a `Date` class:

```
class Date
{
   // All friend function declarations
      public:
   // All member function declarations
      private:
   int month;
   int day;
   int year;
};
```

write the member and functions to read and write a date, increment a date by one day, compare two dates to see which one is greater, etc. Be sure to use operator overloading where applicable.

Chapter 10

Inheritance

10.1   Introduction

Inheritance is the process by which a *derived class* is created as the result of extending, or enhancing, an existing class. This capability saves you from having to "reinvent the wheel", because if a new class greatly resembles an existing class, then *all* of the properties of the existing class can be *inherited* by the new class, and any new features can then be added.

10.2   Terminology

The terms "base class/derived class", or "parent class/child class", are used to refer to the classes involved in the process of inheritance. Other object-oriented languages use the terms "super class/sub class", but they can be misleading because the super class is the base class, and yet for reasons that will soon become apparent, it is still "smaller" than the sub, or derived, class.

10.3   Using Inheritance to Create an "is-a" Relationship

Inheritance allows you to collect related classes into a hierarchy with the classes at the top serving as abstractions for those below. This implies that a derived class is a specialization of its parent class. In other words, the derived class "is a" type of base class, but with more detail added. For this reason, the relationship between a derived class and its base class is called an "is-a" relationship. In other words, a software system designed for a specific project must usually be very specialized, whereas a software system designed as a reusable tool must usually be very general. Inheritance allows you to take a very general software component and specialize it for use in a specific project.

An "is-a" relationship implies that whenever an instance of the base class is needed in some application, the user is free to substitute an instance of some derived class. For example:

■   A car "is a" kind of transportation;

■   A Ford "is a" kind of car;

■   A Mustang "is a" kind of Ford.

The implication is that every place a kind of transportation is needed, it can be replaced with a car, and every place a car is needed, it can be replaced with a Ford, and every place a Ford is needed, it can be replaced with a Mustang. If this cannot be done, then an "is-a" relationship is not present.

10.4   How to Define a Derived Class

A singly inherited derived class is defined by writing:

■   The keyword `class` or `struct`;

■   The name of the derived class;

■   A single colon (:);

■   Optionally, the type of derivation (`private`, `protected`, or `public`);

■   The name of the base class;

■   The remainder of the class definition.

For example, here class `DString` is derived from class `String`. This illustrates the second difference between a class and a structure. When you inherit and create a new class, the compiler assumes that you are doing a *private* derivation. Therefore, if you want to do a *public* derivation, you must explicitly say so. On the other hand, if you create a structure, then the compiler assumes that you are doing a *public* derivation. If you want to do a *private* derivation, you must explicitly say so.

This can be a little confusing, so it's usually best to be consistent in your use of `class` or `struct` in an inheritance hierarchy.

Example 10.1

```
class String
{
   // Class members are private by default
};

class DString : String     // private derivation
{
   // Class members are private by default
};

class DString : public String    // public derivation
{
   // Class members are private by default
};

struct DString : String     // public derivation
{
   // Class members are public by default
};

struct DString : private String     // private derivation
{
   // Class members are public by default
};
```

 Tip

Multiple inheritance, which involves deriving a class from more than one base class, is discussed later in this chapter.

10.5   What Gets Inherited?

In C++ *all* nonstatic data members of a base class are inherited into any instance of the derived class. (Static data members, of course, are not physically encapsulated.) All member functions (non-static and static) of a base class are inherited (for purposes of accessibility) *except* the manager functions (consisting of all constructors, the destructor, and the assignment operator). How the manager functions are handled is discussed later in this chapter.

10.6   Access Privileges

Look at it this way: Just because you inherit your parents' wealth doesn't necessarily mean that you have access to it. And just because a base class member gets inherited, it does not necessarily mean that nonstatic functions in the derived class have access to it.

To be more precise, insofar as new member functions of the derived class are concerned:

In a public derivation:

■   all public class members are inherited as public;

■   all protected class members are inherited as protected;

■   all private class members remain inaccessible.

In a protected derivation:

■   all public class members are inherited as protected;

■   all protected class members are inherited as protected;

■   all private class members remain inaccessible.

In a private derivation:

■   all public class members are inherited as private;

■   all protected class members are inherited as private;

■   all private class members remain inaccessible.

 Tip

This book will focus on public and private derivations only since virtually no one does a protected derivation.

10.7   The Keyword `protected`

Recall that under the principle of data hiding, the only functions that have access to the private members of a class are the class methods and friend functions. This still excludes new methods that a derived class may create. Because every derived instance contains the base class data members, the problem should be obvious: how can new methods in a derived class gain access to these inherited members?

The answer is that the designer of the base class must have declared such members to be *protected*. This means that member functions in a derived class and friends of the derived class may access them. But note that for the member functions, this is true only for the `this` pointer and for an explicit instance of the *same* derived class. For a friend function, it is true only for an explicit instance of the *same* derived class. In other words, what is *not* allowed is for a member function or friend function to gain access to the protected members of an explicitly declared instance of the base class.

 Example 10.2

```
class String
{
   // public interface
       protected:
   char* ptr;
};

class DString : public String
{
   void derived_method(String& b, DString& d);
};

void DString::derived_method(String& b, DString& d)
{
   ptr = 0;        // OK; access via 'this' pointer
   d.ptr = 0;      // OK; explicit instance of DString
   b.ptr = 0;      // Error; access not allowed
}
```

10.8   Changing the Inherited Access

Suppose that you decide to do a private derivation, so that all of the public methods in the base class are inherited as private in the derived class. You have therefore prevented users of the derived class from accessing these methods. But suppose also that there is a particular inherited method that you want to make available to the users, so that its access in the derived class has to be public. How can you do this?

The answer is that the original access privilege of the method in the base class can be "restored" to its original value by declaring the scoped member name in the appropriate access region of the derived class. In the case of member functions, you do this by omitting the return type and formal argument list. For a data member, you omit the type. Note, however, that the access privilege cannot be either increased or decreased.

In the following example, the method `String::upper()` is public, but due to the *private* derivation, it is inherited as *private* in the class `DString`. Nevertheless, the declaration in the derived class changes `String::upper()` back to public access so that the global function `foo()`, using an instance of class `DString`, can call it.

 Example 10.3

```
class String
{
    public:
  String upper() const;
  // Other details omitted
    private:
  char* ptr;
} ;

class DString : String      // private derivation
{
      public:
  DString(const String&);
  String::upper;       // Restores String::upper() to public
  // Other details omitted
} ;

void foo(DString& d)
{
  DString obj(d.upper());    // OK; String::upper() is public
}
```

10.9   Private or Public Inheritance?

Unless you have a good reason for *not* doing so, ensure that you always perform a *public* derivation. As mentioned earlier, with classes the default derivation type is private, and with structures it's public. Only a public derivation can create a true is-a relationship.

Example 10.4

```
class String
{
    public:
  String upper() const;
  // Other details omitted
    private:
  char* ptr;
};

class DString : public String   // public derivation
{
    public:
  DString(const String&);
  // Other details omitted
};

void foo(DString& d)
{
  DString obj(d.upper());    // OK; DString "is a" String
}
```

Once again the String class has a method String::upper() whose purpose is to create and return a new String instance, all of whose letters have been converted into uppercase mode. Since the class DString is publicly derived, you are saying that a DString *is a* String, so the global function foo() has no trouble accessing String::upper().

But look what happens instead if you do a *private* derivation.

Example 10.5

```
class String
{
    public:
  String upper() const;
  // Other details omitted
    private:
  char* ptr;
};

class DString : String       // private derivation
{
    public:
  DString(const String&);
  // Other details omitted
};

void foo(DString& d)
{
  DString obj(d.upper());   // Error; String::upper() is private
}
```

The call to upper() no longer compiles because now the method is *private* inside class DString, and therefore cannot be accessed by the global function foo(). The conclusion is that with a private derivation, an "is-a" relationship has not been achieved because it was just proven that a DString really is *not* a kind of String.

 Tip

The real meaning of private derivation will be discussed shortly.

10.10   Function Hiding

If one or more functions with the same name are declared in a base class, and then are redeclared in a derived class at least once, then *all* of the functions with that name that are inherited into the derived class are *hidden* from consideration by the compiler when it tries to resolve a function call. This is called *function hiding* or *function overriding*. It is *not* function overloading for the simple reason that a base class and a derived class each define a unique scope.

Here's the problem. Suppose you've written a `String` class with a method called `append()` that appends its character input argument onto the end of the invoking object. After this class has been tested and placed into a library, you decide that it would be a good idea to let the users have the option to append a string literal as well. So you derive a new class and add the new `append()` method.

 Example 10.6

```
class String
{
     public:
   void append(char);
   // Other details omitted
     protected:
   char* ptr;
};

class DString : public String
{
     public:
   void append(const char*);
   // Other details omitted
};

void foo(DString& d)
{
   d.append('Z');  // Error; DString::append(char) does
                   // not exist
}
```

Because the method `DString::append(const char*)` has completely hidden the inherited method `String::append(char)`, and the compiler cannot convert a `char` into a `char*`, the result is a compilation error.

Caution

> *When doing a public derivation, you should not change the behavior of an inherited non-virtual function by hiding this function with a new version. Such a technique violates the "is-a" relationship you are asserting because it is no longer true that a derived class instance can be substituted wherever a base class instance is found, and still get the same behavior. (Virtual functions are different, and will be discussed later in this chapter.)*

10.10.1   What If You Have to Do Function Hiding?

Nevertheless, sometimes when a base class must be enhanced, and the source code is not available, it really is necessary to redeclare a function in the derived class with the same name as a function inherited from the base class. The problem now, of course, is that *all* such functions with that name inherited from the base class are *hidden* from the users of the derived class.

 Tip

> *The C++ Draft Working Paper also says that function overloading can be achieved in this situation with a 'using declaration' in the derived class. This feature will be discussed further in Chapter 13, Namespaces.*

10.10.2   The Solution Using Private Inheritance

The solution to this dilemma is to declare the `append(char)` method in the `DString` class, and then simply have its definition invoke the corresponding method in the `String` class. This is called *message passing*.

In addition, you can prevent the user of the derived class from gaining direct access to the bracket operator of the `String` class via an instance or pointer of the `DString` class by doing a *private* derivation. This means that the `append()` method in the `String` class becomes *private* in the `DString` class, and is therefore inaccessible to users of the `DString` class, but still is callable by new methods in the `DString` class. In other words, class `DString` is being implemented "in terms of" class `String`, and merely needs its service(s). This is what a private derivation is all about.

Example 10.7

```
class String
{
    public:
  void append(char);
  // Other details omitted
    protected:
  char* ptr;
};

class DString : private String    // private derivation
{
    public:
  void append(char ch) { String::append(ch); }
  void append(const char*);
  // Other details omitted
};

void foo(DString& d)
{
  d.append('Z'); // OK; calls DString::DString(char)

  // The following line does not compile because
  // String::append() is private in DString
  d.String::append('Z');

  // The following line does not compile because a privately
  // derived class cannot be converted to its base class
  static_cast<String&>(d).append('Z');
}
```

10.10.3   The Solution Using Containment

Because "is implemented in terms of" also applies to a containing relationship, the same effect of a private derivation can be achieved by doing away with inheritance entirely, and simply creating another class that contains an instance of the first class. Then the containing class can work through the public interface of the contained class.

Here is the preceding example using this technique.

 Example 10.8

```
class String
{
    public:
  void append(char);
  // Other details omitted
    protected:
  char* ptr;
};

class DString       // NOT a derived class
{
    public:
  void append(char ch) { obj.append(ch); }
  void append(const char*);
  // Other details omitted
    private:
  String obj;    // Containment
};

void foo(DString& d)
{
  d.append('Z'); // OK; calls DString::append(char)

  // The following line does not compile because
  // obj is private in DString
  d.obj.append('Z');
}
```

10.10.4   Private Inheritance or Containment?

Instead of doing a private derivation, most C++ programmers use containment to achieve "is implemented in terms of". However, with the containing relationship, member functions of the derived class must work through the public interface of the contained instance, and do not have any special privilege to access the protected members. A private derivation is more flexible in this regard because member functions of the derived class do have access to the inherited protected base class members.

10.11   How to Write the Manager Functions

You are responsible for ensuring that the manager functions of a derived class inter-act properly with the corresponding manager functions of the base class. Some-times this is done automatically (e.g., to invoke a base class default constructor or destructor), and sometimes you must write the appropriate syntax (e.g., to invoke a base class copy constructor or assignment operator). As a general rule, always ensure that the derived class manager functions *never* replicate the functionality contained within the base class manager functions.

10.11.1   Constructors Are Not Inherited

First, base class constructors are *not* inherited into a derived class for purposes of accessibility. To prove this, look at the following example.

 Example 10.9

```
class String
{
    public:
  String(const char* = "");
  // Other details omitted
};

class DString : public String;
{
  // Nothing new added
};

void foo()
{
  DString d("Test");   // Error
}
```

Note that the function `String::String(char*)` is *not* invoked by the compiler to satisfy the implicit call to `DString::DString(char*)` as a result of the instan-tiation of `d`. Instead, the compiler insists upon invoking some unambiguous derived class constructor that can accommodate type `char*`. Therefore, a derived class must provide its own constructor(s).

10.11.2   Initializing the Parts of a Derived Object

When a derived class instance comes into existence, it consists of two parts: the inherited instance variables from the base class and any new instance variables that might be added in the derived class definition. A base class constructor is still responsible for initializing the base class instance variables, while a derived class constructor is responsible for initializing the derived class instance variables. So it should be obvious that the instantiation of a derived class must implicitly invoke a constructor in *both* the base class and the derived class.

Fortunately, the compiler guarantees this. Assuming that a suitable unambiguous derived class constructor can be found by the compiler, what happens is that, after the formal arguments have been pushed onto the stack, a call to some base class constructor automatically occurs. After this constructor finishes executing, the compiler again automatically invokes the derived class constructor, and it then executes. This sequence of events corresponds to the layout of the instance variables in memory, in which the base class variables always come before the derived class variables. Isn't that nice?

10.11.3   Using the Base/Member Initialization List

Yes, except for one small thing. The compiler needs to know *which* base class constructor to invoke. If you give it no guidance whatsoever, then it has no choice but to invoke the default constructor. (If the default constructor is missing, or inaccessible, then a compilation error results.) But to have any other constructor invoked, you *must* use the base/member initialization list in the derived class constructor definition. (You should recall that this syntax was first discussed in Chapter 7 when it was used to provide initialization for nonstatic data members of a class.)

To do this, simply write the base class name followed by a parenthesized list of arguments to be passed to the appropriate constructor. This syntax is essentially the same as that of a function-style cast. The base class name followed by an empty set of parentheses invokes the default constructor. Then proceed to initialize any derived class data members. As noted in Chapter 7, the order of items in the base/member initialization list is irrelevant, but it's probably best to specify the base class name first, followed by the derived class data members in declaration order.

The following example shows how the constructors of the `DString` class interact with the corresponding constructors of the `String` class. Also note how the `DString` class contains a constructor that accepts a `String` class object by 'reference-to-`const`'. This is a perfectly reasonable constructor to invoke because frequently a derived class object needs to be constructed from a base class object.

Example 10.10

```
class String
{
    public:
  String(const char* = "");
  String(const String&);
  ~String() { delete [] ptr; }
    protected:
  char* ptr;
  // Other details omitted
};

class DString : public String
{
    public:
  DString() : /* String(), */ length(strlen(ptr)) {}
  DString(const char* p) : String(p), length(strlen(ptr)) {}
  DString(const DString& d) : String(d), length(d.length) {}
  DString(const String& s) : String(s), length(strlen(ptr)) {}
    private:
  unsigned length;
};
```

10.11.4   Derived-to-Base Standard Conversion

What's interesting about the previous example is the derived class copy constructor, and how it invokes the base class copy constructor. Since the actual argument is a derived type, it would appear that you are asking the compiler to find a base class constructor whose one formal argument receives a derived class object by 'reference-to-const'. There's just one small problem with this scenario: a base class knows nothing about any derived classes! So how can it possibly contain a constructor accepting such an argument? The answer is it can't, and really doesn't need to.

C++ solves this dilemma by adding a standard conversion that allows a base class pointer (or reference) to point to (or bind to) a derived class object. This is sometimes called an "upcast" because you are traversing up the inheritance hierarchy. However, the derived class must have been *publicly* inherited for this standard conversion to occur.

Example 10.11

```
class String
{
   // Details omitted
};

class DString : public String   // public derivation
{
   // Details omitted
};

void foo()
{
   DString d;
   String* ptr = &d;    // ptr points to base portion of d
   String& ref = d;     // ref binds to base portion of d
   String obj(d);       // Create obj using String copy ctor
}
```

Therefore, the formal argument in the base class copy constructor automatically refers to the *base portion only* of the derived class object to be copied, and can execute properly. Interestingly, the same standard conversion occurs on the `this` pointer because, in the derived class copy constructor it points to the entire derived object, whereas, in the base class copy constructor, it points only to the base portion of the derived object.

 Caution

> *Do not use a base class pointer to point to an* **array** *of derived class objects. Performing pointer arithmetic on the pointer will not, in all probability, take you to the proper array element because the compiler will only be adding 'sizeof base' each time you add 1 to the pointer.*

10.11.5   Destructor

Just like the base class, there will *always* be a destructor in every derived class (supplied implicitly by the compiler or explicitly by you). After it gains control and runs, it will *automatically* invoke the base class destructor. Obviously, then, the derived class destructor should *never* explicitly invoke the base class destructor.

10.11.6   Assignment Operator

First, like any other class, if you do *not* write an assignment operator in the derived class, the compiler will supply one automatically. In this case, upon gaining control, it will (1) invoke the base class assignment operator, and (2) perform a memberwise copy of any instance variables in the derived class. (A memberwise copy means that each instance variable gets its contents copied into the corresponding instance variable of the object being assigned into. If this instance variable itself is an instance of a class, then its instance variables will also be memberwise-copied.)

However, if you choose to write one, then just like a non-operator function, it hides the base class assignment operator. This means that when it gains control, it must take on the responsibility of explicitly calling the assignment operator in the base class. If not, then you've got a very nice program bug.

There are three ways in which this call can be made, one using functional notation, and two using infix notation.

   Example 10.12

```cpp
class String
{
    public:
    String& operator=(const String&);
    // Other details omitted
};

class DString : public String
{
    public:
    DString& operator=(const DString& d);
    // Other details omitted
    private:
    unsigned length;
};

DString& DString::operator=(const DString& d)
{
    if(this != &d)
    {
        String::operator=(d);                  // Functional notation
        *static_cast<String*>(this) = d;  // Infix notation
        static_cast<String&>(*this) = d;  // Infix notation
        length = d.length;
    }
    return *this;
}
```

Note that like the copy constructor, a derived-to-base standard conversion occurs on the d object and on the this pointer.

10.11.7   Putting It All Together

Here is a complete example using the String class as a base class, from which a derived class called DString is inherited. This derived class adds the data member length to the String abstraction. Observe carefully how the functions of the DString class interact with the corresponding functions of the String class, particularly the overloaded insertion operator and assignment operator.

 Example 10.13

```
// File mystring.h

#ifndef MYSTRING_H
#define MYSTRING_H

#include <iostream.h>
#include <string.h>

class String
{
   friend inline ostream& operator<<(ostream&, const String&);
      public:
   inline String(const char* = "");
   inline String(const String&);
   ~String() { delete [] ptr; }
   inline String& operator=(const String&);
      protected:
   char* ptr;
};

inline ostream& operator<<(ostream& str, const String& s)
{
   const char quote = '"';
   return str << quote << s.ptr << quote;
}

inline String::String(const char* p) : ptr(0)
{
  p = p ? p : "";
  ptr = new char[strlen(p) + 1];
  strcpy(ptr, p);
}

inline String::String(const String& s) : ptr(0)
{
   ptr = new char[strlen(s.ptr) + 1];
   strcpy(ptr, s.ptr);
}
```

(Continued)

```
inline String& String::operator=(const String& s)
{
   if(this != &s)
   {
      unsigned length = strlen(s.ptr);
      if(strlen(ptr) != length)
      {
         delete [] ptr;
         ptr = new char[length + 1];
      }
      strcpy(ptr, s.ptr);
   }
   return *this;
}

#endif

// File dstring.h

#ifndef DSTRING_H
#define DSTRING_H

#include <iostream.h>
#include "mystring.h"

class DString : public String
{
   friend
   inline ostream& operator<<(ostream&, const DString&);
      public:
   DString() : String(), length(strlen(ptr)) {}
   DString(const char* p) : String(p), length(strlen(ptr)) {}
   DString(const DString& d) : String(d), length(d.length) {}
   ~DString() {}
   inline DString& operator=(const DString&);
      private:
   unsigned length;
};

inline ostream& operator<<(ostream& str, const DString& d)
{
   return str << static_cast<const String&>(d)
              << " length = " << d.length;
}
```

(Continued)

```
inline DString& DString::operator=(const DString& d)
{
   if(this != &d)
   {
      String::operator=(d);
      length = d.length;
   }
   return *this;
}

#endif

// File main.cpp

#include <iostream.h>
#include "dstring.h"

int main()
{
   DString n1;
   DString n2("C++ test string");
   DString n3(n2);
   DString n4;
   n4 = "A different string";
   cout << n1 << '\n';
   cout << n2 << '\n';
   cout << n3 << '\n';
   cout << n4 << '\n';
   return 0;
}

/* A typical run would yield:

"" length = 0
"C++ test string" length = 15
"C++ test string" length = 15
"A different string" length = 18

*/
```

10.12   Introduction to Polymorphism

Consider this simple code fragment.

 Example 10.14

```
class String
{
     public:
   void base_method();
};

class DString : public String
{
     public:
   void derived_method();
};

void foo()
{
   String* ptr_base = new DString;
   ptr_base->base_method();      // OK
   ptr_base->derived_method();   // Error; not accessible
   delete ptr_base;
}
```

Remember the derived-to-base standard conversion? That is exactly what is occurring here since the call to `operator new()` returns a pointer of type `DString*`, and the address is being stored into a pointer of type `String*`.

But what good does it do you? After all, since the derived class has a method `derived_method()`, and you attempt to invoke it through the pointer `ptr_base`, you will most certainly get an error for the simple reason that the compiler only "knows" about methods in the *base* class, not the derived class. (Remember: a base class knows nothing about a derived class.) The only method that can be invoked using the pointer is `base_method()`.

Therefore, common sense would seem to tell you that the only type of object that a base class pointer should ever point at is a base class object, and that if you really need to access a derived class method, then you must use a derived class pointer. Of course, since a derived object also contains a base class part, both methods are accessible through a derived class pointer.

Example 10.15

```
class String
{
     public:
   void base_method();
};

class DString : public String
{
     public:
   void derived_method();
};

void foo()
{
   String* ptr_base = new String;
   ptr_base->base_method();          // OK
   delete ptr_base;
   DString* ptr_derived = new DString;
   ptr_derived->base_method();       // OK
   ptr_derived->derived_method();    // OK
   delete ptr_derived;
}
```

Fortunately, your common sense is wrong (at least in this situation). To see why, suppose you are running a used car lot, and your inventory consists of a collection of "pointers" to the various cars on your lot. Each car has an `identify()` method inside of it that says "I am a car", and has another `identify()` method that was added later that says the specific kind of car. Someone then asks you to provide an inventory of all the cars present, so you then proceed to scan your collection of pointers and send some kind of identify message to each car, rightfully expecting that each car will identify itself in some unique fashion. Unfortunately, as things now stand, the only type of response that you will get back from all cars is "I am a car" instead of the message that identifies the specific type of car. Not very useful!

Why did this happen? Simple. Each pointer was of type "car", and therefore, when the `identify()` message was sent, the compiler had no choice except to invoke the method in the "car" part of the object instead of the "specialized" part of the object. Nevertheless, wouldn't it be great if by some magical process the specialized part really could get invoked?

10.12.1   The Meaning of Polymorphism

The answer to the preceding dilemma is found in the concept of *polymorphism* (literally meaning "many forms"). In other words, the same message can be sent to different objects, and that message will take on different "forms" as it is carried out by the methods. In the example above, if the message `identify()` is sent to a Ford, then the method that says "I am a Ford" should be invoked, whereas if the message is sent to a Toyota, then the method that says "I am a Toyota" should be invoked.

10.13   Polymorphism and the Virtual Function

C++ implements polymorphism with the use of a *virtual function*. (In other object-oriented languages, such as Smalltalk and Lisp, polymorphism is done automatically.) The mechanics of a virtual function can be summarized as follows:

> If a function in a base class definition is declared to be virtual, and is declared *exactly* the same way (including the return type, with the exception noted below) in one or more derived classes, then all calls to that function using pointers or references of the base class will invoke the function that is specified by the object being pointed at or referred to, and *not* by the type of the pointer or reference itself.

Insofar as the return type is concerned, C++ allows a virtual function in a base class to return a pointer or reference of its own type, and a derived class to do the same. This would allow, for example, a unary operator such as '++' to be overloaded as a virtual function and to accommodate function chaining by returning its own class type by reference.

The keyword `virtual` is written before the return type (if any) of the function, and can appear *only* inside a class definition. It needs to be written only in the base class because if it's virtual in the base class, then it is automatically virtual in all derived classes. However, it may be a good idea to repeat it in each derived class for better documentation.

A (non-pure) virtual function means that both the function interface and an implementation are inherited. Of course, a derived class may accept this inherited implementation or may choose to define a different implementation.

 Tip

> *The meaning of a "pure" virtual function will appear later in the discussion of abstract base classes.*

Here is a simple example using a virtual function in which two derived classes called `Ford` and `Toyota` are derived from a base class called `Car`. The

`Car::identify()` method in the base class is overridden in each derived class to produce the proper vehicle identification.

 Example 10.16

```
// File car.h

#ifndef CAR_H
#define CAR_H

class Car
{
    public:
  virtual void identify() const;
  ~Car();
};

#endif

// File car.cpp

#include <iostream.h>
#include "car.h"

void Car::identify() const
{
  cout << "I am a car\n";
}

Car::~Car()
{
  cout << "Car destructor\n";
}

// File ford.h

#ifndef FORD_H
#define FORD_H

#include "car.h"

class Ford : public Car
{
    public:
  virtual void identify() const;
  ~Ford();
};

#endif
```

(Continued)

```
// File ford.cpp

#include <iostream.h>
#include "ford.h"

void Ford::identify() const
{
   cout << "I am a Ford\n";
}

Ford::~Ford()
{
   cout << "Ford destructor\n";
}

// File toyota.h

#ifndef TOYOTA_H
#define TOYOTA_H

#include "car.h"

class Toyota : public Car
{
     public:
   virtual void identify() const;
   ~Toyota();
};

#endif

// File toyota.cpp

#include <iostream.h>
#include "toyota.h"

void Toyota::identify() const
{
   cout << "I am a Toyota\n";
}

Toyota::~Toyota()
{
   cout << "Toyota destructor\n";
}
```

(Continued)

```
// File main.cpp

#include "ford.h"
#include "toyota.h"

int main()
{
   Car* inventory[] = { new Car, new Ford, new Toyota };
   const int size = sizeof(inventory) / sizeof(*inventory);
   for(int i = 0; i < size; ++i)
   {
      inventory[i]->identify();
      delete inventory[i];
   }
   return 0;
}

/* The output of this program is:

I am a car
Car destructor
I am a Ford
Car destructor
I am a Toyota
Car destructor

*/
```

 Tip

It doesn't quite make sense to inline a virtual function because using a base class pointer or reference, the compiler cannot possibly perform the code substitution that an inline function implies. It can, however, inline the function if a base class object (not a pointer or reference) is used.

10.13.1   Virtual Destructor

Take a close look at the output of the previous example. While the proper virtual method got invoked, something is terribly wrong with how the two destructors got handled. Notice that the destructors in the derived classes did *not* get called. Obviously this can lead to disaster if the destructors had to perform some real work, such as releasing heap space. Why did this bug happen?

The problem arose during the execution of the `delete` statement which releases the space that each `Car` object occupies. When it gets compiled, the compiler generates a call to the destructor based upon the type of `inventory`, which is an array of pointers to type `Car`. Therefore, the only call is to the destructor of class `Car`, and the destructors of the derived classes `Ford` and `Toyota` are left high and dry.

The solution should be obvious—the destructor in the base class must be declared virtual so that polymorphism can be achieved when a delete statement occurs on a base class pointer. That is, the correct definition for Car should have been:

Example 10.17

```
class Car
{
    public:
    virtual void identify() const;
    virtual ~Car();
};
```

You should now revise Example 10.16 to incorporate this virtual destructor and prove to yourself that you will now get the correct result.

So the question at hand is: Should a base class destructor *always* be declared virtual? The answer is yes if at least one other function in the class is declared virtual. Otherwise, don't declare it virtual because then you will be wasting time (an extra level of indirection) and space (an extra pointer in each object).

The theory is that if no virtual function is present, then the designer does not foresee the possibility that a base class pointer (or reference) will ever be used to point (or refer) to a derived class object. In other words, such a coding technique would only be useful to implement polymorphism, and without at least one virtual function, what's the point of it all?

Tip

A destructor is the only case in which the virtual *keyword may be used with the base class and derived class functions literally having different names.*

10.14 Invoking a Virtual Function from a Base Class Constructor

You cannot invoke a virtual function from a base class constructor and expect polymorphism to come into play because, when the function is executing, the derived class has not been fully constructed, and the code to put the virtual mechanism into effect has not yet been built. The result is that early binding is used, and the base class function is always selected.

The following example proves this. When the base class constructor runs, it selects B::foo() to call instead of D::foo() even though the invoking object is type D.

Example 10.18

```cpp
#include <iostream.h>

class String
{
    public:
  String() { foo(); }
  virtual void foo() { cout << "String::foo called\n"; }
};

class DString : public String
{
    public:
  DString() {}
  virtual void foo() { cout << "DString::foo called\n"; }
};

int main()
{
  DString d;
  return 0;
}

/* The output of this program is:

String::foo called

*/
```

10.15   How to Achieve Polymorphism from a Nonmember Function

The effect of polymorphism via the virtual function mechanism in C++ can be achieved even if a nonmember function is involved. A perfect example would involve an overloaded insertion operator, which is a nonmember function. Thus, given a pointer of reference to some base class, how can the overloaded insertion operator in a derived class gain control? The following example shows how to do this.

Example 10.19

```
#include <iostream.h>

class String
{
   friend ostream& operator<<(ostream&, const String&);
     public:
   String(const char* = "");
   virtual ~String() { delete [] ptr; }
   virtual ostream& display(ostream& = cout) const;
   // Other details omitted
     protected:
   char* ptr;
};

String::String(const char* p) : ptr(0)
{
  p = p ? p : "";
  ptr = new char[strlen(p) + 1];
  strcpy(ptr, p);
}

ostream& operator<<(ostream& str, const String& s)
{
   return s.display(str);
}

ostream& String::display(ostream& str) const
{
  const char quote = '"';
   return str << quote << ptr << quote;
}

class DString : public String
{
    public:
  DString() : String(), length(strlen(ptr)) {}
  DString(const char* p) : String(p), length(strlen(ptr)) {}
  virtual ostream& display(ostream&) const;
    private:
  unsigned length;
};

ostream& DString::display(ostream& str) const
{
   return String::display(str) << "\nlength = " << length;
}
```

(Continued)

```
int main()
{
   String* ptr = new String("Test base class");
   cout << *ptr << '\n';
   delete ptr;
   ptr = new DString("Test derived class");
   cout << *ptr << '\n';
   delete ptr;
   return 0;
}

/* The output of this program is:

"Test base class"
"Test derived class"
length = 18

*/
```

10.16   Abstract Base Classes

An abstract base class (ABC) is used when inheritance involves the process of *specification* (not specialization). In other words, the base class contains only a function declaration, and the derived class must *specify* its implementation.

An ABC is created by the inclusion of at least one *pure virtual function*. This is a virtual function that has the syntax '= 0' appended to the signature within the class definition. By implication, this means you *cannot* declare a base class object. Instead, the class provides the beginnings of a derivation hierarchy, and it is up to the derived class(es) to "fill in the details" via specification. A derived class inherits the interface of the pure virtual function, and must provide the implementation. Otherwise, the derived class itself becomes another ABC.

 Tip

> *A pure virtual function may be defined outside (not inside) the class definition. Note that this implementation is not inherited into the derived classes, which still must provide their own implementations.*

For example, suppose you want to pay a visit to your friendly banker and apply for some kind of loan, the details of which have yet to be determined, including the exact type of loan. Because your banker once had a course in C++, she has already written a very generalized class called Loan that can be used for literally any kind of loan.

Example 10.20

```
// File loan.h

#ifndef LOAN_H
#define LOAN_H

class ostream;
class Loan
{
    friend ostream& operator<<(ostream&, const Loan&);
        public:
    Loan(double, double, int, const char*);
    virtual ~Loan() {}
    virtual void compute() = 0;   // pure virtual function
        protected:
    double principal;
    double yearly_rate;
    int length_in_years;
    double monthly_payment;
    const char* const type;
} ;

#endif

// File loan.cpp

#include <iostream.h>
#include "loan.h"

ostream& operator<<(ostream& str, const Loan& L)
{
    str << L.type << '\n';
    str << "Principal = $" << L.principal << '\n';
    str << "Rate = " << L.yearly_rate * 100 << '%'
        << '\n';
    str << "Length = " << L.length_in_years << '\n';
    str << "Payment = $" << L.monthly_payment << '\n';
    return str;
}

Loan::Loan(double p, double r, int l, const char* t)
          : principal(p), yearly_rate(r),
        length_in_years(l), type(t),
        monthly_payment(0) {}
```

Now you can create some classes of specific loans and implement the `compute()` function for each one.

First, we'll assume that a simple interest loan is one in which you will pay back the full amount in equal monthly payments consisting of both principal and interest. Even though the amount of the principal balance is being reduced each month, the interest being paid does not change. This is how such a loan might be implemented using a class called `Simple`.

Example 10.21

```cpp
// File simple.h

#ifndef SIMPLE_H
#define SIMPLE_H

#include "loan.h"

class Simple : public Loan
{
     public:
   Simple(double, double, int);
   virtual void compute();
};

#endif

// File simple.cpp

#include "simple.h"

Simple::Simple(double prin, double rate, int length)
        : Loan(prin, rate, length,
        "Simple interest loan") {}

void Simple::compute()
{
   // P = Principal
   // R = Monthly rate
   // L = Length in months
   // Monthly payment is: (P * (R * L + 1)) / L

   double monthly_rate = yearly_rate / 12;
   int length_in_months = length_in_years * 12;
   monthly_payment = (principal * (monthly_rate
        * length_in_months + 1)) / length_in_months;
}
```

Next, a fully amortized loan is also one in which equal monthly payments are made. But now the interest is computed on the remaining principal balance, and the difference between the payment and the interest paid is applied toward paying off the principal. Since the remaining principal has been reduced, next month's interest payment will be slightly smaller while the principal reduction will be slightly larger. A class called `Amortizd` will provide this abstraction.

Example 10.22

```
// File amortizd.h

#ifndef AMORTIZD_H
#define AMORTIZD_H

#include "loan.h"

class Amortizd : public Loan
{
     public:
  Amortizd(double, double, int);
  virtual void compute();
};

#endif

// File amortizd.cpp

#include <math.h>
#include "amortizd.h"

Amortizd::Amortizd(double prin, double rate, int length)
       : Loan(prin, rate, length, "Amortized loan") {}

void Amortizd::compute()
{
  // P = Principal
  // R = Monthly rate,
  // L = Length in months
  // Monthly payment is:
  // (P * R * (1 + R)^L) / ((1 + R)^L - 1)

     double monthly_rate = yearly_rate / 12;
     int length_in_months = length_in_years * 12;
     double temp = pow(1 + monthly_rate, length_in_months);
     monthly_payment = (principal * monthly_rate *
        temp) / (temp - 1);
}
```

Now you can create some kind of container object, e.g., an array of pointers, that will be used to point to instances of the two specific types of loans. Let's assume that you're interested in a $300,000 loan, at 8.00% interest, for 30 years. Now it's just a matter of looping through the array, sending the compute() message, displaying the answer, and deleting the loan. Because the compute() function in the base class was declared to be virtual, the compute() function for the proper type of loan is guaranteed to get control.

Example 10.23

```cpp
// File main.cpp

#include <iostream.h>
#include "loan.h"
#include "simple.h"
#include "amortizd.h"

int main()
{
   Loan* portfolio[] =
   {
      new Simple(300000.0, 0.08, 30),
      new Amortizd(300000.0, 0.08, 30)
   };
   const int size = sizeof(portfolio) / sizeof(*portfolio);
   for(int i = 0; i < size; ++i)
   {
      portfolio[i]->compute();
      cout << *portfolio[i] << '\n';
      delete portfolio[i];
   }
   return 0;
}

/* The output of this program is:

Simple interest loan
Principal = $300000
Rate = 8%
Length = 30
Payment = $2833.33

Amortized loan
Principal = $300000
Rate = 8%
Length = 30
Payment = $2201.29

*/
```

10.17   Multiple Inheritance

Multiple inheritance occurs when a derived class is inherited from more than one base class.

For example, let's start with a class called `Appliance` that contains a cost.

 Example 10.24

```
// File applianc.h

#ifndef APPLIANC_H
#define APPLIANC_H

class Appliance
{
    public:
  Appliance(double c);
  double get_cost() const;
    protected:
  double cost;
};

#endif
```

Next, you would certainly have to agree that a radio *is a* kind of appliance, so let's publicly derive a class called `Radio` with some representative data and public interface.

Example 10.25

```
// File radio.h

#ifndef RADIO_H
#define RADIO_H

#include "applianc.h"
class Radio : public Appliance
{
   enum band {AM, FM};
      public:
   Radio(double cost, band am_fm = AM, double station = 810)
      : Appliance(cost), am_fm(am_fm), station(station) {}
   void set_station(double);
   double get_station() const;
   void set_band(band);
      protected:
   band am_fm;
   double station;
};

#endif
```

In preparation for the creation of a clock class, we will need the abstraction of a class called `Time` that can keep time.

 Example 10.26

```
// File time.h

#ifndef TIME_H
#define TIME_H

class ostream;
class Time
{
   friend ostream& operator<<(ostream&, const Time&);
      public:
   Time(int h, int m, int s);
   void set_time();
   Time get_time() const;
      protected:
   int hours, minutes, seconds;
};

#endif
```

A clock also is a kind of appliance, and it contains an instance of the `Time` class.

Example 10.27

```
// File clock.h

#ifndef CLOCK_H
#define CLOCK_H

#include "applianc.h"
class Clock : public Appliance
{
    protected:
  static Time default_time;
    public:
  Clock(double cost, const Time& clock_time = default_time)
    : Appliance(cost), clock_time(clock_time) {}
  void set_clock_time(const Time&);
  Time get_clock_time() const;
    protected:
  Time clock_time;
};

#endif

// File clock.cpp

#include "clock.h"
Time Clock::default_time(12, 0, 0);
```

An alarm clock then *is a* kind of clock with its own time abstraction, and the added capabilities to set the alarm time and retrieve it.

Example 10.28

```
// File alarm.h

#ifndef ALARM_H
#define ALARM_H

#include "clock.h"
class Alarm_clock : public Clock
{
    public:
  Alarm_clock(double cost,
    const Time& alarm_time = default_time)
    : Clock(cost), alarm_time(alarm_time) {}
  void set_alarm_time(const Time&);
  Time get_alarm_time() const;
    protected:
  Time alarm_time;
};

#endif
```

Now the stage is set, because from both the alarm clock and the radio, we can multiply derive a clock-radio class with the added capability to wake up to either music or a buzzing noise. The syntax to write a derived class that is created as the result of multiple inheritance is as follows:

■   The keyword `class` or `struct`;

■   The name of the derived class;

■   A single colon (:);

■   The type of derivation (`private`, `protected` or `public`);

■   The name of the base class;

■   A comma, and a repeat of the preceding two items as many times as required;

■   The remainder of the class definition.

   Example 10.29

```
// File c_radio.h

#ifndef C_RADIO_H
#define C_RADIO_H

#include "alarm.h"
#include "radio.h"
class Clock_radio : public Alarm_clock, public Radio
{
   enum sound {radio, buzz};
      public:
   Clock_radio(double cost, sound sound_type = buzz)
      : Appliance(cost),    // Note this particular call
         sound_type(sound_type) {}
   void set_wakeup(sound = buzz);
      private:
   sound sound_type;
};

#endif
```

A test of all of the these classes might look as follows.

 Example 10.30

```
// File main.cpp

#include <iostream.h>
#include "c_radio.h"

int main()
{
    Clock_radio GE(49.95);
    cout << GE.get_cost() << '\n';    // Error; ambiguous
    cout << GE.get_station() << '\n';
    cout << GE.get_clock_time() << '\n';
    cout << GE.get_alarm_time() << '\n';
    return 0;
}
```

10.17.1   Virtual Base Classes

In the previous example, the problem with the call to the `Appliance::get_cost()` method is that since both the `Radio` and `Clock` classes inherently contain an `Appliance` class, the `Clock_radio` class then has inherited *two* `Appliance` objects, and the compiler doesn't know which one to invoke.

The solution is to make the `Appliance` class a *virtual base class* by adding the keyword `virtual` during the creation of both the `Radio` and `Clock` classes. This word may appear before or after the derivation type, and both derived classes must specify it. The net result is that when the class `Clock_radio` is declared, it will contain only *one* copy of the `Appliance` class.

Thus, the corrected definitions for both the `Radio` and `Clock` classes would be:

 Example 10.31

```
class Radio : virtual public Appliance
{
    // Details omitted
};

class Clock : virtual public Appliance
{
    // Details omitted
};
```

10.17.2 Initializing a Virtual Base Class

Note that since the `Appliance` class needs an argument passed into its constructor in order to initialize the `cost` field, you could reasonably inquire as to which of its derived classes should take on this responsibility, the `Radio` or the `Clock` class. Surprisingly, the answer is neither one, because there really is no reason to prefer one over the other. Instead, this job becomes the responsibility of the constructor of the `Clock_radio` class (the "most derived class"). That is why the base/member initialization list in the `Clock_radio` constructor specifies the `Appliance` class and an argument to be passed to its constructor. This call will occur before the parent classes of `Clock_radio` are constructed, and the initialization that the `Radio` and `Clock` classes do insofar as the `cost` data member is concerned are completely ignored. If the `Clock_radio` class fails to do this initialization explicitly, then the default constructor in the `Appliance` class will be invoked, but because the `Appliance` class does not have a default constructor, the program will fail to compile.

 Tip

> *Multiple inheritance can be very confusing. It's like a parachute—something that is very rarely needed. But when it is needed, aren't you glad you have it?*

Review Questions

1.   What is the advantage of inheritance in C++?

2.   What is the relationship between the base class and the derived class?

3.   Why is the access specifier `protected` needed?

4.   What is the difference between a private, public, and protected derivation?

5.   How does a base class receive its arguments in order to construct its members properly?

6.   What happens if a derived class fails to explicitly provide arguments to the base class constructor?

7.   How can the overloaded assignment operator in a derived class invoke the overloaded assignment operator in the base class?

8.   Why can a base class pointer point to a derived class instance?

9.   When using a base class pointer, why does it not matter that the pointer may be pointing to a derived class instance?

10. What is polymorphism, and how does C++ implement it?

11. Explain how a virtual function works.

 Exercise 10.1

Using the `Card` class that you developed in Chapter 8, Exercise 4, replace the `display()` method with an overloaded insertion operator. You will also need to overload the increment operator for the suit and rank. Then derive a new class called `Better_card` that adds an enumeration for the color of the card (red or black) and an insertion operator that displays this color after invoking the insertion operator for the `Card` class. Encapsulate a deck of 52 cards of this derived type and display the entire deck, making sure to output the suit, rank and color of each card.

 Exercise 10.2

If you haven't already done so, then do Exercise #1 from Chapter 9 to get a working `String` class.

While this class works well to provide an effective enhancement to strings in C, the implementation is inefficient because of the vast amount of heap management that is occurring. For example, when the copy constructor or overloaded assignment operator is called, the string literal to which the class's pointer is pointing must be copied so that each instance has its own private resources on the heap. If this were not done, then two `String` instances would be pointing to the same heap space, and when the constructor functions get called, an attempt would be made to release the same heap space twice.

A better approach to handling the String class would be to use the concept of *reference counting*. In this scheme it is perfectly permissible to have more than one String instance point to the same space on the heap. In other words, if two String instances are identical, then the string literals are also identical and may be shared by the two instances. Of course, this yields some very serious problems that must eventually be addressed.

To implement reference counting, a new field (let's call it ref_count) must be added to each instantiation of the String class. This field maintains a count of the number of instances of another class, the purpose of which is to share the string literal that lives on the heap.

Let's call this new class Ref_string and derive it *privately* from the String class. The private derivation ensures that the public interface of the String class is hidden from the users of the Ref_string class. In the interest of completeness, be sure to define all of the manager functions and have them interface the corresponding function in the String class.

Once the class Ref_string has been written, it must then be "wrapped" inside another class that contains as its one data member (ptr_rs) a pointer to an instance of class Ref_string. Let's call this class Wrapper, and say that it must be granted friendship by the Ref_string class. Now, if two instances of the Wrapper class need to point to the same string literal, then it's just a matter of having both pointers point to the same instance of class Ref_string.

Write the class Wrapper and its member definitions. Note that the field ref_count within the Ref_string class is really for the use of the functions inside the Wrapper class, so that setting, incrementing, and decrementing this field should be done within the Wrapper class, *not* the Ref_string class. Each class should know how to display itself.

Test your program with the following `main()` function:

```
int main()
{
   Wrapper* p1 = new Wrapper("Adam");
   Wrapper* p2 = new Wrapper(*p1);
   cout << *p1 << '\n';
   cout << *p2 << '\n';

   delete p2;
   p2 = new Wrapper(*p1);
   cout << *p1 << '\n';
   cout << *p2 << '\n';

   *p1 = "Eve";
   cout << *p1 << '\n';
   cout << *p2 << '\n';

   *p1 = *p2;
   cout << *p1 << '\n';
   cout << *p2 << '\n';

   delete p1;
   delete p2;

   return 0;
}

/* The output of this program is:

"Adam" count = 2
"Adam" count = 2
"Adam" count = 2
"Adam" count = 2
"Eve" count = 1
"Adam" count = 1
"Adam" count = 2
"Adam" count = 2

*/
```

Exercise 10.3

Given the following main() function:

```cpp
// File main.cpp

#include <iostream.h>
#include "contain.h"
#include "array.h"
#include "list.h"

int main()
{
   Container* ptr[] = { new Array, new List };
   const int size = sizeof(ptr) / sizeof(*ptr);
   for(int i = 0; i < size; ++i)
   {
      const int limit = 2;
      for(int j = 0; j < limit; ++j)
        ptr[i]->add(j * 2);
      cout << *ptr[i];
      for(int k = 0; k < limit * 2; ++k)
        cout << k << " is " << (ptr[i]->holds(k)
                 ? "present\n" : "not present\n");
      delete ptr[i];
      cout << "=================\n";
   }
   return 0;
}

/* The output of this program is:

Array
0
2
0 is present
1 is not present
2 is present
3 is not present
=================
List
0
2
0 is present
1 is not present
2 is present
3 is not present
=================

*/
```

Write an abstract base class called `Container` from which the classes `Array` and `List` are derived. The class `Array` should be implemented as a pointer to an unknown number of `int`s, and the class `List` should be implemented as a linked list of `int`s. The `Container` class declares the methods `add()` and `holds()` to be polymorphic, and retains the description of a derived class in a data member of type `const char* const`.

Chapter 11

Templates

11.1   Introduction to Function Templates

Function templates provide you with the capability to write a single function that serves as a skeleton, or template, for a family of similar functions. In this function at least one formal argument is generic, or parameterized. By writing such a function, you provide the user with a powerful capability to invoke the function with an unlimited range of different types.

11.2   What's Wrong with Function Overloading?

In Chapter 9 you learned a great deal about how to overload functions in C++ and the benefits you may achieve from doing so. The chief advantage to this process is that it relieves someone who is using your functions from having to know about different names for various functions (either at global or class scope) that essentially do the same task. Unfortunately, overloaded functions, while a vast improvement over what's available in C, aren't the ultimate solution to the problem that is inherent in writing functions that are similar in their behavior and differ only in the types of the data upon which they operate.

To understand this better, here is an inline function called `max()` that returns the greater of its two input arguments. Of course, it has to be continually overloaded in order to accommodate the various types of arguments that can conceivably be used to invoke it.

Example 11.1

```cpp
#include <iostream.h>

inline int max(int x, int y)
{
   return (x > y) ? x : y;
}

inline long max(long x, long y)
{
   return (x > y) ? x : y;
}

inline double max(double x, double y)
{
   return (x > y) ? x : y;
}

inline char max(char x, char y)
{
   return (x > y) ? x : y;
}

int main()
{
   int a = 1;
   int b = 2;
   cout << max(a, b) << '\n';     // Invoke max(int, int)

   long c = 4L;
   long d = 3L;
   cout << max(c, d) << '\n';     // Invoke max(long, long)

   double e = 5.62;
   double f = 3.48;
   cout << max(e, f) << '\n';     // Invoke max(double, double)

   char g = 'A';
   char h = 'a';
   cout << max(g, h) << '\n';     // Invoke max(char, char)

   return 0;
}

/* The output of this program is:

2
4
5.62
a

*/
```

Even though function overloading has been used, the problem with this example is that there is still too much repetitious coding because each function is doing essentially the same thing—returning the greater of its two input arguments.

Now, instead of your having to write many similar `max()` functions, wouldn't it be nice to be able to write just *one* `max()` function that returns the greater of its two input arguments and can accommodate virtually any type of input argument?

11.3   Why Not Use a Macro?

Certainly you can write a macro to "solve" this problem. The trouble is:

- You've lost the ability to ensure that you are not comparing arguments of different, but compatible types;

- Macros are handled by the preprocessor which makes debugging more difficult;

- It's easy to make a mistake when writing a macro, such as forgetting a set of parentheses;

- Macros can have nasty side effects, such as applying an increment or decrement operator more than once.

11.4   How to Write a Function Template

As you have probably figured out by now, a function template solves the problem quite nicely. First, function templates should be written at the start of your program in the global area, or you may place them into a header file. All function templates include a template declaration, which has the following syntax:

- The C++ keyword `template`;

- A left angle bracket (<);

- A list of generic types. If there is more than one type, then each one is separated by a comma. A generic type consists of two parts:

  1. The keyword `class` or `typename` (Note: this use of the word `class` has nothing to do with the keyword `class` that is used to create a user-defined type. Instead, it should be interpreted as meaning "type".);

  2. An identifier that represents some generic type, and that will be used whenever this type needs to be written in the function definition. Typically the name `T` is used (as in Template), but any valid C++ name will do.

- A right angle bracket (>).

Tip

> *Borland 5.0 supports the use of the keyword* `typename` *instead of the keyword* `class` *in a template declaration. For purposes of backward compatibility, however, it will not be used in this book. Another use for* `typename` *is shown later in this chapter.*

Then you continue with the function declaration or definition itself, preceded by any of the normal modifiers, e.g., `inline`, `extern`, `static`, etc.

Now let's solve the `max()` problem by writing a function template that takes two generic types and returns the greater of its two input values. Of course, if `T` represents a user-defined type, then it is the responsibility of the designer of class `T` (or an enumeration of type `T`) to ensure either that the appropriate operators have been properly overloaded, i.e., `operator>()` and `operator<<()`, or that a suitable user-defined conversion function exists.

Example 11.2

```
#include <iostream.h>

template <class T>
inline const T& max(const T& x, const T& y)
{
   return (x > y) ? x : y;
}

int main()
{
   int a = 1;
   int b = 2;
   cout << max(a, b) << '\n'; // Instantiate with type int

   long c = 4L;
   long d = 3L;
   cout << max(c, d) << '\n'; // Instantiate with type long

   double e = 5.62;
   double f = 3.48;
   cout << max(e, f) << '\n'; // Instantiate with type double

   char g = 'A';
   char h = 'a';
   cout << max(g, h) << '\n'; // Instantiate with type char

   return 0;
}

/* The output of this program is:

2
4
5.62
a

*/
```

When a function template is called, the compiler deduces the type of the actual argument and substitutes it for the generic type, thereby instantiating what is called a *generated function*. In the previous example, the compiler will instantiate generated functions with types `int`, `long`, `double`, and `char`, respectively.

Note that the actual arguments are being received in the function template by reference, and the answer is returned by reference, *not* by value. This saves three calls to the copy constructor in case T represents a user-defined type. On the other hand, for fundamental types, passing by reference is slightly more inefficient than passing by value.

Caution

In versions of Borland C++ prior to 5.0, if you include `<stdlib.h>` *and want the capability to define your own* `min()` *and* `max()` *functions, then ensure that you have defined the preprocessor variable:* `__MINMAX_DEFINED`

11.5   Explicitly Specifying the Type

The type that the template parameter takes on at instantiation time can be explicitly specified by writing it between angle brackets immediately after the function name. If the angle brackets are empty, then it has no effect because the type will be deduced from the actual argument anyway. But if you write the type, then the deduced type is superseded.

Example 11.3

```
// File max.h

#ifndef MAX_H
#define MAX_H

template <class T>
const T& max(const T& x, const T& y)
{
   return (x > y) ? x : y;
}

#endif

// File main.cpp

#include <iostream.h>
#include "max.h"

int main()
{
   double a = 6.5;
   double b = 4.3;
   cout << max<>(a, b) << '\n';              // type double
   cout << max<double>(a, b) << '\n';        // type double
   cout << max<int>(a, b) << '\n';           // type int
   return 0;
}

/* The output of this program is:

6.5
6.5
6

*/
```

This technique of explicitly specifying the types is useful when at least one of the parameterized types is not a formal argument in the function, and therefore cannot be deduced. For example, if you want to have the `max()` function return a type that is different from the type of the input argument, then you could do this.

 Example 11.4

```
// File max.h

#ifndef MAX_H
#define MAX_H

template <class T, class U>
T max(const U& x, const U& y)
{
    return (x > y) ? x : y;
}

#endif

// File main.cpp

#include <iostream.h>
#include "max.h"

int main()
{
    double a = 6.5;
    double b = 4.3;
    // cout << max(a, b) << '\n';    // Error; what is type T?
    cout << max<int>(a, b) << '\n';// OK; T == int,
                                   // U == double
    cout << max<int, double>(a, b) << '\n';// Same as above
    return 0;
}

/* The output of this program is:

6
6

*/
```

11.6   Make Function Templates Available to the Compiler

Function template definitions must be available to the compiler when the call to the function is encountered, so they usually are stored in a header file that is included. In other words, to keep things as simple as possible, do not use modularity with function templates by segregating the declaration (in a header file) from the actual definition (in a definition file) because if you do, then the linker will never know anything about the function template definition since this definition cannot be compiled into object format like non-template function definitions. This situation is shown in the following example in which the linker cannot find the definition of `max(int, int)` to satisfy the call.

 Example 11.5

```cpp
// File max.h

#ifndef MAX_H
#define MAX_H

template <class T>
const T& max(const T& x, const T& y);

#endif

// File max.cpp

template <class T>
const T& max(const T& x, const T& y)
{
    return (x > y) ? x : y;
}

// File main.cpp

#include <iostream.h>
#include "max.h"

int main()
{
    int a = 1;
    int b = 2;
    cout << max(a, b) << '\n';  // Linker error
    return 0;
}
```

11.7   Including a Function Template in Two Different Compilation Units

Normally, when two different compilation units include the same definition (data or function), the linker will complain about encountering a duplicate definition. But in the case of a function template, if both compilation units happen to instantiate the function template with the same type, then the two object files that are passed on to the linker will *not* cause a duplicate definition error.

This is proven by the following example in which the function max() gets instantiated with type char in two definition files.

 Example 11.6

```
// File max.h

#ifndef MAX_H
#define MAX_H

template <class T>
inline const T& max(const T& x, const T& y)
{
    return (x > y) ? x : y;
}

#endif

// File funct1.cpp

#include <iostream.h>
#include "max.h"

void funct1(char x, char y)
{
    cout << "max = " << max(x, y) << '\n';
}
```

(Continued)

```cpp
// File funct2.cpp

#include <iostream.h>
#include "max.h"

void funct2(char x, char y)
{
   cout << "max = " << max(x, y) << '\n';
}

// File main.cpp

void funct1(char, char);
void funct2(char, char);

int main()
{
   char a = 'A';
   char b = 'B';
   char c = 'C';
   char d = 'D';
   funct1(a, b);
   funct2(c, d);
   return 0;
}

/* The output of this program is:

max = B
max = D

*/
```

11.8   Instantiating With Different Types

If the generic type T is deduced to be different for any of the actual arguments, then the generated function cannot be instantiated. For example, the following program will not compile because the first argument is an int and the second is a double.

 Example 11.7

```
#include <iostream.h>

template <class T>
inline const T& max(const T& x, const T& y)
{
   return (x > y) ? x : y;
}

int main()
{
   int a = 5;
   double b = 6.1;
   cout << max(a, b) << '\n';  // Error; different types
   return 0;
}
```

11.9   Mixing Parameterized and Non-parameterized Types

There is no problem in writing a function template in which the formal argument list contains a mixture of parameterized and non-parameterized types. Here is an example of a function template that returns the largest element of an array consisting of literally any type of data. Of course, the function assumes that the 'greater than' operator has meaning for type T, whatever that might be.

 Example 11.8

```
#include <iostream.h>

template <class T>
const T& largest(const T* ptr, unsigned size)
{
   unsigned answer = 0;
   for(unsigned i = 1; i < size; ++i)
      if(ptr[i] > ptr[answer])
         answer = i;
   return ptr[answer];
}

int main()
{
   const int array[] = { 4, 7, -3, 32, 0 };
   const unsigned size = sizeof(array) / sizeof(*array);
   cout << "Largest value = " << largest(array, size) << '\n';
   return 0;
}

/* The output of this program is:

Largest value = 32

*/
```

11.10   Specializing a Function Template

Sometimes a function template just can't handle all of the possible instantiations that you might want to do. In this case you must specialize the function template by declaring the function and specifying fixed argument types. Pointers are a good example of where you need to specialize a function template because pointers always consist of two parts: the pointer itself and the object to which it points. And, as you know, pointers always need special handling.

Consider the `max()` function template called with two pointers, each of which points to a string literal.

 Example 11.9

```
#include <iostream.h>

template <class T>
inline const T& max(const T& x, const T& y)
{
   return (x > y) ? x : y;
}

int main()
{
   const char* p1 = "A";
   const char* p2 = "B";
   cout << max(p1, p2) << '\n';
   return 0;
}
```

Do you see the problem here? The compiler replaces the parameterized type with type `char*`, and the generated function now is in the dubious position of comparing two *addresses* instead of comparing the two string literals to which the addresses point. Not good.

To fix the problem, you need to write a specialized `max()` function that is specifically designed to accommodate strings. So this is what the revised example now looks like.

Example 11.10

```cpp
#include <iostream.h>
#include <string.h>

template <class T>
inline const T& max(const T& x, const T& y)
{
   return (x > y) ? x : y;
}

// template <>
inline const char* max(const char* x, const char* y)
{
   return strcmp(x, y) > 0 ? x : y;
}

int main()
{
   const char* p1 = "A";
   const char* p2 = "B";
   cout << max(p1, p2) << '\n';  // call max(const char*...

   int a = 4;
   int b = 2;
   cout << max(a, b) << '\n';     // call max(const T&...
   return 0;
}

/* The output of this program is:

B
4

*/
```

Note the commented line in the example above. According to the C++ Draft, this is the correct way to indicate that a template is being *specialized*, i.e., by writing the keyword `template` followed by empty angle brackets. Otherwise, a call to `max()` using type `char*` would result in a duplicate definition error. In other words, without the specialization syntax, the compiler would deduce a generated function (with type `T` being `char*`) from the function template, and then not know which function to call. Unfortunately, Borland C++ 5.0 does not yet support this syntax, so it will continue to be shown as a commented line.

11.11   Declaring a Function

In order to get the correct answer, sometimes it is only necessary to *declare* a function (as opposed to defining it) that has the same modifiers in its declaration as those of an existing function template.

For example, here the `max()` function has been declared to accept two `int` arguments by reference-to-`const`, and to return the same type. Note how this signature corresponds to the function template. When a call is made to `max()` with different types, the compiler has no problem in converting the `unsigned` into type `int` in order to match the declaration, and will automatically provide a definition of the function template to the linker that accommodates two `int`'s by reference-to-`const`.

 Example 11.11

```
#include <iostream.h>

template <class T>
inline const T& max(const T& x, const T& y)
{
   return (x > y) ? x : y;
}

inline const int& max(const int& x, const int& y);

int main()
{
   int a = -6;
   unsigned b = 12;
   cout << max(a, b) << '\n';
   return 0;
}

/* The output of this program is:

12

*/
```

11.12   Specializing vs. Overloading a Function Template

You must be careful to differentiate between *overloading* a function template vs. *specializing* a function template. Overloading means that a function with another signature has been entered into the overloading list in addition to any form that can get instantiated by argument deduction. As shown in the example above, this allows normal conversions to be used when calling the function. Using the special-ization syntax `template <>` does *not* cause the function to be declared. It merely says that if the generic type `T` should happen to be deduced to type `int`, then use the specialized form of the function rather than generating one from the template. Again returning to the example above, if this had been done, then a compilation error would have resulted because there is no function available that can accept the two different types `int` and `unsigned`.

 Caution

> *You can only* declare *a function when overloading a function template. If you* define *it, then you will get a duplicate definition error.*

11.12.1   Overloading Parameterized Pointer and Non-pointer Types

You may overload a function template if the only difference is that one function receives its argument by value and the other receives its argument by pointer. If the function is called with a non-pointer type, then the compiler has no choice except to generate a function from the template accepting a non-pointer type.

However, if the function is called with a pointer type, then both template functions are callable. But according to Section 14.10.6 of the C++ Draft, since the function accepting a pointer type is more specialized than the one not accepting a pointer type, the pointer type will be called. In simple English, retaining the pointer associated with the actual argument to deduce that type `T` is really type `int` constitutes a better match than discarding the pointer in order to deduce that type `T` is really type `int *`.

 Example 11.12

```
template <class T>
void foo(T);

template <class T>
void foo(T*);

void g(int a, int* b)
{
   foo(a);    // OK; calls foo(T)
   foo(b);    // OK; calls foo(T*)
}
```

 Caution

> *Borland 5.0 incorrectly yields an ambiguity error on the call with the pointer type.*

11.13   `const` **vs. non-**`const` **Arguments**

Unlike non-parameterized functions, a function template with a parameter of type T can bind to either a `const` or non-`const` instance. For example, in the following program *all* of the function calls are valid.

 Example 11.13

```
template <class T>
void foo(T& arg);

template <class T>
void bar(const T& arg);

void f(int a, const int b)
{
   foo(a);       // OK; T == int, arg == int
   bar(a);       // OK; T == int, arg == const int
   foo(b);       // OK; T == const int, arg == const int
   bar(b);       // OK; T == int, arg == const int
}
```

The ramification is that you should probably not attempt to overload a function template based upon `const` vs. non-`const` arguments received by pointer or reference.

 Example 11.14

```
template <class T>
void foo(T&);

template <class T>
void foo(const T&);

void bar(int a, const int b)
{
   foo(a);    // OK; call foo(T&)
   foo(b);    // Ambiguous; can call foo(T&) or foo(const T&)
}
```

Per Section 13.3.1 of the C++ Draft, for the argument a of type int, the compiler deduces two signatures: `foo(int&)` and `foo(const int&)`. Both rank as "exact match", but are distinguishable because the second adds a `const` modifier, thereby making the first a better choice. Therefore, calling `foo()` with an int calls `foo(T&)`.

For the second argument `b` of type `const int`, the compiler deduces two signatures, both of which are `foo(const int&)` (since `T` is type `const int` in the first case and type `int` in the second case). Since the signatures are the same, the call is ambiguous.

Caution

Borland 5.0 incorrectly yields an ambiguity error on the call with type `int`.

Since this overloading does not work in all cases, you must decide whether or not to write the keyword `const` in front of your formal arguments. In Example 11.2 this was done in order to support constants which, as you know, cannot be bound to non-constant types. The only "problem" is that the function can never be used to create a modifiable object, which might be useful if, for example, you want to store a value into the greater of the two input arguments.

Example 11.15

```
#include <iostream.h>

template <class T>
inline const T& max(const T& x, const T& y)
{
    return (x > y) ? x : y;
}

void f()
{
    cout << max(1, 2) << '\n';      // OK
    int a = 1;
    int b = 2;
    max(a, b) = 0;    // Compilation error; not modifiable
}
```

Of course, if the `max()` function had received its arguments by value, then the problem goes away, except for the fact that now you are in danger of invoking the copy constructor many times for user-defined types.

If this is not already confusing enough, consider the `const`/`volatile` (cv) qualifiers on the actual and formal arguments when the compiler tries to determine if a function template constitutes an acceptable match.

Example 11.16

```
template <class T>
void f1(T&, T&);

template <class T>
void f2(T&, const T&);

template <class T>
void f3(const T&, T&);

template <class T>
void f4(const T&, const T&);

void g(int a, const int b)
{
    f1(a, b);      // Error; T == int, T == const int
    f2(a, b);      // OK; T == int, T == int
    f3(a, b);      // Error; T == int, T == const int
    f4(a, b);      // OK; T == int, T == int
}
```

■ The call to f1() is invalid because T becomes type int for the first argument and type const int for the second argument, and of course it cannot be both types at the same tine.

■ The call to f2() is valid because T becomes type int for both arguments.

■ The call to f3() is invalid because T becomes type int for the first argument and type const int for the second argument.

■ The call to f4() is valid because T becomes type int for both arguments.

In summary:

■ For a formal argument of type const T&, the compiler infers (deduces) that T is the type of the actual argument without the const-qualification.

■ For a formal argument of type T&, the compiler honors any const-qualified actual argument by making T const-qualified. The formal argument still cannot be bound to a constant actual argument (as opposed to a const-qualified actual argument).

11.14 Argument Matching Rules

When a function template has been overloaded with at least one other function having the same name but with non-parameterized arguments, the C++ Draft says that the function template yields a generated function for purposes of argument matching. In other words, you may view function templates as non-parameterized functions for overloading resolution.

Let's look at an example to see what this means.

 Example 11.17

```
template <class T>
void foo(const T&, char);
void foo(char, double);

template <class T>
void bar(const T*);
void bar(double);

void test(float fl, char ch)
{
    foo(0, fl);    // Invalid
    bar(ch);       // Calls non-template bar(double)
}
```

When the call to foo() is made, the compiler deduces that a foo() exists whose formal arguments are const int& and char. Thus, since the first actual argument is type int, the deduced function is the better choice (since this call merely adds a const qualifier, whereas the non-template foo() requires an integral conversion. The second actual argument of type float prefers the non-template function because the conversion of a float to a double is a promotion, and this is better than the floating pointer conversion of a float to a char. Since the intersection of the two sets of callable functions is empty, the call is invalid.

For the call to bar(), the function template requires a pointer type, and since there is no conversion from a char into any pointer type, no generated function can be deduced. Therefore, the compiler chooses the non-template bar().

 Caution

Borland 5.0 incorrectly chooses the function template for the call to foo().

11.15   Default Function Arguments

It is certainly possible to specify default function arguments in a function template. The only problem is that if the default is a parameterized type, then what is the compiler supposed to deduce?

 Example 11.18

```
#include <iostream.h>

template <class T>
void foo(const T& x = T())
{
    cout << "x = " << x << '\n';
}

int main()
{
    foo();          // Error; what type is T?
    return 0;
}
```

By the way, note carefully the use of a function-style cast of type T as the default argument value. Assuming that the type of T is known to the compiler, such a cast for a fundamental type will produce whatever value this type would take on if an instance were defined in the global space with no explicit value (i.e., zero). If, however, T is a user-defined type, then the expression T() will invoke the default constructor for type T.

As noted earlier, C++ solves the problem of not having an explicit argument from which to deduce the type by giving you the capability to *explicitly* specify the type.

Example 11.19

```
#include <iostream.h>

template <class T>
void foo(const T& x = T())
{
   cout << "x = " << x << '\n';
}

int main()
{
   foo<int>();  // OK; now T is type int
   return 0;
}

/* The output of this program is:

x = 0

*/
```

Of course, you always have the option to override the default argument. In this case the actual argument gets converted to whatever type you have explicitly stated.

 Example 11.20

```
#include <iostream.h>

template <class T>
void foo(const T& x = T())
{
   cout << "x = " << x << '\n';
}

int main()
{
   foo<int>(5.67);  // OK; convert 5.67 to type 'int'
   return 0;
}

/* The output of this program is:

x = 5

*/
```

If you omit the type between the angle brackets *and* specify an explicit argument, then it's the same as not having the angle brackets in the first place. Of course, the formal argument is then deduced to the same type as that of the actual argument.

 Example 11.21

```
#include <iostream.h>

template <class T>
void foo(const T& x = T())
{
    cout << "x = " << x << '\n';
}

int main()
{
    foo<>(5.67);
    foo(5.67);
    return 0;
}

/* The output of this program is:

x = 5.67
x = 5.67

*/
```

Caution

The technique of explicitly specifying the type for a function template is not available in Borland compilers prior to version 5.0.

11.16   Introduction to Class Templates

A *class template* is a class with at least one type that is parameterized, and thus provides the framework for a family of similar classes. By writing such a class, you provide the user with the capability to instantiate the class with an unlimited range of different types. For example, a class template representing the abstraction of some container type (array, linked list, stack, queue, etc.) can then hold objects of literally any type.

Tip

Class templates accepting non-parameterized (value) types are discussed later.

11.17   How to Define a Class Template

A class template, like a function template, always begins with the keyword `template` followed by the list of parameterized types. You then write the class definition in the normal way, using the parameterized types where appropriate.

For example, here is the start of the class `Complex` whose `real` and `imag` members are now generic. As was the case with a default argument in a function template, note how the default constructor takes two default arguments, both of which use a function-style cast to accommodate both fundamental and user-defined types.

 Example 11.22

```
template <class T>
class Complex
{
    public:
    Complex(const T& = T(), const T& = T());  // Def. const.
    // Remainder of the public interface
    private:
    T real;
    T imag;
};
```

11.18   Parameterizing the Class Name

Once the first line of the class definition has been seen by the compiler, you have a choice of whether to *parameterize* the class name whenever it appears inside the class definition (except when specializing a class member). Parameterization of the class name is done by writing the class name followed by the parameterized type between angle brackets. In the case of a constructor, you also have a choice to parameterize the function name (just for the sake of consistency).

For example, this is how the default and copy constructors of the `Complex` class would be declared.

Example 11.23

```
template <class T>
class Complex
{
    public:
  Complex(const T& = T(), const T& = T());  // Def. const.
  // Complex<T>(const T& = T(), const T& = T());    // same
  Complex(const Complex&);        // Copy constructor
  // Complex<T>(const Complex<T>&);   // same
  // Remainder of the public interface
    private:
  T real;
  T imag;
};
```

11.19   Defining Members Outside the Class Definition

Each class member function, static data member, and friend function definition that is defined outside the class definition must be written as a template declaration. In addition, when scoping a class member name, you *must* parameterize the name.

Example 11.24

```
template <class T>
class Complex
{
    public:
  Complex(const T& = T(), const T& = T());  // Def. const.
  Complex(const Complex<T>&);   // Copy constructor
  // Remainder of the public interface
    private:
  T real;
  T imag;
  static int counter;
};

template <class T>
Complex<T>::Complex(const T& r, const T& i)
          : real(r), imag(i) {}

template <class T>
Complex<T>::Complex(const Complex<T>& c)
          : real(c.real), imag(c.imag) {}

template <class T>
int Complex<T>::counter = 0;
```

11.20   Instantiating a Class Template

While the specific types of a function template are (usually) deduced by the compiler as a result of a call to the function, in the case of a class template you are responsible for explicitly specifying the name of the type that is to be used. This is done when the class template is instantiated (thereby yielding a *generated class*) by following the class name with the specific types written between angle brackets. If no instance is actually created, e.g., you just want to declare a pointer, then no instantiation occurs.

   Example 11.25

```
template <class T>
class Complex
{
   // Class members
};

void foo()
{
   // No instantiation done
   Complex<int>* ptr;

   // Instantiate with type int
   Complex<int> c1(1, 2);

   // Instantiate with type double
   typedef Complex<double> Complex_double;
   Complex_double c2(3.4, 5.6);
}
```

Of course, it is possible to instantiate a class template with a type that itself is the specialization of another class template.

Example 11.26

```
template <class T>
class Complex
{
   // Class members
};

template <class T>
class Array
{
   // Class members
};

void foo()
{
   // Instantiate Array with type int
   Array<int> a1;

   // Instantiate Array with type Complex<double>
   Array<Complex<double> > a2;

   // Instantiate Array with type Complex<double>
   typedef Complex<double> Complex_double;
   typedef Array<Complex_double> Array_Complex_double;
   Array_Complex_double a3;
}
```

 Caution

Note the space between the right angle brackets in the instantiation of a2. *This space is required in order to avoid the creation of a right-shift operator token. That's why you're always better off using a* typedef *in these situations.*

11.21   Specializing a Class Template

In a manner similar to the way in which you specialize a function template, a class template can be specialized by writing a class definition and its member definitions with the generic type replaced by a specific type.

For example, suppose that the Complex class instantiated with type int needs a default constructor whose default values are both 1 instead of 0. Then this is how it could be written.

Example 11.27

```
template <class T>
class Complex
{
    public:
  Complex(const T& = T(), const T& = T()); // Def. const.
  Complex(const Complex<T>&) ; // Copy constructor
  // Other details omitted
    private:
  T real;
  T imag;
} ;

template <class T>
Complex<T>::Complex(const T& r, const T& i)
    : real(r), imag(i) {}

template <class T>
Complex<T>::Complex(const Complex<T>& c)
    : real(c.real), imag(c.imag) {}

// template <>
class Complex<int>
{
    public:
  Complex(int = 1, int = 1) ;
  Complex(const Complex<int>&);
    private:
  int real;
  int imag;
};

// template <>
Complex<int>::Complex(int r, int i)
  : real(r), imag(i) {}

// template <>
Complex<int>::Complex(const Complex<int>& c)
  : real(c.real), imag(c.imag) {}

void foo()
{
  Complex<double> c1;
  Complex<int> c2;
}
```

11.22   Make Class Templates Available to the Compiler

Recall in the discussion on function templates that you should never segregate a function template declaration from the definition using modularization. The reason is that if the user includes only the header file (containing the declaration), then the compiler will never have the chance to compile the definition (in its own file), and the linker will complain.

The same principle applies to class templates. Be sure to include all of the template definitions in the same header file that contains the class definition itself. Then, when the user includes this header file, all of the template definitions will be instantiated and compiled into object format.

11.23   Default Template Arguments

Borland C++ 5.0 supports default template arguments. They look very similar to the default arguments that are specified in a function's formal argument list. To write default template arguments, just follow the generic type name with the symbol '=' and the default type. All such defaults must appear last in the template declaration. When you instantiate the class, simply write empty angle brackets in order to accept the default value(s).

 Example 11.28

```cpp
template <class T = double>
class Complex
{
    public:
  Complex(const T& = T(), const T& = T()); // Def. const.
  Complex(const Complex<T>&) ; // Copy constructor
  // Other details omitted
    private:
  T real;
  T imag;
};

void foo()
{
  // Instantiate Complex with type int
  Complex<int> c1(1, 2);

  // Instantiate Complex with default type
  Complex<> c2(3.4, 5.6);
}
```

11.24   Complex Number Example

Here is a complete example using a parameterized complex number class. Note that the default type is double.

 Example 11.29

```cpp
// File complex.h

#ifndef COMPLEX_H
#define COMPLEX_H

#include <iostream.h>

template <class T = double>
class Complex
{
   friend ostream& operator<<(ostream&, const Complex<T>&);
      public:
   Complex(const T& = T(), const T& = T());
   Complex(const Complex<T>&);
   ~Complex();
   Complex<T>& operator=(const Complex<T>&);
   static void total(ostream& = cout);
      protected:
   T real;
   T imag;
   static int counter;
};

template <class T>
ostream& operator<<(ostream& str, const Complex<T>& obj)
{
   return str << obj.real << " + " << obj.imag << 'i';
}

template <class T>
Complex<T>::Complex(const T& r, const T& i) : real(r), imag(i)
{
   ++counter;
}

template <class T>
Complex<T>::Complex(const Complex<T>& obj)
        : real(obj.real), imag(obj.imag)
{
   ++counter;
}

template <class T>
Complex<T>::~Complex()
{
   --counter;
}
```

(Continued)

```
template <class T>
Complex<T>& Complex<T>::operator=(const Complex<T>& obj)
{
   real = obj.real;
   imag = obj.imag;
   return *this;
}

template <class T>
void Complex<T>::total(ostream& str)
{
     str << counter << " instantiation"
         << (counter == 1 ? "" : "s") << '\n';
}

template <class T>
int Complex<T>::counter = 0;

#endif

// File main.cpp

#include "complex.h"

int main()
{
   typedef Complex<int> Complex_int;
   Complex_int c1(1, 2);
   cout << c1 << '\n';
   Complex_int c2(3, 4);
   cout << c2 << '\n';
   Complex_int c3(c2);
   cout << c3 << '\n';
   Complex_int::total();

   typedef Complex<> Complex_default;
   Complex_default c4(5.6, 9.34);
   cout << c4 << '\n';
   Complex_default::total();

   return 0;
}

/* The output of this program is:

1 + 2i
3 + 4i
3 + 4i
3 instantiations
5.6 + 9.34i
1 instantiation

*/
```

11.25   Granting Friendship

A parameterized class may give friendship to another class template. For example, here is a parameterized node class giving friendship to a linked list class.

 Example 11.30

```
// File node.h

#ifndef NODE_H
#define NODE_H

#include <iostream.h>

template <class U>
class List;

template <class T>
class Node
{
   friend class List<T>;
   friend ostream& operator<<(ostream&, const Node<T>&);
   Node(const T&);
   T data;
   Node<T>* next;
};

#endif

// File list.h

#ifndef LIST_H
#define LIST_H

#include "node.h"

template <class U>
class List
{
   // public interface
      private:
   Node<U>* head;
   Node<U>* tail;
};

#endif
```

 Tip

Borland C++ version 5.0 requires that the class receiving the friendship be forward-declared. This declaration had been optional in previous versions of the compiler.

A class template may also grant friendship to a non-parameterized class, but unlike the List class above, the non-parameterized class can contain only generated class instances of the class template, not parameterized instances.

 Example 11.31

```
template <class T>
class Complex
{
   friend class Array;
   // Class members
};

class Array
{
   Complex<int> c;   // Generated class instance
   // Other details
};
```

Finally, a non-parameterized class may not give friendship to a parameterized class.

 Example 11.32

```
class Complex
{
   friend class Array<T>;    // Error
};

template <class T>
class Array
{
   // Class members
};
```

11.26   Non-Type Template Arguments

A class template may be instantiated with non-type template arguments. These must consist of constant non-floating point values whose types themselves may be generic. A template declaration may freely combine generic and non-type arguments. When the class template is instantiated, the specific value must be known to the compiler, and is written between the angle brackets.

In the following example the non-type template argument dim is used to provide the dimension of the generic array.

 Example 11.33

```
template <class T, int dim>
class Array
{
     public:
   Array();
     private:
   T array[dim];    // OK; dim is known at compilation time
};

template <class T, int dim>
Array<T, dim>::Array()
{
   for(int i = 0; i < dim; ++i)
     array[i] = T();
}

void foo()
{
   Array<int, 5> obj;
}
```

As another example of non-type arguments, the following program computes the factorial of 10 (the hard way!).

Example 11.34

```cpp
#include <iostream.h>

template <long value>
class Fact : Fact<value - 1>
{
    public:
  long eval() const {return value * Fact<value - 1>::eval();}
};

// template <>
class Fact<0L>
{
    public:
  long eval() const { return 1L; }
};

int main()
{
  const long value = 10L;
  const Fact<value> fact;
  cout << value << "! = " << fact.eval() << '\n';
  return 0;
}

/* The output of this program is:

10! = 3628800

*/
```

11.27   Inheritance

A class template can serve as a base class for a derived class that itself is either another class template or a specialization of the base class. In the following example, a new template class called DComplex has been derived from the Complex class shown in Example 11.29 in order to add an overloaded '+' operator. All of the manager functions are shown.

 Example 11.35

```cpp
template <class T = double>
class DComplex : public Complex<T>
{
  friend
  DComplex<T> operator+(const DComplex<T>&, const DComplex<T>&);
    public:
  DComplex() {}
  DComplex(const T& r) : Complex<T>(r) {}
  DComplex(const T& r, const T& i) : Complex<T>(r, i) {}
  DComplex(const DComplex<T>& arg) : Complex<T>(arg) {}
  ~DComplex() {}
  inline DComplex<T>& operator=(const DComplex<T>&);
};

template <class T>
inline
DComplex<T>& DComplex<T>::operator=(const DComplex<T>& arg)
{
  Complex<T>::operator=(arg);
  return *this;
}
```

11.28   typename **Keyword**

The C++ Draft says that "a name used in a template is assumed not to name a type unless it has been explicitly declared to refer to a type in the context enclosing the template declaration or is qualified by the keyword typename". This situation can be illustrated by the following example.

 Example 11.36

```
template <class T>
class X : public T
{
    Int data;        // Error; Int is not a valid type
};
```

When the template is parsed, the compiler has no idea if Int is or is not a valid type. After all, it could have been made valid as the result of a typedef in class T that is inherited, thus making it valid in the context of class X. But according to the rule above, the compiler chooses to assume that it is not valid, and issues an error.

The solution is to tell the compiler explicitly that T::Int is a valid type. This is done by preceding the declaration of data with the keyword typename, and then scoping type Int within class T.

 Example 11.37

```
template <class T>
class X : public T
{
    typename T::Int data;    // OK
};
```

Of course, when class X gets instantiated, it must be with some user-defined type that does indeed provide a suitable typedef to replace the unknown type Int.

Example 11.38

```
template <class T>
class X : public T
{
   typename T::Int data;    // OK
};

class ADT1
{
   // empty
};

class ADT2
{
   typedef int Int;
};

void foo()
{
   X<double> x1;  // Error
   X<ADT1> x2;    // Error
   X<ADT2> x3;    // OK
}
```

11.29   How to Write a Callback Using Templates

A callback is the process by which a function is registered with a caller function or object, which then calls back the function when an appropriate condition is encountered.

For example, an elevator contains a variety of methods and a collection of buttons which are responsible for calling back these methods.

Example 11.39

```
// File elevator.h

#ifndef ELEVATOR_H
#define ELEVATOR_H

#include <iostream.h>

class Elevator
{
    public:
  void Schedule_floor()
    {cout << "Floor has been scheduled" << '\n';}
};

#endif

// File button.h

#ifndef BUTTON_H
#define BUTTON_H

template <class T>
class Button
{
    public:
  Button(const T& ref) : functor_obj(ref) {}
  void press() { functor_obj(); }
    private:
  const T& functor_obj;
};

#endif
```

(Continued)

```cpp
// File functor.h

#ifndef FUNCTOR_H
#define FUNCTOR_H

template <class T>
class Functor
{
     public:
   typedef void (T::*Ptr_mem_func)();
   Functor(T& ref, Ptr_mem_func ptr)
        : client(ref), callback(ptr) {}
   void operator()() const { (client.*callback)(); }
     private:
   T& client;
   Ptr_mem_func callback;
};

#endif

// File main.cpp

#include "elevator.h"
#include "button.h"
#include "functor.h"

int main()
{
   typedef Functor<Elevator> ElevatorFunctor;
   typedef Button<ElevatorFunctor> ElevatorButton;
   Elevator Otis;
   ElevatorFunctor functor(Otis, &Elevator::Schedule_floor);
   ElevatorButton button(functor);
   button.press();
   return 0;
}

/* The output of this program is:

Floor has been scheduled

*/
```

Review Questions

1. What is a function template, and why would you ever need one?

2. How do you tell the compiler that a function is a template?

3. How does the compiler deduce the types of the function arguments when a call to that function is made?

4. Why would you need to overload a function template?

5. Why would you need to specialize a function template?

6. How can you explicitly specify the parameterized types when calling a function template?

7. What role does the `const` keyword play when it qualifies an actual argument?

8. What role does the `const` keyword play when it qualifies a formal argument?

9. How can you explicitly specify the parameterized types when instantiating a class template?

10. What are non-type parameters, and why would you ever use them?

11. What is wrong with the following template declarations?

```
<class T> T f(T arg);
template <T> T f(T arg);
template <class T> T f();
template <class T, class T> T f(T arg);
template <class T, U> void f(T arg1, U arg2);
```

Exercise 11.1

Write a function template called `swap()` that swaps the contents of its two input arguments. Test this function by using several different instantiations of fundamental types. Then create a user-defined type (e.g., a complex number) and apply the `swap()` function to this type.

Exercise 11.2

Using your `swap()` function, write a function template that takes as its two arguments a parameterized type representing a pointer to an array and an `int` representing the length of the array. The function must bubble sort the array into ascending sequence and then print the array.

Exercise 11.3

Write a function template called `count ()` that accepts three arguments: a parameterized type representing a pointer to an array, the length of the array, and some value of the array type. Count the number of occurrences of the value within the array and return the resulting count. Instantiate the function using several different types.

 Exercise 11.4

Modify Exercise #3 so that a string can be searched for the number of occurrences of a specified substring.

 Exercise 11.5

Modify Exercise #3 from Chapter 6 so that the `Array` class can accommodate literally any type of data.

 Exercise 11.6

Write a generic class called `Stack` that emulates typical stack operations such as push and pop. Let the user instantiate the `Stack` class with a specific type and the length of the stack (using a value-based template argument). Also, be sure to check for stack overflow and underflow.

 Exercise 11.7

Write a smart pointer class called `Pointer` that emulates the behavior of a C-style pointer that points to a single object of an unknown type. Assume that this object has been allocated from the heap, and that the class then takes ownership of it. Be sure to write all of the manager functions, paying special attention to the copy constructor and assignment operator. Also write an overloaded insertion operator. Of course, you must overload the '*' and '->' operators. If the user attempts to use an "uninitialized" `Pointer` object, then display an error message and terminate the program. Test your class with both fundamental and user-defined types.

Chapter 12

Exception Handling

12.1 Introduction

Exception handling in C++ provides a better method by which the caller of a function can be informed that some error condition has occurred. Previous methods proved to be inadequate because of the semantics of the language itself, and the inability of the function to know what the caller wanted to do after the error had been detected. You will now see how exception handling can solve these problems.

12.2 The Problem

Suppose you want to write a function called `quadratic()` that computes and returns one value of X in the quadratic equation $AX^2+BX+C = 0$. Here is one way it can be done, including a `main()` to test the function:

Example 12.1

```cpp
#include <iostream.h>
#include <math.h>

double quadratic(int A, int B, int C)
{
   double discriminant = (B * B) - (4 * A * C);
   double numerator = -B + sqrt(discriminant);
   double denominator = 2 * A;
   return numerator / denominator;
}

int main()
{
   cout << "Enter the coefficients: ";
   int A;
   int B;
   int C;
   while(!(cin >> A >> B >> C).eof())
   {
      double x1 = quadratic(A, B, C);
      cout << "The first root is " << x1 << '\n';
      cout << "Enter the coefficients: ";
   }
   cout << "End-of-file\n";
   return 0;
}

/* A typical run would yield:

Enter the coefficients: 1 5 4
The first root is -1
Enter the coefficients: 1 1 1
sqrt: DOMAIN error
The first root is +NAN
Enter the coefficients: 0 1 1
Floating point error: Stack fault.
Abnormal program termination

*/
```

Obviously, there are two bugs in the `quadratic()` function: (1) it fails to check for a denominator equal to zero, and (2) it fails to check for a negative discriminant. Both situations result in an error condition.

So you might reasonably conclude that a few validity checks are in order. But assuming that either one of these error conditions is detected, the problem now is to determine exactly what the function should do to handle them.

One solution might be to execute that old standby `exit(1)`.

Example 12.2

```
#include <stdlib.h>
double quadratic(int A, int B, int C)
{
   if(A == 0)
   {
      cout << "The first coefficient is equal to 0\n";
      exit(1);
   }
   double discriminant = (B * B) - (4 * A * C);
   if(discriminant < 0)
   {
      cout << "Imaginary roots\n";
      exit(1);
   }
   double numerator = -B + sqrt(discriminant);
   double denominator = 2 * A;
   return numerator / denominator;
}
```

Unfortunately, the user of this function will not be very happy with you because there really is no justification for exiting a program merely on account of a keying error in which the coefficient A is equal to zero, or for having coefficients that yield a negative discriminant. So exit(1) is not a viable solution.

On the other hand, since the function has been declared to return a variable of type double, then in lieu of issuing an exit(1), the compiler will ensure that you return an expression of this type, even for the error cases. So the only question is the particular value of the expression that will be returned for each error case. But now you're stuck because no matter what pseudo value you might choose to use, e.g., zero, it could legitimately be a valid value for X, so this doesn't work. And any other solution, such as setting a global flag, is awkward and imposes an unwanted burden upon the user to monitor this flag after each call to the function.

The overall problem can be summarized by the following table. In order to effectively check for error conditions and handle them properly, the function that is called must check for the various error conditions, but *not* handle them. Nevertheless, it still must signal the caller that some disastrous error occurred. The caller has just the opposite responsibility, so that there is a very distinct line drawn between the responsibilities of the caller of the function and the function itself.

Table 12-1   Error Handling Responsibilities

	Check for errors?	Process?
Caller	NO	YES
Function	YES	NO

12.3   The Solution

Exception handling (EH) in C++ provides a solution to the preceding dilemma because it allows a function to notify its caller that some disastrous condition has occurred in a manner that is completely independent of the function's return type (or lack thereof in the case of a constructor or destructor). EH is supported by these three C++ keywords: `throw`, `try`, and `catch`.

Other examples of where you could use EH:

- A constructor cannot allocate enough heap space, and must inform the routine doing the instantiation that an object could not be successfully created.

- A constructor for some `Fraction` class detects that the denominator is equal to zero.

- An overloaded `operator[]()` function for some class detects that the subscript value is out of range.

- A `pop()` method of some `Stack` class determines that there is nothing to be popped.

- A function designed to open a disk file fails for some reason.

12.4   `throw` **Keyword**

Using EH, a function notifies its caller that some disastrous situation has occurred by "throwing", i.e., raising an exception. This is done by writing the keyword `throw` followed by any valid C++ object, including a user-defined object. A copy of this object is made and no more processing within the function occurs. Remember: the type of the object that is thrown is completely independent of the return type of the function in which the throw occurs. In addition, a function may throw more than one type.

For example, the preceding `quadratic()` function can now be rewritten as:

Example 12.3

```
double quadratic(int A, int B, int C)
{
   if(A == 0)
      throw 0;   // Throw an int
   double discriminant = (B * B) - (4 * A * C);
   if(discriminant < 0)
      throw "Imaginary roots";   // Throw a string
   double numerator = -B + sqrt(discriminant);
   double denominator = 2 * A;
   return numerator / denominator;
}
```

12.5   Exception Specifications

A function (definition or declaration) can explicitly document the exceptions it could possibly throw by writing an *exception specification* after its signature. This entails writing the keyword throw followed by a parenthesized list of formal argument types. In addition to documentation, if, at execution time, the function throws an object in violation of the promise made in its exception specification, then a run-time error will occur (discussed later in this chapter). In the case of a derivation hierarchy, if a base class name is listed, then any derived object of that base class may also be thrown. (Of course, if the base class is an abstract base class (ABC), then it cannot be instantiated and thrown.)

Of course, it should be obvious that it's a poor idea to use an exception specification with a function template because the function has no idea of the type with which it will eventually be instantiated, and therefore has no idea what it will or will not be throwing.

Example 12.4

```
// quadratic() can throw an 'int' or a 'char*'
double quadratic(int A, int B, int C) throw(int, char*);

// quadratic() promises not to throw anything
double quadratic(int A, int B, int C) throw();

// User has no idea what quadratic() may or may not throw
double quadratic(int A, int B, int C);

// quadratic() can throw a Quadratic_error object or any
// object derived from Quadratic_error
double quadratic(int A, int B, int C) throw(Quadratic_error);
```

 Caution

Exception specifications do not participate in overloading resolution. This means that a function in object format may have been compiled with a different exception specification than what is found in the function declaration. Therefore, always make sure that a function declaration and its definition are consistent in their use of an exception specification.

12.6   `try` Keyword

The `try` keyword enables the EH mechanism and starts what is called a *try block*. This consists of the keyword `try` followed by a pair of braces, similar to a function body. If the user never bothers to write a try block, then any exceptions that are thrown will cause the program to terminate. In other words, the `throw` keyword may only appear within a try block or within a function called from a try block, or from another function that itself was invoked from the first function called from the try block, etc.

12.7   `catch` Keyword

In order for the caller to handle an object that is thrown, the object must be "caught" by writing one or more *catch blocks* immediately after the try block. A catch block consists of the keyword `catch` followed by a formal argument list that contains exactly *one* entry, somewhat similar to a function's formal argument list that contains just one entry. The formal argument name is, of course, always optional.

For example, a try block and two catch blocks to accommodate the `quadratic()` function might be written as follows. Remember that if the coefficient A is equal to

Example 12.5

```
try
{
    double x1 = quadratic(A, B, C);
    cout << "The first root is " << x1 << '\n';
}

catch(int)
{
    cout << "The coefficient A is equal to 0\n";
}

catch(const char* message)
{
    cout << message << '\n';
}
```

At execution time, if no exception is thrown, then the try block executes normally and all following catch blocks are bypassed automatically. On the other hand, if an exception is thrown, the type of the thrown expression is matched consecutively against all catch blocks that follow the try block. As soon as a match occurs, the catch block is entered and executed, after which all remaining catch blocks are bypassed. If an exception is thrown and no suitable catch block can be found, then the function `terminate()` is called and the program terminates.

A catch block with ellipsis (3 dots) as its one argument serves as a default handler, i.e., it can accommodate literally any type of object that might be thrown. If coded, it must be the last catch block after a try block. This is useful when the caller really doesn't care what is being thrown.

Example 12.6

```
try
{
    double x1 = quadratic(A, B, C);
    cout << "The first root is " << x1 << '\n';
}

catch(...)
{
    cout << "First root cannot be computed\n";
}
```

Here is the complete listing to invoke the `quadratic()` function and accommodate EH.

Example 12.7

```cpp
#include <iostream.h>
#include <math.h>

double quadratic(int A, int B, int C) throw(int, char*)
{
   if(A == 0)
      throw 0;
   double discriminant = (B * B) - (4 * A * C);
   if(discriminant < 0)
      throw "Imaginary roots";
   double numerator = -B + sqrt(discriminant);
   double denominator = 2 * A;
   return numerator / denominator;
}

int main()
{
   cout << "Enter the coefficients: ";
   int A;
   int B;
   int C;
   while(!(cin >> A >> B >> C).eof())
   {
      try
      {
         double x1 = quadratic(A, B, C);
         cout << "The first root is " << x1 << '\n';
      }

      catch(int)
      {
         cout << "The first coefficient is equal to 0\n";
      }

      catch(const char* message)
      {
         cout << message << '\n';
      }

      cout << "Enter the coefficients: ";
   }
   cout << "End-of-file\n"
   return 0;
}
```

(Continued)

```
/* A typical run would yield:

Enter the coefficients: 1 5 4
The first root is -1
Enter the coefficients: 1 1 1
Imaginary roots
Enter the coefficients: 0 1 1
The coefficient A is equal to 0
Enter the coefficients: ^Z
End-of-file

*/
```

12.8   Matching Process for Catch Blocks

If an object of type T is thrown, then any catch block that takes an argument of type C constitutes an acceptable match if:

■   T and C are the same type (e.g., int can be caught by int);

■   C adds a const qualifier (e.g., int can be caught by const int and int* can be caught by const int*);

■   C adds a reference qualifier (e.g., int can be caught by int&);

■   C is an accessible base class of T (e.g., Derived can be caught by Base);

■   T and C are pointer types, and a standard conversion exists from T to C (e.g., int* can be caught by void*).

Promotions and all other standard conversions are not done. For example, a char object cannot be caught by type int, and an int object cannot be caught by type double.

12.9   Error Conditions

The EH mechanism can result in two different kinds of errors. The first occurs if (1) an exception is thrown from outside the context of a try block, or (2) no suitable catch block can be found to handle a thrown exception. In both cases the global function terminate() is called, which then calls the function abort().

If you want to gain some measure of control, you can provide your own termination function (it must take no arguments and return nothing), and pass its address to the function set_terminate() (declared in the file except.h). In addition, it should call abort().

Example 12.8

```
#include <iostream.h>
#include <except.h>

void my_terminate()
{
   cout << "EH terminate error\n" ;
   abort();
}

int main()
{
   set_terminate(my_terminate);
   throw 1;    // No try block present
   return 0;
}

/* The output of this program is:

EH terminate error
Abnormal program termination

*/
```

The second type of error occurs if the type of an object that is thrown from a function violates the promise made by the exception specification. This error will also occur if the object is thrown from a second function called by this function, and propagates through without being caught. Note that this constitutes a run-time (not compile-time) error, and the global function `unexpected()` will be called, followed by a call to the function `terminate()`.

If you want to intercept this call, you can provide your own unexpected function (it must take no arguments and return nothing), and pass its address to the function `set_unexpected()` (declared in the file `except.h`). Unlike the termination handler, it is perfectly acceptable to have the unexpected function throw (or re-throw) an exception.

Example 12.9

```
#include <iostream.h>
#include <except.h>

void my_unexpected()
{
    cout << "EH unexpected error\n";
    throw -1;
}

void f() throw(int)
{
    throw 'A';      // Error; cannot throw a char
}

int main()
{
    set_unexpected(my_unexpected);
    try
    {
        f();
    }
    catch(int n)
    {
        if(n >= 0)
            cout << n << '\n';
    }
    return 0;
}

/* The output of this program is:

EH unexpected error

*/
```

12.10   Propagation of Thrown Objects

Note that if an exception propagates through a function that promises that it may throw a different type, or promises to throw nothing at all, then it is still an unexpected error unless the function catches the exception.

In the following example g() promises the user that it will never throw an exception, and then calls f(), which throws an int. Because the user (presumably) has no idea of how g() works, the last thing the user expects to happen is an exception being thrown. In point of fact, the int that is thrown by f() propagates its way back through g(), which detects the fact that its own exception specification is being violated, and invokes my_unexpected().

Example 12.10

```
#include <iostream.h>
#include <except.h>

void my_unexpected()
{
   cout << "EH unexpected error\n";
   terminate();
}

void f() throw(int)
{
   throw 1;
}

void g() throw()
{
   f();
}

int main()
{
   set_unexpected(my_unexpected);
   g();
   cout << "Success!\n";
   return 0;
}

/* The output of this program is:

EH unexpected error
Abnormal program termination

*/
```

Now let's change the program so that `g()` catches the exception thrown by `f()`. Since nothing is now being thrown to `main()`, the program ends successfully.

Example 12.11

```
#include <iostream.h>
#include <except.h>

void my_unexpected()
{
   cout << "EH unexpected error\n";
   terminate();
}

void f() throw(int)
{
   throw 1;
}

void g() throw()
{
   try
   {
      f();
   }
   catch(int) {}
}

int main()
{
   set_unexpected(my_unexpected);
   g();
   cout << "Success!\n";
   return 0;
}

/* The output of this program is:

Success!

*/
```

If an exception is thrown that cannot be handled by any of the catch blocks in function g(), then it will propagate to the next higher try/catch pair. If all such pairs are exhausted, then the function terminate() will be called.

In the following example, the int that is thrown by f() cannot be caught by g(), so it propagates back to main() where it is successfully caught.

Example 12.12

```cpp
#include <iostream.h>
#include <except.h>

void my_unexpected()
{
   cout << "EH unexpected error\n";
   terminate();
}

void f() throw(int)
{
   throw 1;
}

void g() throw(int)
{
   try
   {
      f();
   }
   catch(char)
   {
      cout << "Caught char in g()\n";
   }
}

int main()
{
   set_unexpected(my_unexpected);
   try
   {
      g();
   }
   catch(int)
   {
      cout << "Caught int in main()\n";
   }
   return 0;
}

/* The output of this program is:

Caught int in main()

*/
```

12.11   Re-Throwing an Exception

A function can "re-throw" an exception by coding the keyword throw without specifying any C++ expression whatsoever. Now function g() catches the int thrown by function f(), and re-throws it to main().

 Example 12.13

```
#include <iostream.h>
#include <except.h>

void my_unexpected()
{
   cout << "EH unexpected error\n";
   terminate();
}

void f() throw(int)
{
   throw 1;
}

void g()
{
   try
   {
      f();
   }
   catch(...)
   {
      cout << "Caught in g()\n";
      throw;    // Re-throw
   }
}
```

(Continued)

```
int main()
{
    set_unexpected(my_unexpected);
    try
    {
        g();
    }
    catch(int)
    {
        cout << "Caught int in main()\n";
    }
    return 0;
}

/* The output of this program is:

Caught in g()
Caught int in main()

*/
```

12.12   Throwing a User-Defined Object

If two or more values are to be thrown, then these values must be encapsulated within a class, and an instance of this class may subsequently be thrown. In addition, exceptions that are related may be grouped together in some inheritance hierarchy. These classes may be caught by writing separate catch blocks, or may be caught by writing just one catch block that specifies the base class and employs the virtual function mechanism to invoke the proper function for each class.

Let's return to the quadratic function example. In the following program, an abstract base class called Quadratic_error has been written, from which two derived classes, Non_quadratic, and Imaginary_roots, have been derived. The quadratic() function now throws an instance of these two classes if the appropriate error is encountered.

The catch block catches an instance of the base class Quadratic_error by reference so that the virtual function display() can be invoked.

Example 12.14

```cpp
#include <iostream.h>
#include <math.h>
#include <string.h>

class Quadratic_error
{
   friend
   ostream& operator<<(ostream&, const Quadratic_error&);
      public:
   Quadratic_error(const char*);
   virtual ostream& display(ostream& = cout) const = 0;
      private:
   char message[256];
};

ostream& operator<<(ostream& str, const Quadratic_error& qe)
{
   return qe.display(str);
}

Quadratic_error::Quadratic_error(const char* m)
{
   strcpy(message, m);
}

ostream& Quadratic_error::display(ostream& str) const
{
   return str << message;
}

class Non_quadratic : public Quadratic_error
{
      public:
   Non_quadratic(const char* m) : Quadratic_error(m) {}
   virtual ostream& display(ostream& = cout) const;
};

ostream& Non_quadratic::display(ostream& str) const
{
   return Quadratic_error::display(str);
}
```

(Continued)

```
class Imaginary_roots : public Quadratic_error
{
      public:
   Imaginary_roots(const char* m, double d)
        : Quadratic_error(m), discriminant(d) {}
   virtual ostream& display(ostream& = cout) const;
      private:
   double discriminant;
};

ostream& Imaginary_roots::display(ostream& str) const
{
   return Quadratic_error::display(str) << "\ndiscriminant = "
          << discriminant;
}

double quadratic(int A, int B, int C) throw(Quadratic_error)
{
   if(A == 0) throw Non_quadratic("Non-quadratic equation");
   double discriminant = (B * B) - (4 * A * C);
   if(discriminant < 0)
      throw Imaginary_roots("Imaginary roots", discriminant);
   double numerator = -B + sqrt(discriminant);
   double denominator = 2 * A;
   return numerator / denominator;
}

int main()
{
   cout << "Enter the coefficients: ";
   int A;
   int B;
   int C;
   while(!(cin >> A >> B >> C).eof())
   {
      try
      {
        double x1 = quadratic(A, B, C);
        cout << "The first root is " << x1 << '\n';
      }

      catch(const Quadratic_error& qe)
      {
        cout << qe << '\n';
      }

      cout << "Enter the coefficients: ";
   }
   cout << "End-of-file\n";
   return 0;
}
```

(Continued)

```
/* A typical run would yield:

Enter the coefficients: 1 5 4
The first root is -1
Enter the coefficients: 1 1 1
Imaginary roots
discriminant = -3
Enter the coefficients: 0 1 1
Non-quadratic equation
Enter the coefficients: ^Z
End-of-file

*/
```

12.13   Unwinding the Stack

Envision a function that throws an exception after locally-defined objects have been created on the stack, either from within the try block or within the function itself. In addition, assume that a constructor has allocated heap space, so that it's up to the destructor to release this space. But if and when an exception is thrown, the closing brace of the function is never reached, and theoretically the auto objects never get popped off the stack, so that the destructor never gets called.

Fortunately, this is not the case, since the compiler guarantees that such auto objects will indeed get popped from the stack, thereby precluding the possibility of memory leakage. Of course, if the function itself should happen to have allocated heap space, then it's the function's responsibility to release that space before throwing the exception.

 Tip

The use of a "smart pointer" class would negate the need to use pointers and ensure that the heap space gets released. The class called auto_ptr *defined in the header file* memory.h *performs this task.*

12.14   What If `operator new()` Fails?

Recall that when you write the keyword `new`, the compiler generates a call to the function `operator new()` (or `operator new[]()` if you are requesting an array), and passes the actual number of bytes that will be needed. But if the allocation fails, then an exception of type `xalloc` (defined in the header file `except.h`) will be thrown. If desired, you may call the method `xalloc::why()` that will return a `string` object by 'reference-to-`const`' that tells you the reason for the failure.

 Tip

> *The class* `string` *is the built-in string class from the standard C++ library (defined in the header file* `cstring.h`*).*

 Caution

> *The C++ Draft now calls for* `operator new()` *to throw an exception of type* `bad_alloc` *if it fails for any reason. The method* `xalloc::why()` *has been replaced with the method* `bad_alloc::what()` *to determine the exact reason for the exception.*

12.15   What If a Constructor Fails?

If a constructor should fail to execute properly (e.g., `operator new()` fails), then an exception must be thrown back to whoever performed the instantiation. If this routine fails to catch the exception, then an abort will automatically occur, but now it's no longer the problem of the constructor. (Note that whenever a constructor fails to run to completion, the destructor for the (presumed) object will not be called.)

Here is an example of how to handle the failure of `operator new()` within a constructor. Note how the base/member initialization list is used to initialize the pointer values to zero *before* any heap allocation is attempted. This ensures that a stable object has been created before anything can go wrong, and guarantees that `operator delete()` will not cause an abort.

Example 12.15

```
// File x.h

#ifndef X_H
#define X_H

class X
{
      public:
   X(int = 0, int = 0) throw(const char*);
   X(const X&) throw(const char*);
   inline ~X();
      private:
   int* px;
   int* py;
   int x_length;
   int y_length;
   void allocate(const char*) throw(const char*);
   inline void release();
};

inline X::~X()
{
   release();
}

inline void X::release()
{
   delete [] px;
   delete [] py;
}

#endif
```

(Continued)

```
// File x.cpp

#include <iostream.h>
#include <except.h>
#include <cstring.h>
#include "x.h"

X::X(int x, int y) throw(const char*)
        : px(0), py(0), x_length(x), y_length(y)
{
   allocate("Default ctor failed");
}

X::X(const X& obj) throw(const char*) : px(0), py(0),
        x_length(obj.x_length), y_length(obj.y_length)
{
   allocate("Copy ctor failed");
}

void X::allocate(const char* s) throw(const char*)
{
   try
   {
      px = new int[x_length];
      py = new int[y_length];
   }
   catch(xalloc& obj)
   {
      cout << obj.why() << '\n';
      release();
      throw s;
   }
}
```

(Continued)

```
// File main.cpp

#include <iostream.h>
#include "x.h"

int main()
{
   cout << "Enter 2 values for the heap space: ";
   int a;
   int b;
   while(!(cin >> a >> b).eof())
   {
      try
      {
         X x1(a, b);
         X x2(x1);
         cout << "Success!\n";
      }
      catch(const char* message)
      {
         cout << message << '\n';
      }
      cout << "Enter 2 values for the heap space: ";
   }
   cout << "End-of-file\n";
   return 0;
}

/* A typical run of the program would yield:

Enter 2 values for the heap space: 15000 15000
Out of memory
Default ctor failed
Enter 2 values for the heap space: 13000 13000
Out of memory
Copy ctor failed
Enter 2 values for the heap space: 6000 6000
Success!
Enter 2 values for the heap space: ^Z
End-of-file

*/
```

 Tip

Your compiler may produce different results depending upon the amount of heap space that is available.

12.16   How to Disable the EH Mechanism in `operator new()`

If you want to disable the EH mechanism in `operator new()`, then include the file `new.h` and call the function `set_new_handler()` with either an argument of 0 or the address of your own handler function. Now you are responsible for checking for failure by examining the content of the pointer for the value zero.

12.17   Exception Specifications with Virtual Functions

If a virtual function in a base class specifies an exception specification, then a function in a derived class that hides the base class function is only allowed to make this specification more restrictive, i.e., reduce the number of types that the function can legally throw.

 Example 12.16

```
class B
{
   virtual void f() throw(int);
   virtual void g();
};

class D : public B
{
   virtual void f();                // Error
   virtual void g() throw(int);     // OK
};
```

12.18   How to Throw an Exception From the Base/Member Initialization List

Consider this very simple abstraction of a `Person` class whose key data element is called `name`, which itself is an instance of the `String` class. The constructor for `Person` receives a `String` object by reference-to-`const` and correctly proceeds to initialize the `name` object in the base/member initialization list.

Example 12.17

```
class Person
{
      public:
    Person(const String& S) : name(S) {}
    // Other details omitted
      private:
    String name;
};
```

Because a `String` object (`name`) is being initialized with another `String` object (`S`), there is no doubt that the copy constructor in the `String` class will be invoked. But if that constructor requests heap space, and the request fails, then presumably it will catch the exception that is thrown and re-throw it back to the caller, which in this case is the `Person` constructor. On the assumption that the `Person` constructor wishes to catch what is thrown, it's obvious that it will not happen for the simple reason that no try block was written. But how can any try block be written to encompass the base/member initialization list?

The answer is that the syntax for a try block has been enhanced to allow you to write the keyword `try` after the formal argument list and before the colon. In effect, the base/member initialization list and the body of the constructor together constitute the entire try block.

With this change, the previous example would be written:

 Example 12.18

```
class Person
{
      public:
    Person(const String& S) try : name(S) {}
    catch(...)
    {
        // Process the error
    }
    // Other details omitted
      private:
    String name;
};
```

 Caution

Borland C++ 5.0 does not yet support this enhanced try block feature.

Review Questions

1. What is the purpose of exception handling?

2. What error recovery techniques are available without exception handling?

3. What is meant by "throwing an exception"?

4. What is a try block?

5. What is meant by "catching" an exception?

6. What is a catch block?

7. What is an "exception specification"?

 Exercise 12.1

Write a global function that takes an integer as its one formal argument and does a table look-up on an array of elements, each of which consists of an integer and a string. If there is an exact match on the integer input, then the function returns a pointer to the string verbiage of the number itself, e.g., "One" for 1, "Five" for 5, etc. If the number cannot be found in the array, then throw an exception. Loop until the operator enters end-of-file.

 Exercise 12.2

Modify the `Fraction` class from Chapter 9, Exercise 2, so that if the constructor detects a denominator of zero, it throws an exception.

Chapter 13

Namespaces

13.1   Introduction

Namespaces provide a way to partition the global space into individually named scopes to avoid naming conflicts that can arise when including files from many different sources.

13.2   What's the Problem?

In both the C and C++ languages, there is just one global scope. It's the place where a lot of names get dumped, e.g., all of your global functions and variable declarations, along with the libraries that you use to build your applications. This is called "namespace pollution", and obviously leads to conflicts in naming conventions.

Example 13.1

```
// File a.h

#ifndef A_H
#define A_H

void f(int);

#endif

// File b.h

#ifndef B_H
#define B_H

void f(char);

#endif

// File foo.cpp

#include "a.h"
#include "b.h" // Oops...now overloading f()
```

Clearly both header files cannot be included in `main()` because of the conflict in names. Even as shown in the following example, it is impractical (and ugly) to expect each person who writes a header file to invent unique names.

Example 13.2

```
// File a.h

#ifndef A_H
#define A_H

void A_f(int);

#endif

// File b.h

#ifndef B_H
#define B_H

void B_f(char);

#endif

// File foo.cpp

#include "a.h"
#include "b.h"   // OK now
```

13.3   The Solution

C++ solves this dilemma by providing a new mechanism, called the namespace, that partitions the global space into individually named scopes. Such scopes can be named by writing the keyword `namespace` followed by some arbitrary name, and then a pair of braces that defines the scope.

 Example 13.3

```
// File a.h

#ifndef A_H
#define A_H

namespace A
{
   void f(int);
   extern int x;
   // etc.
}

#endif
```

The names declared within the scope of A do not collide with global names or with names in any other namespace.

 Caution

You should only declare, not define, members within a namespace, if that namespace is part of a header file. A definition of data or a function is likely to produce a duplicate definition error from the linker.

13.4   How to Access Namespace Members

The members of the namespace can be referred to by using the traditional notation for class members, i.e., the scope resolution operator.

 Example 13.4

```
// File a.h

#ifndef A_H
#define A_H

namespace A
{
    void f(int);
    extern int x;
    // etc.
}

#endif

// File foo.cpp

#include "a.h"

void foo()
{
    int y = A::x;
    A::f(1);
}
```

Thus, to solve the preceding problem with the two header files, you might code:

Example 13.5

```
// File a.h

#ifndef A_H
#define A_H

namespace A
{
   void f(int);
}

#endif

// File b.h

#ifndef B_H
#define B_H

namespace B
{
   void f(char);
}

#endif

// File foo.cpp

#include "a.h"
#include "b.h"

void foo()
{
   A::f(1);
   B::f('A');
}
```

13.5   Namespace Continuation

If the compiler encounters more than one namespace having the same name, it merges the namespaces together. Of course, duplicate names are not allowed unless they are functions whose signatures constitute unambiguous overloading.

 Example 13.6

```
// File a.h

#ifndef A_H
#define A_H

namespace A
{
   void f(int);
}

namespace A     // Same namespace name
{
   void f(char);
}

#endif

// File foo.cpp

#include "a.h"

void foo()
{
   A::f(1);
   A::f('A');
}
```

13.6   Namespace Aliases

Obviously the names of the various namespaces themselves must be unique. In
order to avoid any possibility of duplication, they might have to be comprised of
many characters. This, of course, could mean burdensome coding.

 Example 13.7

```
// File att.h

#ifndef ATT_H
#define ATT_H

namespace AmericanTelephoneAndTelegraph
{
    void f(int);
}

#endif

// File gmc.h

#ifndef GMC_H
#define GMC_H

namespace GeneralMotorsCorporation
{
    void f(int);
}

#endif

// File foo.cpp

#include "att.h"
#include "gmc.h"

void foo()
{
    AmericanTelephoneAndTelegraph::f(1);
    GeneralMotorsCorporation::f(1);
}
```

A solution is for the user to create a namespace alias. This is done by writing the
keyword namespace, the alias name, an '=' sign, and the namespace name to
which the alias is to be bound.

Example 13.8

```
// File att.h

#ifndef ATT_H
#define ATT_H

namespace AmericanTelephoneAndTelegraph
{
   void f(int);
}

#endif

// File gmc.h

#ifndef GMC_H
#define GMC_H

namespace GeneralMotorsCorporation
{
   void f(int);
}

#endif

// File foo.cpp

#include "att.h"
#include "gmc.h"

void foo()
{
   namespace ATT = AmericanTelephoneAndTelegraph;
   namespace GMC = GeneralMotorsCorporation;
   ATT::f(1);
   GMC::f(1);
}
```

13.7   `using` **Declaration**

The names of members within a namespace can be referenced without the need to scope them if they have been declared with a *using declaration*. This is done by writing the keyword `using`, followed by the particular namespace member name. This inserts the name into the local scope, as though it had actually been declared there.

 Example 13.9

```
// File a.h

#ifndef A_H
#define A_H

namespace A
{
   void f(int);
}

#endif

// File b.h

#ifndef B_H
#define B_H

namespace B
{
   void f(char);
}

#endif

// File foo.cpp

#include "a.h"
#include "b.h"

void foo()
{
   using A::f;   // Bring A::f(int) into scope
   f(1);         // OK
   B::f('A');    // OK
}
```

But note that if you attempt to create an ambiguous situation by including two or more functions with the *same declaration*, then any calls to this function that are not scoped will result in a compilation error. For example, if `B::f()` is changed to accept an `int` instead of a `char`, then the second call to `f()` is ambiguous.

Example 13.10

```
// File a.h

#ifndef A_H
#define A_H

namespace A
{
   void f(int);
}

#endif

// File b.h

#ifndef B_H
#define B_H

namespace B
{
   void f(int);   // Same declaration as A::f(int)
}

#endif

// File foo.cpp

#include "a.h"
#include "b.h"

void foo()
{
   using A::f;  // Bring A::f(int) into scope
   f(1);        // OK; call A::f(int)
   using B::f;  // Bring B::f(int) into scope
   f(1);        // Error; ambiguous call
}
```

The effect of a using declaration can be negated if it is contained in its own scope. In other words, once the scope ends, those declarations inserted into the local scope then go out of scope.

Example 13.11

```cpp
// File a.h

#ifndef A_H
#define A_H

namespace A
{
   void f(int);
}

#endif

// File b.h

#ifndef B_H
#define B_H

namespace B
{
   void f(int);
}

#endif

// File foo.cpp

#include "a.h"
#include "b.h"

void foo()
{
   {
     using A::f;   // Bring A::f(int) into scope
     f(1);         // OK; call A::f(int)
   }
   {
     using B::f;   // Bring B::f(int) into scope
     f(1);         // OK; call B::f(int
   }
}
```

13.8   using **Directive**

A *using directive* says that all names from a given namespace are available for use without qualification, in effect dumping them back into the global space. In other words, just imagine the namespace scope being stripped away, and envision how the members would then be accessed.

A using directive is written with the two keywords using namespace followed by the name of the namespace. Obviously, the possibility for duplicate definitions exists if you do this, in which case explicit scoping must be used.

 Caution

> *A using directive is not an "all-inclusive using declaration", so be careful not to confuse a using declaration with a using directive.*

 Example 13.12

```
void f(int);  // Global declaration

// File a.h

#ifndef A_H
#define A_H

namespace A
{
   void f(int);
}

#endif

// File foo.cpp

#include "a.h"

void foo()
{
   f(1);          // OK; call ::f(int)
   using namespace A; // Make A::f(int) available
   f(1);          // Error; ambiguous -- ::f(int) or A::f(int) ?
   ::f(1);        // OK
   A::f(1);       // OK
}
```

If you have more than one using directive within a function, and each namespace has a duplicate member, then an ambiguity error will occur when that member is referenced.

Example 13.13

```
// File a.h

#ifndef A_H
#define A_H

namespace A
{
    void f(int);
}

#endif

// File b.h

#ifndef B_H
#define B_H

namespace B
{
    void f(char);
    void f(int);
}

#endif

// File foo.cpp

#include "a.h"
#include "b.h"

void foo()
{
    using namespace A;
    using namespace B;
    f('A');        // Calls B::f(char)
    f(1);          // Ambiguous; A::f(int) or B::f(int)?
}
```

The call to `f(char)` uses the normal rules of function overloading. The call to `f(int)` is obviously ambiguous.

As with a using declaration, the only way to negate the effect of a `using` directive is to exit the scope in which it was first encountered.

Example 13.14

```
// File a.h

#ifndef A_H
#define A_H

namespace A
{
   void f(int);
}

#endif

// File b.h

#ifndef B_H
#define B_H

namespace B
{
   void f(char);
   void f(int);
}

#endif

// File foo.cpp

#include "a.h"
#include "b.h"

void foo()
{
   {
      using namespace A;
      f(1);    // OK; call A::f(int)
   }
   {
      using namespace B;
      f(1);    // OK; call B::f(int)
   }
}
```

 Tip

There is no way to insert the members of an entire namespace into the local scope with just one statement. You must insert each one individually via a using declaration.

13.9   Unnamed Namespaces

If you omit the identifier in a namespace definition, then you create an unnamed namespace. This namespace is unique for that compilation unit, and a `using` directive for it is automatically assumed. The net result is that if two different compilation units include this namespace, each one will have its own copy of the members, and the linker will *not* subsequently yield a duplicate definition error. In effect, it is a substitute for declaring global members to have `static` (internal) linkage.

    Example 13.15

```
// File header.h

#ifndef HEADER_H
#define HEADER_H

namespace        // Unnamed namespace created
{
    int x;
}

#endif

// File foo1.cpp

#include "header.h"

void foo1()
{
    x = 1;
}

// File foo2.cpp

#include "header.h"

void foo2()
{
    x = 1;
}
```

13.10   Friend Functions

If a class within a namespace definition declares a friend function, then this function has namespace, not global, scope. The same is true for any variable declared `extern`.

 Example 13.16

```
// File a.h

#ifndef A_H
#define A_H

namespace A
{
   extern int x;
   class C
   {
      friend void f();
   };
}

#endif

// File foo.cpp

#include "a.h"

void foo()
{
   x = 1;        // Error; x is not declared
   A::x = 1;     // OK
   f();          // Error; f() is not declared
   A::f();       // OK
   using namespace A;
   x = 1;        // OK
   f();          // OK
}
```

13.11   A Class is a Namespace

A class definition itself constitutes a namespace. By writing a `using` declaration in a derived class, you can achieve the effect of overloading the functions in the derived class with those in the base class that have the same name.

 Example 13.17

```
class B
{
    public:
  void f(char);
  void f(double);
};

class D : public B
{
  using B::f;   // Brings all B::f methods into scope of D
    public:
  void f(int) { f('A'); } // Calls B::f(char)
};

void foo(D& d)
{
  d.f(1);      // Calls D::f(int)
  d.f('A');    // Calls B::f(char);
  d.f(2.3);    // Calls B::f(double);
}
```

Review Questions

1. What is the purpose of the namespace mechanism?

2. What is a using declaration?

3. What is a using directive?

4. What is an unnamed namespace, and why would you ever create one?

Chapter 14

Runtime Type Information

14.1 Introduction

Runtime type information (RTTI) is a mechanism by which the type of an object can be determined at execution time as opposed to compilation time. It consists of two parts: dynamic casting and the `typeid` operator.

 Tip

> *Some books may refer to this topic as "Runtime type* identification*", but it's the same thing.*

14.2 Dynamic Casting

If you have a pointer or reference of some base class type, it may, of course, be pointing or referring to either a base class or to a derived class object. If you wish to invoke a certain function with this pointer or reference, and this function has been declared virtual in the base class, then there is absolutely no problem since polymorphism will automatically take effect.

But suppose that this function is unique to some derived class so that it cannot be declared in the base class. In this case, the compiler does not allow you to call the function using a base class pointer or reference. Instead, you must use a pointer or reference of the specific derived class type in order to invoke the function.

But if all you have is an array of base class pointers, then how do you know if any given pointer does, in fact, point to an instance of the derived class? Can you safely cast the base class pointer to a derived class pointer (called a "downcast")? Maybe, and maybe not. This is where you need the `dynamic_cast` keyword.

14.2.1   Syntax

The format of a dynamic cast is identical to the new style of casting you learned in Chapter 1. Here is a simple example to illustrate its use.

 Example 14.1

```
class B
{
     public:
   virtual ~B() {}
};

class D : public B
{
     public:
   void bar();
};

void bar(B* ptr_B)
{
   D* ptr_D = dynamic_cast<D*>(ptr_B);
   if(ptr_D)
      ptr_D->bar();
}
```

Since `ptr_B` represents a base class pointer, and `ptr_D` represents a derived class pointer, if `ptr_B` does, in fact, point to an object of type D, `ptr_D` will point to the derived object (and contain the same address that `ptr_B` contains). Therefore, the call to `D::bar()` can safely be made, and is perfectly valid. On the other hand, if `ptr_B` does not point to an object of type D, then, `ptr_D` will contain zero, and the call to `D::bar()` cannot safely be made.

In addition to pointers, the `dynamic_cast` keyword may be used with a reference.

Example 14.2

```
class B
{
    public:
  virtual ~B() {}
};

class D : public B
{
    public:
  void bar();
};

void foo(B& ref_B)
{
  try
  {
      D& ref_D = dynamic_cast<D&>(ref_B);
      ref_D.bar();
  }
  catch(...) {}
}
```

If `ref_B` does, in fact, refer to an object of type D, then `ref_D` will refer to that same object, and the method `D::bar()` may safely be called. Otherwise, an exception of type `bad_cast` will be thrown.

 Caution

> *Since the dynamic cast mechanism uses the compiler's table of virtual function pointers, the base class must contain at least one virtual function.*

14.2.2   Example of a Dynamic Cast

Suppose that you have a base class called `Vehicle`, from which the classes `Car` and `Truck` are derived. Further, suppose that a `Truck` object has a data member called `capacity` that, for whatever reason, doesn't exist in the `Car` class. If you then have a container class called `Collection`, which can contain both `Car` and `Truck` objects, and iterate across all `Vehicle` objects, you have to know if each pointer is really pointing to a `Truck` object so that the `Truck::get_capacity()` message can legally be sent.

Example 14.3

```cpp
#include <iostream.h>

class Vehicle
{
    public:
  virtual ~Vehicle() {}
  // Other details omitted
};

class Car : public Vehicle
{
  // Details omitted
};

class Truck : public Vehicle
{
    public:
  Truck(int c) : capacity(c) {}
  int get_capacity() const { return capacity; }
    private:
  int capacity;
};

class Collection
{
    public:
  Collection(int n);
  ~Collection();
  void start();
    private:
  Vehicle** ptr;
  int number;
};

Collection::Collection(int n) : ptr(0), number(n)
{
  ptr = new Vehicle*[number];
  for(int i = 0; i < number; ++i)
  {
    if(i % 2 == 0)
      ptr[i] = new Truck(i);  // Even number means a truck
    else
      ptr[i] = new Car;       // Odd number means a car
  }
}
```

(Continued)

```
Collection::~Collection()
{
    for(int i = number - 1; i >= 0; --i)
        delete ptr[i];
    delete [] ptr;
}

void Collection::start()
{
    for(int i = 0; i < number; ++i)
    {
        Truck* p = dynamic_cast<Truck*>(ptr[i]);
        if(p)
            cout << "capacity = " << p->get_capacity() << '\n';
    }
}

int main()
{
    Collection vehicles(7);
    vehicles.start();
    return 0;
}

/* The output of this program is:

capacity = 0
capacity = 2
capacity = 4
capacity = 6

*/
```

14.3   `typeid` Keyword

Unlike the `dynamic_cast` keyword that is used to perform a safe downcast, the `typeid` keyword may be used with non-polymorphic types (such as fundamental types and expressions).

The syntax for `typeid` is shown in the following example.

 Example 14.4

```
typeid(expression)
```

where `expression` is any valid type, object, or C++ expression. Polymorphism is honored in the sense that if the expression is a base class pointer or reference, and the object to which the expression points or refers is a class derived from the base class, then this derived class will be the resultant type. If you use a pointer, and it contains 0, then `typeid` will throw an exception of type `bad_typeid`. Of course, the base class must contain at least one virtual function; otherwise, the resultant type is always that of the base class.

14.3.1   Header File `typeinfo.h`

The use of the `typeid` keyword results in the return a temporary object of type `const type_info&`. The header file `typeinfo.h` contains the definition of the class `type_info`, as follows:

 Example 14.5

```
class type_info
{
      private:
    type_info(const type_info&);
    type_info& operator=(const type_info&);
      public:
    virtual ~type_info();
    bool operator==(const type_info&) const;
    bool operator!=(const type_info&) const;
    bool before(const type_info& rhs) const;
    const char* name() const;
};
```

The most useful function, `name()`, returns a string literal that describes the type of the object, whether the type is primitive, user-defined, pointer, reference, etc. The function `before()` returns a non-zero value if the value of `this->name()` precedes that of `rhs.name()` in the collating sequence. You may also compare two `type_info` objects for equality or inequality by using the overloaded operators that are shown.

14.3.2   **Examples of** typeid

Here is a simple example that uses the name() method to infer the type of the object that was used to perform the instantiation of the function f().

 Example 14.6

```
#include <iostream.h>
#include <typeinfo.h>

class B
{
    public:
  virtual void g(short) {}
};

class D : public B {};

template <class T>
void f(const T& arg)
{
  cout << "T is type " << typeid(T).name() << '\n';
  cout << "arg is type " << typeid(arg).name() << '\n';
  cout << "----------------------------\n";
}

int main()
{
  f(1 == 1);
  f(1);
  f(2.3);
  f('A');
  f("B");
  const char* str = "C";
  f(str);
  f(&B::g);
  double (*p)(int);
  f(p);
  B* ptr;
  f(ptr);
  ptr = new B;
  f(*ptr);
  delete ptr;
  ptr = new D;
  f(*ptr);
  delete ptr;
  return 0;
}
```

(Continued)

```
/* The output of this program is:

T is type bool
arg is type const bool
----------------------------
T is type int
arg is type const int
----------------------------
T is type double
arg is type const double
----------------------------
T is type char
arg is type const char
----------------------------
T is type char *
arg is type char * const
----------------------------
T is type const char *
arg is type const char * const
----------------------------
T is type void (B::*)(short)
arg is type void (B::* const)(short)
----------------------------
T is type double (*)(int)
arg is type double(* const)(int)
----------------------------
T is type B *
arg is type B * const
----------------------------
T is type B
arg is type B
----------------------------
T is type B
arg is type D
----------------------------

*/
```

 Caution

Although the C++ Draft specifies the name type_info, *Borland 5.0 supports the name* typeinfo *(no underscore).*

Here is another example in which the typeid keyword is used to prompt the terminal operator for the right type of object to be input. Two tests are run, one using type int, and the other using an instance of the standard library's string class.

Example 14.7

```
#include <iostream.h>
#include <typeinfo.h>
#include <cstring.h>

template <class T>
const T& input(T& object)
{
   cout << "Input data for an object of type "
        << typeid(T).name() << " :";
   cin >> object;
   return object;
}

int main()
{
   int number;
   cout << "You entered: " << input(number) << '\n';
   string str;
   cout << "You entered: " << input(str) << '\n';
   return 0;
}

/* A typical run of this program is:

Input data for an object of type int: 12
You entered: 12
Input data for an object of type string: Testing...
You entered: Testing...

*/
```

Review Questions

1. What are the two parts of runtime type information?
2. Why would you ever need to perform a safe downcast?
3. Name two ways in which the `dynamic_cast` keyword can be used.
4. Why would you ever use the `typeid` keyword?
5. What is the class `type_info`?
6. What does the method `type_info::name()` do?
7. How does polymorphism work with the `typeid` keyword?

 Exercise 14.1

Given the following function declarations, display what the types of T and `arg` are when the functions are called with both const-qualified and non-const-qualified arguments.

```
template <class T>
void foo(T& arg);
template <class T>
void bar(const T& arg);
```

 Exercise 14.2

Modify Example 14.3 to use the `typeid` and `reinterpret_cast` keywords instead of doing a `dynamic_cast`.

Chapter 15

Iostream Output

15.1   Introduction

In Chapter 2 you learned the fundamentals of how to do input and output using iostream methods. Of course, there is a lot more to it than was covered there, and in this chapter you will learn how to format your output so that it is more readable to the user of your programs.

15.2   The Instances `cerr` **and** `clog`

In addition to the instance `cout`, C++ provides you with two other instances of the class `ostream` called `cerr` and `clog`. They are used for any error messages that you may wish to direct to the terminal operator. The output of `cerr` is unbuffered, while the output of `clog` is buffered.

Although the output of both the `cerr` and `clog` instances will normally be shown on the screen, if redirection is used, say to a printer or disk file, then the results of `cout` will be redirected, while the results of `cerr` and `clog` will continue to be shown on the screen.

15.3   Formatting the Output

Think about a `printf()` function call. It usually consists of a control string argument and, optionally, a list of expressions to be output. The control string contains literals which will be output exactly as shown, and conversion specifications that indicate exactly how an expression from the list of expressions is to appear. Each conversion specification starts with a '%' and ends with a conversion character, e.g., `"%d"` or `"%i"` for decimal format, `"%c"` for character format, `"%s"` for a string, etc. Between the start and end you may enter various flags, the field width, base formatting, justification, floating point precision, and so forth. Each conversion specification stands on its own; there is no connection to any other one.

Now, however, you are working with the `cout` object that has some state, and it's this state that governs how your output data will appear on the screen. For example, if the state of `cout` is set to hexadecimal, then all integer output will appear in hexadecimal. If the state of `cout` is set to left-justify, then all fields from now on will appear left-justified.

15.3.1   Bit Format Flags

Most of the states of the `cout` object are represented by a `long` (protected) field inherited from the class `ios`. (This class represents general properties of a stream, such as whether it's open for reading and whether it is a binary or a text stream.) Since each state is a binary representation of some 'on' or 'off' condition, all it needs is one bit. Therefore, this `long` integer can uniquely represent at most 32 different binary conditions. For example, the output state of decimal is either on or off. Similarly, the state of left-justification is either on or off.

The value for each binary state is represented by a constant value in an unnamed public enumerated type within the class `ios`. No two fields of this type have the same bit on. Using a mutator function, these bits are then bitwise ORed into the long integer that reflects the state of the `cout` object.

Each binary value also has a name associated with it that you may reference. The complete list of all enumerated values is shown below. Don't forget that because these names exist within the class `ios`, this class must be specified in conjunction with the scope resolution operator (::) to unambiguously access a specific value. These are the names and values that Borland C++ 5.0 uses.

Table 15-1 Bit Format Flags

Name	Value	Meaning
ios::skipws	0x0001	Skip whitespace on input
ios::left	0x0002	Left-justification of output
ios::right	0x0004	Right-justification of output
ios::internal	0x0008	Pad after sign or base indicator
ios::dec	0x0010	Show integers in decimal format
ios::oct	0x0020	Show integers in octal format
ios::hex	0x0040	Show integers in hexadecimal format
ios::showbase	0x0080	Show the base for octal and hex numbers
ios::showpoint	0x0100	Show the decimal point for all floats
ios::uppercase	0x0200	Show uppercase hex numbers
ios::showpos	0x0400	Show + for positive numbers
ios::scientific	0x0800	Show exponential notation on floats
ios::fixed	0x1000	Show fixed decimal output on floats
ios::unitbuf	0x2000	Flush all streams after insertion
ios::stdio	0x4000	Flush stdout and stderr after insertion
ios::boolalpha	0x8000	Insert/extract bools as text or numeric

 Caution

> *Because the type* `bool` *is not supported for Borland versions prior to 5.0, the bit* `ios::boolalpha` *does not exist for those versions.*

15.3.2   How to Turn On the Bit Format Flags

In order to change the state of the `cout` object, you must be able to change the bits that represent its state. Within the class `ios` several mutator member functions are provided to allow this to be done.

 Tip

> *Different C++ compilers will generate code that provides different default settings for these bits. For Borland C++, it will turn on the* `ios::skipws` *and* `ios::unitbuf` *bits at the start of each program. All other bits will be off.*

15.3.2.1   The Method `ios::setf()`

The first of these mutator methods is called `ios::setf()`. As you can see, it is inherited from the class `ios`. To call it, you must first specify the instance name (`cout`), the dot operator, and then the method name.

 Example 15.1

```
cout.setf( /* arguments */ );
```

The `ios::setf()` method also returns the previous value of the format flags.

For example, to turn on the `ios::showpos` bit, you would code:

 Example 15.2

```
cout.setf(ios::showpos);
```

The function `ios::setf()` works by bitwise ORing its one argument with the existing values, thereby leaving any other bits undisturbed. This means that it's possible to turn on more than one bit with just one call to `ios::setf()` by using an expression for the first argument that contains several bits ORed together.

For example, to turn on the `ios::showpos` and the `ios::uppercase` bits, you would code:

 Example 15.3

```
cout.setf(ios::showpos | ios::uppercase);
```

 Caution

Do not confuse the bitwise OR (single vertical bar) with the Boolean OR (two vertical bars).

Unfortunately, ambiguous situations can arise. For example, from a logical perspective, you should never set the state of the `cout` object to specify that output should appear in decimal *and* in hexadecimal *and* in octal. But there is nothing to prevent you from doing this.

To help you guard against this possibility, `ios::setf()` has been overloaded to accept two arguments. In this case, the first argument specifies which bits are to be turned ON, whereas the second argument specifies those bits that are to be turned off first. Thus, for example, before specifying that output is to appear in octal, you can easily specify that the decimal and hexadecimal bits are to be turned off first. To do this, you would code:

Example 15.4

```
cout.setf(ios::oct, ios::dec | ios::oct | ios::hex);
```

Caution

Note that even though the ios::oct *bit is to be set on, it is still mandatory that you specify it in the second argument. The reason is that the bit to be turned on is the result of doing a bitwise AND of the first and second arguments.*

15.3.2.2   The Method ios::unsetf()

In order to turn the formatting bits off, you may use the mutator function ios::unsetf(). This function takes exactly one argument—the bit pattern to be turned off. Thus, to turn off the bit ios::showpos, you would code:

Example 15.5

```
cout.unsetf(ios::showpos);
```

Like ios::setf(), more than one bit at a time can be turned off by bitwise ORing the enumerated values together in the argument field. For example, to turn off the ios::showpos and ios::uppercase bits, you would code:

Example 15.6

```
cout.unsetf(ios::showpos | ios::uppercase);
```

15.3.2.3   The Method ios::flags()

Because the field in the class ios that represents the bit settings is protected, you cannot access it directly. However, there is a public accessor member function called ios::flags() that will return this field to you as a long. In addition, if you provide a long as an argument to ios::flags(), then the existing value will be returned to you *after* your argument is used to provide a new setting for the field.

In this example the initial value of the bit settings is returned and printed in upper-case hexadecimal notation.

 Example 15.7

```
#include <iostream.h>

int main()
{
    long value = cout.flags();
    cout.setf(ios::uppercase);
    long new_value = cout.setf(ios:: hex, ios::dec |
        ios::oct | ios::hex);
    cout << "Initial value = " << value << '\n';
    cout << "New value = " << new_value << '\n';
    return 0;
}

/* The output of this program is:

Initial value = 2001
New value = 2201

*/
```

15.3.3   How to Display Integers in the Proper Base

Output formatting is important because you want to have complete flexibility in the manner in which your data appears. Let's start with the base in which integers will be shown.

In a `printf()` function call, you have three choices: decimal, octal, and hex. You can get decimal output by using a conversion specification of `"%d"` or `"%i"`, an octal by using `"%o"`, and hex by using either `"%x"` or `"%X"`. (How to emulate lower vs. upper case will be discussed later.) In C++, there are three bits in the enumerated values shown in Table 15-2 that control the base setting:

Table 15-2   Base Setting

Name	Value	Meaning
ios::dec	0x0010	Show integers in decimal format
ios::oct	0x0020	Show integers in octal format
ios::hex	0x0040	Show integers in hexadecimal format

To guarantee that decimal output is used, you must turn on the bit `ios::dec`, and *ensure that the remaining 2 bits are turned off.* The same reasoning applies to octal and hex output.

The interesting aspect about the output base setting is that in Borland C++, all three bits shown in Table 15-2 are initially off. Therefore, the logical question is, which base will be used? The answer is that Borland (and probably other C++ compilers) will default to decimal output. Remember: once the base has been set, it stays set for all future integers unless it is subsequently changed.

15.3.3.1   The Field `ios::basefield`

Recall from Example 15.4 the form of the `ios::setf()` function that you must use in order to turn on one of the three base setting bits and ensure that the other two bits are off. Since the second argument entails a lot of coding on your part, the iostream library has conveniently provided a `static const` variable that is the bitwise OR of the three base setting bits. This field is called `ios::basefield`, and has the following definition:

Example 15.8

```
const long ios::basefield = ios::dec | ios::oct | ios::hex;
```

The following example runs a test on all three base settings.

Example 15.9

```
#include <iostream.h>

int main()
{
   int x = 65;
   cout << "Decimal: " << x << '\n';
   cout.setf(ios::oct, ios::basefield);
   cout << "Octal: " << x << '\n';
   cout.setf(ios::hex, ios::basefield);
   cout << "Hex: " << x << '\n';
   cout.setf(ios::dec, ios::basefield);
   cout << "Decimal: " << x << '\n';
   return 0;
}

/* The output of this program is:

Decimal: 65
Octal: 101
Hex: 41
Decimal: 65

*/
```

15.3.4   How to Show the Base Setting of Integers

In a `printf()` function call, the use of the flag '#' causes the base of an octal or hexadecimal number to appear as 0 and 0x, respectively. The same effect can be achieved in C++ by setting on the bit `ios::showbase`. To revert back to not showing the base setting, use the `ios::unsetf()` method.

Table 15-3   Showing the Base Setting

Name	Value	Meaning
ios::showbase	0x0080	Show the base for octal and hex numbers

Here is Example 15.9 again with the `ios::showbase` bit turned on.

 Example 15.10

```
#include <iostream.h>

int main()
{
   int x = 65;
   cout.setf(ios::showbase);
   cout << "Decimal: " << x << '\n';
   cout.setf(ios::oct, ios::basefield);
   cout << "Octal: " << x << '\n';
   cout.setf(ios::hex, ios::basefield);
   cout << "Hex: " << x << '\n';
   cout.setf(ios::dec, ios::basefield);
   cout << "Decimal: " << x << '\n';
   return 0;
}

/* The output of this program is:

Decimal: 65
Octal: 0101
Hex: 0x41
Decimal: 65

*/
```

15.3.5   How to Display the Sign of an Integer

Note that on positive decimal output, a '+' sign is assumed, and by default will not appear. In a `printf()` function call, you can force the '+' sign to appear if you use the flag '+'.

Using iostream methods, if you want this sign to appear, you must turn on the bit ios::showpos. (Of course, if the number is negative, the '–' sign will always appear.) To revert back to not showing the '+' sign, use the ios::unsetf() method.

Table 15-4 Showing the Plus Sign

Name	Value	Meaning
ios::showpos	0x0400	Show + for positive numbers

Here is Example 15.10 again with the ios::showpos bit turned on.

 Example 15.11

```
#include <iostream.h>

int main()
{
    int x = 65;
    cout.setf(ios::showbase | ios::showpos);
    cout << "Decimal: " << x << '\n';
    cout.setf(ios::oct, ios::basefield);
    cout << "Octal: " << x << '\n';
    cout.setf(ios::hex, ios::basefield);
    cout << "Hex: " << x << '\n';
    cout.setf(ios::dec, ios::basefield);
    cout << "Decimal: " << x << '\n';
    return 0;
}

/* The output of this program is:

Decimal: +65
Octal: 0101
Hex: 0x41
Decimal: +65

*/
```

 Tip

There is no bit available with which to emulate the 'blank' flag in a printf() *statement. This flag causes a blank to appear in the sign position of a positive number.*

15.3.6   How to Display Output in Uppercase

There is one other option you can employ with hexadecimal numbers. By default any hex digit, as well as the 'x' in the base, appears in lowercase. The same rule applies to the 'e' when printing in scientific notation. In a printf() function call, you would code a capital 'X' to obtain hex digits in uppercase, or a capital 'E' to show the 'E' in scientific notation in uppercase.

Using iostream, if you want to see uppercase, turn on the bit ios::uppercase. To revert back to lowercase, use the ios::unsetf() method.

Table 15-5   Showing Uppercase

Name	Value	Meaning
ios::uppercase	0x0200	Show uppercase hex numbers

The following example prints the hex number abc in hexadecimal, and shows the base setting and all hex digits in uppercase.

    Example 15.12

```cpp
#include <iostream.h>

int main()
{
   cout.setf(ios::uppercase | ios::showbase);
   cout.setf(ios::hex, ios::basefield);
   cout << 0xabc << '\n';
   return 0;
}

/* The output of this program is:

0XABC

*/
```

15.3.7   How to Display a Character

If you want to display a character, there is no problem since the compiler will use argument matching to invoke the insertion operator that takes a char as its one explicit argument. If you want to display a character as some other type, e.g., an integer, then you must cast it using the static_cast keyword (in lieu of using a C-style or function-style cast).

Example 15.13

```
#include <iostream.h>

int main()
{
    char ch = 'A';
    cout << "char: " << ch << '\n';
    cout << "int: " << static_cast<int>(ch) << '\n';
    return 0;
}

/* The output of this program is:

char: A
int: 65

*/
```

15.3.7.1   The Method `ostream::put()`

In addition to using the insertion operator to output a character, the member function called `ostream::put()` provides a way to guarantee that any value gets shown in its character format (think of the C function `putchar()`.) This function also returns the invoking instance by reference, so it can be chained to a subsequent function call.

Example 15.14

```
#include <iostream.h>

int main()
{
    char ch1 = 'A';
    cout.put(ch1) << '\n';
    int ch2 = 66;
    cout.put(static_cast<char>(ch2)) << '\n';
    return 0;
}

/* The output of this program is:

A
B

*/
```

Caution

> *If the argument is not a character type* (char, signed char, *or* unsigned char), *then you must cast it to a character type to avoid an ambiguity error.*

15.3.8   How to Set the Field Width

The field width in C++ works in a manner similar to that in C. If the total number of characters needed for output is less than the specified width, then the extra spaces will be filled with the current fill character. If the number of characters is greater than the specified width, then the width is "expanded" to accommodate the entire field. (In C, the fill character in a printf() function call can be only either a zero or a space; using iostream methods, it can be any character you desire.)

If no width is ever specified, then the default value of zero is assumed (just as it is in C). To change the field width, use the member function ios::width() with one argument: the width value itself. Then the next field to be output will use this value.

In addition to setting the field width, the ios::width() function returns the value of the width that existed prior to the function call. If you wish to return this value and make no modification to it, then call the ios::width() function with no argument specified.

For example, this program prints the number 1 right-justified and preceded by 4 blanks.

 Example 15.15

```
#include <iostream.h>

int main()
{
    int x = 1;
    cout.width(5);
    cout << x << " is the answer\n";
    return 0;
}

/* The output of this program is:

^^^^1 is the answer

(where ^ is a blank)

*/
```

15.3.8.1   The Width Does Not "Stick"

The `ios::width()` method is unusual in the sense that it is an exception to the "set it and forget it" rule that applies to other aspects of formatting. That is, once the width is "consumed" by a field, it reverts back to its default value of zero immediately. If you want to set the width for some subsequent field, then you must call `ios::width()` again.

 Tip

> *Is something bothering you here? Does it seem like you're being forced into a lot of detailed coding just to do some simple formatting? And wouldn't it be nice to be able to perform all of the formatting in one statement? Well, you're absolutely right—it is a lot of work, and it doesn't read very well. That's the bad news. The good news is that your job will become much easier with the introduction of manipulators in Chapter 17. For now, however, you have to learn how to walk before you learn how to run.*

15.3.9   How to Specify the Fill Character

If the total number of characters needed to display a field is less than the current field width, the extra output spaces will be filled with the current fill character. In a `printf()` function call, the default fill character is a blank, and you have only the option to change it to a zero.

Using iostream methods, however, you now have the option for *any* character to serve as the fill character. As before, the default is a blank. The member function `ios::fill()` is used to specify a new fill character. Once it is specified, it remains as the fill character unless it is subsequently changed. The function takes a single argument: the new fill character, and returns the previous fill character. As with `ios::width()`, it may be called with no actual argument if you merely want to return the previous fill character.

Example 15.16

```
#include <iostream.h>

int main()
{
   cout.width(5);
   cout.fill('0');
   cout << 1 << '\n';
   cout.width(5);
   cout.fill('*');
   cout << 23 << '\n';
   return 0;
}

/* The output of this program is:

00001
***23

*/
```

15.3.10   How to Specify Field Justification

In a `printf()` function call, whenever a field is output, the data is always right-justified. If you want to left-justify a field, you must use the '–' formatting flag.

In the iostream library there are three bits which are used to specify the field justification:

Table 15-6   Field Justification

Name	Value	Meaning
ios::left	0x0002	Left-justification of output
ios::right	0x0004	Right-justification of output
ios::internal	0x0008	Pad after sign or base indicator

15.3.10.1   The Field `ios::adjustfield`

If no bit is ever specified, then the justification defaults to right. As with the integer base setting, if one of the bits is on you must ensure that the remaining two bits are off. To this end, the field called `ios::adjustfield` has been defined with all three justification bits turned on.

Example 15.17

```
const long ios::adjustfield = ios::left | ios::right |
        ios::internal;
```

The following example prints a number using all three justifications. The justification `ios::internal` means that padding with the fill character, if any, will occur after the base of the number has been shown (for octal and hexadecimal numbers) and before the number itself. This is also true if a sign for the number is shown, i.e., the padding will occur between the sign and the number itself.

 Example 15.18

```
#include <iostream.h>

int main()
{
    int x = 65;
    cout.fill('*');
    cout.setf(ios::showpos);
    cout.setf(ios::left, ios::adjustfield);
    cout.width(5);
    cout << x << '\n';
    cout.setf(ios::right, ios::adjustfield);
    cout.width(5);
    cout << x << '\n';
    cout.setf(ios::internal, ios::adjustfield);
    cout.width(5);
    cout << x << '\n';
    return 0;
}

/* The output of this program is:

+65**
**+65
+**65

*/
```

15.3.11   How to Format Floating Point Numbers

Floating point numbers are output in C++ just like any other type of number. However, the formatting is certainly different, and default values are not the same as you would get from using a `printf()` function call. Your goal then is to emulate the `"%f"` and `"%e"` conversion specifications.

In the following example, some floating point constants are output with no special formatting.

 Example 15.19

```
#include <iostream.h>

int main()
{
    cout << 1.23456789 << '\n';    // #1
    cout << 4.00 << '\n';          // #2
    cout << 5.678E2 << '\n';       // #3
    cout << 0.0 << '\n';           // #4
    return 0;
}

/* The output of this program is:

1.23457
4
567.8
0

*/
```

For line #1, note that no more than six digits are shown. For line #2, not only do the trailing zeroes *not* show, but even the decimal point does not appear. For line #3, the number prints in fixed point notation despite being keyed in scientific notation. For line #4, even though the value is zero, at least one significant digit will always appear.

15.3.11.1   The Bit `ios::showpoint`

The first step in formatting floating point numbers is to turn on the bit `ios::showpoint`. This will cause a decimal point to appear, and six digits at most will be shown. (If more than six digits are needed, the output will be shown in scientific notation.)

Table 15-7   Showing the Decimal Point

Name	Value	Meaning
ios::showpoint	0x0100	Show the decimal point for all floats

Here is the previous example with the `ios::showpoint` bit now turned on.

Example 15.20

```
#include <iostream.h>

int main()
{
    cout.setf(ios::showpoint);
    cout << 1.23456789 << '\n';
    cout << 4.00 << '\n';
    cout << 5.678E2 << '\n';
    cout << 0.0 << '\n';
    return 0;
}

/* The output of this program is:

1.23457
4.00000
567.800
0.00000

*/
```

15.3.11.2   The Method `ios::precision()`

The next step is to specify the number of positions to be shown after the decimal point. To do this, use the method `ios::precision()` in which the one argument is the number of decimal positions to be shown.

If it is called without an argument, it merely returns the current value of the precision, and does not alter it. If it is called with an argument, the precision is set using this argument, and the prior value for the precision is returned. If the precision is never specified, then it defaults to the value 0.

Here is the previous example again with the precision now set to 2.

Example 15.21

```
#include <iostream.h>

int main()
{
   cout.setf(ios::showpoint);
   cout.precision(2);
   cout << 1.23456789 << '\n';
   cout << 4.00 << '\n';
   cout << 5.678E2 << '\n';
   cout << 0.0 << '\n';
   return 0;
}

/* The output of this program is:

1.2
4.0
5.7e+02
0.0

*/
```

15.3.12   The Bits `ios::scientific` and `ios::fixed`

The output of the previous example shows that the precision is still not right, and sometimes the floating output appears in scientific, rather than fixed point notation. To fix these problems, turn on the bit `ios::scientific` or the bit `ios::fixed`.

Table 15-8 Fixed-Point vs. Scientific

Name	Value	Meaning
ios::scientific	0x0800	Show exponential notation on floats
ios::fixed	0x1000	Show fixed decimal output on floats

If neither bit is turned on, then the compiler emulates the "`%g`" conversion specification in a `printf()` function call.

15.3.12.1   The Field `ios::floatfield`

As you have probably suspected, there is a constant already created that is the bit-wise OR of the bits `ios::scientific` and `ios::fixed`. This field is called `ios::floatfield`, and should be used as the second argument in an `ios::setf()` function call. Note that when the output stream is set to either `ios::fixed` or `ios::scientific`, then the precision setting applies to the number of positions after the decimal point.

Example 15.22

```
const long ios::floatfield = ios::scientific | ios::fixed;
```

Here is Example 15.21 again, now with both notations used.

Example 15.23

```cpp
#include <iostream.h>

int main()
{
   cout.setf(ios::showpoint);
   cout.precision(2);
   // Guarantee fixed decimal
   cout.setf(ios::fixed, ios::floatfield);
   cout << 1.23456789 << '\n';
   cout << 4.00 << '\n';
   cout << 5.678E2 << '\n';
   cout << 0.0 << "\n\n";
   // Guarantee scientific
   cout.setf(ios::scientific, ios::floatfield);
   cout << 1.23456789 << '\n';
   cout << 4.00 << '\n';
   cout << 5.678E2<< '\n';
   cout << 0.0 << '\n';
   return 0;
}

/* The output of this program is:

1.23
4.00
567.80
0.00

1.23e+00
4.00e+00
5.68e+02
0.00e+00

*/
```

15.4   How to Display a `bool` Type

Recall that a variable of type `bool` intrinsically has the value `true` or `false`. When this value is displayed, `true` will appear as a 1, and `false` will appear as a 0.

 Example 15.24

```
#include <iostream.h>

int main()
{
   bool b = false;
   cout << b << '\n';
   b = true;
   cout << b << '\n';
   return 0;
}

/* The output of this program is:

0
1

*/
```

If you turn on the flag `ios::boolalpha`, then the alphabetic representation of these values will appear instead of the numeric representation.

 Example 15.25

```
#include <iostream.h>

int main()
{
   cout.setf(ios::boolalpha);
   bool b = false;
   cout << b << '\n';
   b = true;
   cout << b << '\n';
   return 0;
}

/* The output of this program is:

false
true

*/
```

15.5   How to Print an Address

The address of a variable or object can be generated by using the address operator (&). Because this operator can be applied to a wide variety of types (both built-in and user-defined), the type of argument can theoretically be pointer-to-int or pointer-to-float or even pointer-to-my-class-type. To accommodate all of these various types, the class ostream contains an operator insertion function whose one explicit argument is type void*. Since any pointer type can be converted to a void* under rule #3 of the argument matching rules (as specified in Chapter 9), a match with a void* is guaranteed.

In Borland C++, this address is always shown in 16-bit (2 byte) or 32-bit (4 byte) hexadecimal form.

     Example 15.26

```
#include <iostream.h>

int main()
{
   int x = 0;
   cout << "&x = " << &x << '\n';
   return 0;
}

/* The output of this program is:

&x = 0xfff4

*/
```

Of course, the actual address on your computer will probably be different.

Because the insertion operator to display an address takes a void* instead of a const void*, virtually all C++ compilers have a bug in the sense that they cannot print the address of a constant object because the compiler will not implicitly cast away the const part of an object. Therefore, you need to cast away the const part of the address of each const-qualified object, or write an overloaded insertion operator that does this for you. This operator is shown in the following example.

Example 15.27

```
#include <iostream.h>

ostream& operator<<(ostream& str, const void* ptr)
{
   return str << const_cast<void*>(ptr);
}

int main()
{
   const int x = 0;
   cout << "&x = " << &x << '\n';
   return 0;
}

/* The output of this program is:

&x = 0xfff4

*/
```

15.5.1   Taking the Address of a String

Note that in the case of a string literal, which is type char[], or a pointer-to-a-character, which is type char*, the class ostream contains an operator insertion function accepting type const char* that matches the actual argument type. This is fine if your intent is to print the literal to which the pointer is pointing. However, if you wish to print the content of the pointer variable itself, (i.e., the address of the first character being pointed at), then you must cast this address into a void* type. Of course, don't forget to get rid of the const-qualification, if it's present.

Example 15.28

```
#include <iostream.h>

int main()
{
    const char* ptr = "C++";
    cout << ptr << '\n';
    char* temp_ptr = const_cast<char*>(ptr);
    cout << static_cast<void*>(temp_ptr) << '\n';
    return 0;
}

/* The output of this program is:

C++
0x00a8

*/
```

15.6   Unformatted Output

You may take any internal representation of a C++ type and output it as though it were just an array of characters. That is, whatever the bit representation of the type is in memory, that pattern will be written to the output device with no formatting performed. In C, this is accomplished with the function fwrite(). In C++, the name of the function is ostream::write(). This function takes two arguments: (1) The address of the data to be output, and (2) the number of bytes to be written. Note that in the case of a string, the null byte is treated just like any other byte.

Because the function ostream::write() is declared to accept an argument of type const char*, if the item you wish to print is not of this type, then its address must be cast.

For example, the following program writes the first three bytes of a string literal to the screen, followed by the 4-byte long. Note the reinterpret_cast keyword that is needed in ordert to perform a cast from type long* into type char*.

Example 15.29

```cpp
#include <iostream.h>

int main()
{
   char buffer[] = "C++";
   cout.write(buffer, 3);
   cout << '\n';
   long value = 0x41424344L;
   cout.write(reinterpret_cast<char*>(&value), 4);
   cout << '\n';
   return 0;
}

/* The output of this program is:

C++
DCBA

*/
```

Tip

The output of this program may vary with different compilers depending upon how data is stored internally.

15.7   How to Output to a Memory Buffer

In C, you can send output to a memory buffer of type char* instead of to the screen by using the function sprintf(), where the first argument specifies the address of the buffer area where the data is to be stored. Here is an example.

 Example 15.30

```
#include <stdio.h>

int main(void)
{
   char buffer[80];
   int x = 65;
   sprintf(buffer, "x = %d", x);
   printf("buffer = \"%s\"\n", buffer);
   return 0;
}

/* The output of this program is:

buffer = "x = 65"

*/
```

In order to accomplish the same result in C++, you must first include the header file `strstream.h`. This file contains the definition of the class `ostrstream`, which you then use to perform instantiation. At the time of creation, you must provide two arguments: (1) the address of the buffer where the data is to be written, and (2) the maximum size of this buffer (which normally is the `sizeof` the buffer).

After this has been done, the instance `output` is used where you would normally use `cout`. All of the data is thus sent to the `buffer` area. If you subsequently want to send this `buffer` area to the screen, don't forget to append a null byte to make the `buffer` a legitimate string object. If you subsequently wish to place more output into this buffer area starting back at character position 0, you must use the (inherited) member function `ostream::seekp()` with an argument of 0. Finally, the method `strstreambuf::str()` returns a pointer to the underlying buffer area.

 Example 15.31

```
#include <iostream.h>
#include <strstream.h>

int main()
{
   const char quote = '"';
   char buffer[80];
   ostrstream output(buffer, sizeof buffer);
   int number = 65;
   output << "number = " << number << '\0';
   cout << quote << output.str() << quote << '\n';
   output.seekp(0L);
   output << "A new buffer stream " << "of characters" << '\0';
   cout << quote << output.str() << quote << '\n';
   return 0;
}

/* The output of this program is:

"number = 65"
"A new buffer stream of characters"

*/
```

 Tip

You may also instantiate an `ostrstream` *object and let the compiler provide you with a dynamically allocated buffer area on the heap. This technique, however, entails the use of the* `strstreambuf::freeze()` *function, and will not be covered in this book.*

15.8   The Method `ostream::flush()`

If, at any time, you want to explicitly flush the output buffer, you may do so by calling the member function `ostream::flush()`. For screen output, this is not necessary since all output is flushed automatically. However, in the case where one disk file is being copied to another, you may have to flush the output buffer prior to rewinding the output file for continued use.

 Example 15.32

```
#include <iostream.h>

int main()
{
    cout << "Good-bye world\n";
    cout.flush();
    return 0;
}

/* The output of this program is:

Good-bye world

*/
```

Tip

The function `ostream::flush()` *does not have anything to do with flushing the input buffer.*

15.9   Mixing `stdio` and `iostream` Output

As a general rule, you should not mix `stdio` functions and `iostream` output methods. The reason is that they flush their buffers at different times, so that the order of the output cannot be guaranteed. However, if you are determined to do so, then you must first call the static function `ios::sync_with_stdio()` which will coordinate the two output systems.

Exercise 15.1

Write four global functions that are designed to print an integer in these four ways:

- Decimal within a field width of 10 with leading blanks;

- Hexadecimal within a field width of 10 with leading asterisks and with the base and uppercase of the number shown;

- Octal within a field width of 10 with leading carets and with the base of the number shown;

- Character within single quotes. However, if the number represents a non-printable character (as determined by the `ctype.h` library function `isprint()`), then output the word `NON-PRINTABLE` instead of the character itself.

Then write a `main()` function that calls upon each class function using the internally generated numbers 0 through 50.

For example, the output for the numbers 31 and 32 would be:

```
DEC - 31
HEX - ******0X1F
OCT - ^^^^^^^037
CHR - Non-printable

DEC - 32
HEX - ******0X20
OCT - ^^^^^^^040
CHR - '^'

(where ^ represents a blank)
```

Exercise 15.2

Given the following class definition:

```
class Mult_table
{
      public:
  Mult_table(int);
  void display() const
  {
     title();
     body();
  }
      private:
  int base;
  void title() const;
  void body() const;
};
```

and the `main()` function:

```
int main()
{
  const int start = 2;
  const int end = 10;
  for(int base = start; base <= end; ++base)
  {
     Mult_table table(base);
     table.display();
  }
  return 0;
}
```

write the member functions `title()` and `body()` that display the title and body, respectively, of a multiplication table of size `base`. All entries must align on the units position. Have the `main()` function use an instance of the class to generate tables for all bases in the range 2 through 10, inclusive.

For example, the multiplication table for the base 5 should appear as:

```
    Multiplication Table For Base 5

        0    1    2    3    4

0       0    0    0    0    0
1       0    1    2    3    4
2       0    2    4   11   13
3       0    3   11   14   22
4       0    4   13   22   31
```

Chapter 16

Iostream Input

16.1 Introduction

In addition to being able to use classes to control output, C++ stream I/O classes also handle all input. Just as output consists of a stream of characters being sent to some device, input consists of characters coming in from some device and being translated into their proper defined type. Unlike output, the realm of possibilities for "formatting" simply does not exist when inputting data.

16.2 How to Check for Errors

Unfortunately, we live in an imperfect world. People don't smile, cars crash, checks bounce, and data entry operators sometimes make mistakes. This means that as a programmer, you are responsible for making sure your code is as robust as possible. In other words, no matter what the user may enter as "data", your program must capture it and successfully trap all error conditions to avoid such catastrophes as "garbage in, garbage out", aborts, hangs, endless loops, etc.

16.2.1 Input Status Bits

The condition of any input object, including `cin`, is represented by a collection of public enumerated values inherited from the class `ios`.

Table 16-1   Input Status Bits

Name	Value	Meaning
ios::goodbit	0x0000	Good condition, all bits off
ios::eofbit	0x0001	End-of-file detected
ios::failbit	0x0002	Last input operation failed
ios::badbit	0x0004	Invalid operation attempted
ios::hardfail	0x0080	Unrecoverable error

Each value is a single bit, and the state of an input object is represented as a collection of these values in a protected integer within class istream. This integer may be accessed by using the method ios::rdstate().

16.2.2   Accessor Methods

The easiest way to test the status of an input object such as cin is to use any of the following four accessor methods.

Table 16-2   Accessor Methods

Function	Returns true if:
ios::good()	All bits are off
ios::eof()	ios::eofbit is on
ios::fail()	ios::failbit or ios::badbit or ios::hardfail is on
ios::bad()	ios::badbit or ios::hardfail is on

Since these methods have been inherited into the istream class, you can call them using the cin object.

 Tip

> *These methods do* **not** *return type* bool, *but rather type* int *that will implicity be converted into type* bool *when used as a Boolean expression.*

16.2.3   Testing the Input Object Directly

Another way to check for an input error is to use the overloaded function operator!() (Boolean 'not') on the instance cin. This operator will return an int value of Boolean true if an error occurred, and return false otherwise. Similarly, testing the instance cin itself as a Boolean value will return true if the input was good, and return false otherwise.

The following program is designed to test the cin instance in every possible way. Note that ios::good() and cin always return the same value, as do ios::fail() and !cin.

Example 16.1

```
#include <iostream.h>

void examine(ostream& str = cout)
{
   str << "eof = " << static_cast<bool>(cin.eof()) << '\n';
   str << "good = " << static_cast<bool>(cin.good()) << '\n';
   str << "fail = " << static_cast<bool>(cin.fail()) << '\n';
   str << "bad = " << static_cast<bool>(cin.bad()) << '\n';
   str << "cin = " << static_cast<bool>(cin) << '\n';
   str << "!cin = " << static_cast<bool>(!cin) << '\n';
}

int main()
{
   cout.setf(ios::boolalpha);
   cout << "Enter a number: ";
   int number;
   while(!(cin >> number).eof())
   {
      examine();
      cout << "\nNext number: ";
   }
   examine();
   return 0;
}

/* A typical run of the program would yield:

Enter a number: 123
eof = false
good = true
fail = false
bad = false
cin = true
!cin = false
```

(Continued)

```
Next number: Junk eof = false
good = false
fail = true
bad = false
cin = false
!cin = true
(endless loop follows)

Next number: ^Z
eof = true
good = false
fail = true
bad = false
cin = false
!cin = true

*/
```

16.2.4   The Method `ios::clear()`

Once the `cin` object detects a bit pattern that is not valid (e.g., a non-numeric entry when a numeric is expected), it turns on the fail bit and refuses to extract any more characters from the input stream. Therefore, the first step in recovering from this error condition is to turn off the fail bit (and possibly any other error bits).

To do this, use the method `ios::clear()`. If you call it with no argument, then all of the error bits will be turned off. If you call it with an argument, then the value will be interpreted as the entire bit pattern for the four status flag bits. What this means is that if you wish to turn on just one bit, then you should do a bitwise OR with the remaining bits.

For example, this function turns on the fail bit and ensures that the remaining bits stay the same.

Example 16.2

```
// File fail.h

#ifndef FAIL_H
#define FAIL_H

#include <iostream.h>

inline istream& Fail(istream& str)
{
   str.clear(rdstate() | ios::failbit);
   return str;
}

#endif
```

 Tip

The Fail() *function was coded so that it can be used as a manipulator. This concept will be discussed in Chapter 17.*

16.2.5   How to Flush the Input Stream Buffer

The next problem is how to eliminate any and all "garbage" characters from the input stream. This is analogous to calling the function fflush(stdin) (assuming that fflush() is defined and valid). The following function called Flush() shows how this can be done.

 Example 16.3

```
// File flush.h

#ifndef FLUSH_H
#define FLUSH_H

#include <iostream.h>

inline istream& Flush(istream& stream)
{
   stream.clear();
   int chars_to_skip = stream.rdbuf()->in_avail();
   return stream.ignore(chars_to_skip);
}

#endif
```

The first task it performs is to use `ios::clear()` to allow characters to be extracted from the input stream. Then the method `ios::rdbuf()` is used to return a pointer to the `streambuf` object, which proceeds to call the method `streambuf::in_avail()` that returns the number of characters in the input stream buffer. Finally the method `ios::ignore()` is used to ignore (jump over) this number of characters.

 Tip

> *Like the* `Fail()` *function, the* `Flush()` *function was also coded so that it can be used as a manipulator.*

Thus, a "crash-proof" program that loops while reading numbers and checking for end-of-file and garbage input might resemble this:

 Example 16.4

```
#include <iostream.h>
#include "flush.h"

int main()
{
   cout << "Enter a number: ";
   int number;
   while(!(cin >> number).eof())
   {
      if(!cin)// Test for a bad number
         cout << "Input error!\n";
      else// Process a good number
         cout << "You entered: " << number << '\n';
      Flush(cin);// Clear out the input buffer
      cout << "Next number: ";
   }
   cout << "End-of-file\n";
   return 0;
}

/* A typical run of the program would yield:

Enter a number: 12
You entered: 12
Next number: a
Input error!
Next number: 5 6
You entered: 5
Next number: ^Z
End-of-file

*/
```

One note about the logic of this program. If two *valid* numbers are entered before the operator presses <ENTER>, then only the first number will be processed; the second will be flushed. You may or may not want this to happen, depending upon your design philosophy.

16.3   How to Input into Type `bool`

If you input into a variable of type `bool`, be aware that the only way to create a value of `true` is to enter the value 1, and the only way to create a value of `false` is to enter the value 0. Anything else is considered to be an input error.

 Example 16.5

```
#include <iostream.h>
#include "flush.h"

int main()
{
   cout.setf(ios::boolalpha);
   cout << "Enter a bool value: ";
   bool b;
   while(!(cin >> b).eof())
   {
      if(cin)
         cout << b << endl;
      else
         cout << "Input error\n";
      Flush(cin);
      cout << "Next bool value: ";
   }
   cout << "End-of-file\n";
   return 0;
}

/* A typical run of this program would yield:

Enter a bool value: 1
true
Next bool value: 0
false
Next bool value: 5
Input error
Next bool value: junk
Input error
Next bool value: ^Z
End-of-file

*/
```

Tip

The flag `ios::boolalpha` *may also be set for the* `cin` *object so that the terminal operator is forced to enter the string literals "true" or "false".*

16.4   Integer Input

Recall from the discussion on output in Chapter 15 that the base setting for integer output is, by default, decimal. This setting can, of course, be changed by using the `ios::setf()` function.

In a similar manner, the default base setting for integer input is decimal. This means that for any integral variable, only valid integer data is acceptable, and any attempt to violate this rule will cause an error condition to occur. For example, entering `ABC12` for an integer value will cause an error. However, entering `12ABC` will cause the number `12` to be stored into the integer, and the letters `ABC` to remain in the input stream buffer, so that this is not necessarily an error condition; it depends on what you do next.

Even though the default input base setting is decimal, it is still possible to override this default if you wish to input either an octal or hexadecimal number. This can be done by explicitly entering the base of these numbers (i.e., 0 for octal and 0x (or 0X) for hex). This is analogous in C to writing a `scanf()` with a conversion specification of `"%i"`.

Example 16.6

```
#include <iostream.h>
#include "flush.h"

int main()
{
   cout << "Enter a number: ";
   int number;
   while(!(cin >> number).eof())
   {
      if(cin)
         cout << "You entered: " << number << '\n';
      else
         cout << "Input error\n";
      Flush(cin);
      cout << "Next number: ";
   }
   cout << "End-of-file\n";
   return 0;
}

/* A typical run of the program would yield:

Enter a number: 20
You entered: 20
Next number: 024
You entered: 20
Next number: 0x14
You entered: 20
Next number: ^Z
End-of-file

*/
```

16.4.1   Forcing Decimal Input

However, note what happens when the input base setting is *explicitly* set to decimal via a function call to `ios::setf()`. In this case only *decimal input* is allowed. This is analogous in C to writing `scanf()` with a conversion specification of `"%d"`. Here is Example 16.6 again with the base setting explicitly specified.

 Example 16.7

```
#include <iostream.h>
#include "flush.h"

int main()
{
   cin.setf(ios::dec, ios::basefield);
   cout << "Enter a number: ";
   int number;
   while(!(cin >> number).eof())
   {
      if(cin)
         cout << "You entered: " << number << '\n';
      else
         cout << "Input error\n";
      Flush(cin);
      cout << "Next number: ";
   }
   cout << "End-of-file\n";
   return 0;
}

/* A typical run of the program would yield:

Enter a number: 20
You entered: 20
Next number: 024
You entered: 24
Next number: 0x14
You entered: 0
Next number: ^Z
End-of-file

*/
```

16.4.2   Forcing Octal and Hex Input

In a similar manner, you can hard code the program to accept octal or hexadecimal input values by turning on the `ios::oct` or `ios::hex` bit, respectively. In this situation the terminal operator no longer needs to explicitly enter the base setting for the number (0 for octal and 0x for hexadecimal). Essentially, this is how the `"%o"` and `"%x"` conversion specifications in a `scanf()` function call can be emulated.

 Example 16.8

```
#include <iostream.h>
#include "flush.h"

int main()
{
    cin.setf(ios::oct, ios::basefield);  // octal input
    cout << "Enter an octal number: ";
    int number;
    while(!(cin >> number).eof())
    {
        if(cin)
            cout << "You entered: " << number << '\n';
        else
            cout << "Input error\n";
        cout << "Next octal number: ";
        Flush(cin);
    }
    cout << "End-of-file\n";
    return 0;
}

/* A typical run of the program would yield:

Enter an octal number: 20
You entered: 16
Next octal number: 99
Input error
Next octal number: ^Z
End-of-file

*/
```

16.5   Character Input

Certainly you can use the extraction operator to get character input from the keyboard. Another way is provided by the member function `istream::get()`. It takes a single argument, the character itself, and returns a reference to the invoking instance so that the function calls can be chained together. The difference between `istream::operator>>()` and `istream::get()` is that the latter will honor any and all whitespace characters.

 Example 16.9

```
#include <iostream.h>
#include "flush.h"

int main()
{
   const char quote = '\'';
   cout << "Enter 2 characters: ";
   char ch1, ch2;
   while(!cin.get(ch1).get(ch2).eof())
   {
      cout << "You entered: " << quote << ch1 << quote
         << " and " << quote << ch2 << quote << '\n';
      Flush(cin);
      cout << "Next 2 characters: ";
   }
   cout << "End-of-file\n";
   return 0;
}

/* A typical run of the program would yield:

Enter 2 characters: A B
You entered: 'A' and ' '
Next 2 characters:  C D
You entered: ' ' and 'C'
Next 2 characters: ^Z
End-of-file

*/
```

 Caution

After entering the first two characters, note that 'B' and a newline character remain in the system buffer, so that the buffer must be flushed in order to have the next iteration of the loop stop and wait for more operator input.

The `istream::get()` function has also been overloaded so that it can take no input argument (just like `getchar()` in C). In this form it returns a value of type `int`, which represents the character just read, or the `EOF` constant if either (1) end-of-file was detected, or (2) no character could be read. Because the return type is `int`, no chaining of this form of `istream::get()` is possible.

In the following example, `istream::get()` is used to read in a character, after which a check for end-of-file is made. Because the variable `ch` must be defined as type `int`, don't forget the cast in order to display it as a character.

 Example 16.10

```
#include <iostream.h>
#include "flush.h"

int main()
{
   const char quote = '\'';
   cout << "Enter a character: ";
   int ch;
   while((ch = cin.get()) != EOF)
   {
      cout << "You entered: " << quote
         << static_cast<char>(ch) << quote << '\n';
      Flush(cin);
      cout << "Next character: ";
   }
   cout << "End-of-file\n";
   return 0;
}

/* A typical run of the program would yield:

Enter a character: A
You entered: 'A'
Next character: ^Z
End-of-file

*/
```

 Caution

Once again notice how the newline character remains in the system buffer, and must therefore be flushed.

16.6   String Input Using the Extraction Operator

Strings may also be entered using the extraction operator. Don't forget that leading whitespace is bypassed, and the first whitespace encountered terminates the input. This acts just like the function `scanf()` with the conversion specification `"%s"`.

 Example 16.11

```
#include <iostream.h>
#include "flush.h"

int main()
{
   const char quote = '"';
   cout << "Enter a string: ";
   const int max = 128;
   char string[max];
   while(!(cin >> string).eof())
   {
      cout << "Your string: " << quote << string
         << quote << '\n';
      Flush(cin);
      cout << "Next string: ";
   }
   cout << "End-of-file\n";
   return 0;
}

/* A typical run of the program would yield:

Enter a string:    Hello world
Your string: "Hello"
Next string: C++
Your string: "C++"
Next string: ^Z
End-of-file

*/
```

16.6.1   Limiting the Number of Input Characters

Just as with `scanf()`, you could have a program hang or crash if the operator enters more characters than can safely be accommodated by a string array. To guard against this disaster, you may set the width of the input stream to physically limit the number of characters that can be stored. This is done by using the member function `ios::width()` in conjunction with the `cin` instance. The result is that only the number of characters (less 1) specified by the argument to `ios::width()` will be extracted from the input stream; the remaining characters are left alone. Of course, the first whitespace character encountered will still terminate the input. And don't forget—just like the `ios::width()` function used for output, the input `ios::width()` function only applies to the next item to be input.

For example, in the following program, the terminal operator can input any number of characters, but only the first nine will be stored into the buffer area.

 Example 16.12

```cpp
#include <iostream.h>
#include "flush.h"

int main()
{
   const char quote = '"';
   const int max = 10;
   cout << "Enter a string no longer than " << max - 1
        << " characters\n";
   cin.width(max);
   char string[max];
   while(!(cin >> string).eof())
   {
      cout << "Your string: " << quote << string
         << quote << '\n';
      Flush(cin);
      cout << "Next string: ";
   }
   cout << "End-of-file\n";
   return 0;
}

/*

A typical run of the program would yield:

Enter a string no longer than 9 characters
ThisIsALongString
Your string: "ThisIsALo"
Next string: ^Z
End-of-file

*/
```

16.7   String Input Using `istream::getline()`

Another way to read in strings is to use the member function `istream::getline()`. In this form it takes three arguments.

- The first argument is the address of the string area;

- The second argument is the maximum number of characters (less 1) that will be stored into your buffer area;

- The third argument specifies the terminating character (the one that will stop the transfer of characters from the system buffer into your string array). This third argument defaults to the value '\n', which is the <ENTER> key. Note, however, that if it is changed to some other character, then the <ENTER> key must still be pressed for the input action to cease.

Note the similarity to the C function `fgets()`. The advantage to using `istream::getline()` as opposed to `istream::operator>>()` is that now both leading whitespace and embedded whitespace are retained as part of the string value.

Example 16.13

```
#include <iostream.h>
#include "flush.h"

int main()
{
   const char quote = '"';
   const int max = 10;
   cout << "Enter a string less than " << max
        << " characters: ";
   char string[max];
   while(!cin.getline(string, max).eof())
   {
      cout << "Your string: " << quote << string
         << quote << '\n';
      Flush(cin);
      cout << "Next string: ";
   }
   return 0;
   cout << "End-of-file\n";
}

/* A typical run of the program would yield:

Enter a string less than 10 characters: ___Hello world
Your string: "  Hello "
Next string: ^Z
End-of-file

*/
```

16.7.1   String Input Using `istream::get()`

A slight variation on using the method `istream::getline()` to read a string is
the method `istream::get()`. The only difference is that `istream::getline()`
extracts the newline character ('\n') from the system input buffer and discards it,
whereas `istream::get()` leaves it alone (and, presumably, it must then be
flushed by you before you attempt to read another string). You're probably much
better off sticking with `istream::getline()`.

16.8   The Member Function `istream::gcount()`

It's also possible to find out exactly how many characters were extracted from the system input buffer after an `istream::get()` or `istream::getline()` operation. The member function `istream::gcount()` returns this value.

Here is the previous example with a call to `istream::gcount()`.

 Example 16.14

```
#include <iostream.h>
#include "flush.h"

int main()
{
   const char quote = '"';
   const int max = 10;
   cout << "Enter a string less than " << max
        << " characters";
   char string[max];
   while(!cin.getline(string, max).eof())
   {
      cout << "Your string: " << quote << string
         << quote << '\n';
      cout << "You extracted " << cin.gcount()
         << " characters\n";
      Flush(cin);
      cout << "Next string: ";
   }
   cout << "End of file\n";
   return 0;
}

/* A typical run of the program would yield:

Enter a string less than 10 characters: Hello world
Your string: "Hello wor"
You extracted 9 characters
Next string: ^Z
End of file

*/
```

16.9   Unformatted Input

In Chapter 15 you learned how to write data using the function `ostream::write()` so that its internal representation was preserved on the output device. In a similar fashion, the function `istream::read()` can be used to read in this data from an input device exclusive of any formatting.

In the following program, the keyboard will be used to read in characters. Of course, in most other cases you would want to read from a disk file.

    Example 16.15

```
#include <iostream.h>

int main()
{
   const char quote = '"';
   const int size = 3;
   char buffer[size + 1];
   cout << "Enter " << size << " characters: ";
   cin.read(buffer, size);
   buffer[size] = '\0';
   cout << "buffer: " << quote << buffer << quote << '\n';
   return 0;
}

/* A typical run of the program would yield:

Enter 3 characters: ABC
buffer: "ABC"

*/
```

16.10   How to Input from a Memory Buffer

In C, you can read input from a memory buffer of type `char*` instead of from the
keyboard by using the function `sscanf()`, where the first argument specifies the
address of the buffer area from which the data is to be read.

    Example 16.16

```
#include <stdio.h>

int main(void)
{
    const char quote = '"';
    char buffer[] = "ABC 1.234 5";
    char string[100];
    float f;
    int n;
    sscanf(buffer, "%s%f%d", string, &f, &n);
    printf("string = %c%s%c\n", quote, string, quote);
    printf("float = %f\n", f);
    printf("int = %d\n", n);
    return 0;
}

/* The output of this program is:

string = "ABC"
float = 1.234000
int = 5

*/
```

In order to accomplish the same result using iostream methods, you must first
include the header file `strstream.h` (Note: DOS only honors the first eight characters of the file name.) This file contains the definition of the class `istrstream`,
which you then use to create some instance. At the time of creation, you must provide two arguments: (1) the address of the buffer from which the data is to be read,
and (2) the maximum size of this buffer (which normally is the `sizeof` the buffer).

    Example 16.17

```
char buffer[80];
istrstream input(buffer, sizeof buffer);
```

After this has been done, the instance `input` is used where you would normally use `cin`. All of the data is thus read from the `buffer` area. If you subsequently wish to read this buffer area starting back at character position 0, you must use the member function `ios::seekg()` with an argument of 0.

 Example 16.18

```cpp
#include <iostream.h>
#include <strstream.h>

int main()
{
   const char quote = '"';
   char buffer[] = "ABC 1.234 5";
   char string[100];
   float f;
   int n;

   istrstream input(buffer, sizeof buffer);

   input >> string >> f >> n;
   cout << "string = " << quote << string << quote << '\n';
   cout << "float = " << f << '\n';
   cout << "int = " << n << '\n';

   // Let's do it again
   input.seekg(0);    // return to position 0
   input >> string >> f >> n;
   cout << "string = " << quote << string << quote << '\n';
   cout << "float = " << f << '\n';
   cout << "int = " << n << '\n';

   return 0;
}

/* The output of this program is:

string = "ABC"
float = 1.234000
int = 5
string = "ABC"
float = 1.234000
int = 5

*/
```

16.10.1   Combining Input and Output

If you wish to do both input and output using a memory buffer, one way is to create an instance of the class `strstream`, but with no arguments. When the instance `both` is used, data is stored in an internal buffer area. The extraction operator may then be used with the instance to read from this buffer area. In addition, the function `ios::rdbuf()` returns the address of the buffer area.

  Example 16.19

```cpp
#include <iostream.h>
#include <strstream.h>

int main()
{
   const char quote = '"';
   strstream both;

   // Put data into the internal buffer
   both << "ABC" << " " << 1.234 << " " << 5 << '\0';

   // The data so far:
   cout << both.rdbuf() << '\n';

   // Don't forget this
   both.seekg(0);

   // Extract data from 'buffer'
   char string[100];
   float f;
   int n;
   both >> string >> f >> n;

   // Verify the data
   cout << "string = " << quote << string << quote << '\n';
   cout << "float = " << f << '\n';
   cout << "int = " << n << '\n';

   return 0;
}

/* The output of this program is:

ABC 1.234 5
string = "ABC"
float = 1.234
int = 5

*/
```

16.10.2   Creating Your Own Buffer Area

If you wish to create your own buffer area, then you may do so provided that you open the internal file in both input and output modes (see Chapter 18 on file I/O for more information on file modes).

 Example 16.20

```
#include <iostream.h>
#include <strstream.h>

int main()
{
   const char quote = '"';
   char buffer[100];
   strstream both(buffer, sizeof buffer, ios::in | ios::out);

   // Put data into 'buffer'
   both << "ABC" << " " << 1.234 << " " << 5 << '\0';

   // The data so far:
   cout << buffer << "\n";

   // Don't forget this
   both.seekg(0);

   // Extract data from 'buffer'
   char string[100];
   float f;
   int n;
   both >> string >> f >> n;

   // Verify the data
   cout << "string = " << quote << string << quote << '\n';
   cout << "float = " << f << '\n';
   cout << "int = " << n << '\n';

   return 0;
}

/* The output of this program is:

ABC 1.234 5
string = "ABC"
float = 1.234
int = 5

*/
```

16.11   The Method `ios::tie()`

Chapter 15 talked about the function `flush()` which causes everything in the output buffer to be sent to the output device. In point of fact, you probably will never need to use this function, for several reasons. First, recall that the bit `ios::unitbuf` in the class `ios` is on by default. This causes all output streams to be flushed automatically whenever there is data in them. Second, the stream `ostream` is "tied" to the stream `istream` by the function call:

Example 16.21

```
cin.tie(&cout);
```

This statement has already been executed for you, and means that whenever the operator needs to enter some data from the keyboard, any prompting information in the output stream is guaranteed to appear on the terminal screen. To "untie" these streams, you may call the `tie()` function with a value of zero.

Therefore, if you really want to avoid flushing the output stream, you must (1) turn off the bit `ios::unitbuf`, and (2) untie the streams.

In this example, the prompt does *not* appear before the operator must enter a number.

Example 16.22

```cpp
#include <iostream.h>

int main()
{
    cout.unsetf(ios::unitbuf);
    cin.tie(0);
    cout << "Enter a number: ";
    int number;
    cin >> number;
    cout << "You entered: " << number << '\n';
    return 0;
}

/* A typical run of the program would yield:

12
Enter a number: You entered: 12

*/
```

Note that the prompt did not appear until after the number was entered. Now let's add the `ostream::flush()` function so that the prompt again appears.

 Example 16.23

```
#include <iostream.h>

int main()
{
   cout.unsetf(ios::unitbuf);
   cin.tie(0);

   cout << "Enter a number: ";
   cout.flush();
   int number;
   cin >> number;
   cout << "You entered: " << number << '\n';
   return 0;
}

/* A typical run of the program would yield:

Enter a number: 12
You entered: 12

*/
```

Exercise 16.1

Modify Exercise #1 in Chapter 15 so that the number that is displayed is obtained from the terminal operator (as an `int`) instead of being hard coded. Be sure to check for:

■ End-of-file (which terminates the program);

■ Valid numeric input;

■ A number in the range 0 through 255, inclusive.

 Exercise 16.2

Write a class called `Format` that contains member functions to prompt the user for:

■ A floating point number;

■ The number of positions after the decimal point;

■ The width of the field;

■ Left or right justification;

■ The fill character;

■ Fixed or scientific output.

Check all responses for numerics (if appropriate) and valid data. Then call another member function that will output the number between angle brackets (<>) according to all of the specifications. In the main program, use a `while` loop so that many tests can be run. Terminate the program when end-of-file is encountered.

Exercise 16.3

Write a class called `Loan` that first computes the monthly payment due on a fully amortized loan, and then optionally prints the corresponding complete amortization table. The class definition follows:

```
// File loan.h

#ifndef LOAN_H
#define LOAN_H

#include <iostream.h>
class Loan
{
    friend ostream& operator<<(ostream&, const Loan&);
        public:
    Loan(double principal, double rate, int length);
    void compute_payment(ostream& = cout);
    bool want_schedule() const;
        private:
    double principal;
    double rate;
    double payment;
    int length;
};

#endif
```

The monthly payment is computed as a function of the beginning principal balance, the yearly interest rate, and the length of the loan expressed in years, and is expressed by the following formula:

$$M = (P * I * (1 + I)^L) / ((1 + I)^L - 1)$$

where P is the principal, I is the *monthly* interest rate (yearly rate / 12), L is the length of the loan in *months* (years * 12), and M is the *monthly* payment due. Note: that's (1 + I) raised to the Lth power.

The method `Loan::compute_payment()` computes the monthly payment and displays it to the user.

The method `Loan::want_schedule()` asks the user if she wants to see the entire loan amortization table. If the answer is yes, then display the table using an overloaded insertion operator. This function must print all three input values (with the yearly interest rate shown to three decimal positions followed by a percent sign) plus your monthly payment as a heading for the full amortization table.

Next, print column headings and data as follows:

1. *The payment number*, which starts at 1 and increments by 1 for each line (month) of data shown;

2. *The principal remaining*, which, for the first line, is the original principal balance for the loan, and for all subsequent months is the new principal balance (item 5) obtained from the previous month;

3. *The interest paid*, which is the principal remaining multiplied by the monthly interest rate;

4. *The principal paid*, which is the monthly payment less the monthly interest paid;

5. *The new principal balance*, which is the principal remaining less the principal paid. This figure then becomes the principal remaining for the next month.

All money figures should be printed with two decimal positions. Print the interest rate to three decimal positions.

After every 12 months' worth of data, print "YEAR #nn TOTALS", where 'nn' is the year number, followed by the total interest paid for that one year under the "interest paid" column, and the total principal paid for that one year under the "principal paid" column.

At the end of the table, print the grand total interest paid for the loan under the "interest paid" column, and the grand total principal paid for the loan under the "principal paid" column.

Then print the error amount for the loan schedule by multiplying the monthly payment by the number of months in the loan and subtracting the original principal plus the total interest amount paid. The final principal remaining for the loan should be $0.00 or within a few cents thereof.

Use the following `main()` function to test your class:

```
// File main.cpp

#include <iostream.h>
#include "loan.h"

int main()
{
   cout << "Enter the principal, yearly interest rate "
        "e.g., .08), and length in years\n";
   double principal, rate;
   int length;
   while(!(cin >> principal >> rate >> length).eof())
   {
      if(!cin || principal < 0 || rate < 0 || length < 0)
         cout << "Input error\n";
      else
      {
         Loan L(principal, rate, length);
         L.compute_payment();
         if(L.want_schedule())
            cout << L << '\n';
      }
      Flush(cin);
      cout << "Next loan: \n";
   }
   return 0;
}
```

Make your output look professional, i.e., something you would be proud to show to either your lender or the bankruptcy judge.

Chapter 17

Manipulators

17.1   Introduction

Manipulators provide you with the capability to facilitate and encapsulate the formatting that you must do with the input and output streams. Up to now all such formatting has been painstakingly tedious and very error-prone. That is about to change with the use of manipulators. The term itself comes from the fact that a manipulator does just what the name implies—it manipulates, or changes, the state of the I/O stream object.

17.2   The Format of a Manipulator

Because of the way in which a manipulator is called, it must conform to a certain pattern. This pattern dictates that the function must take as an argument an instance of class ostream by reference (assuming an output manipulator), and return an instance of class ostream by reference. To allow the chaining of manipulators with other calls to the insertion operator, the function must terminate by returning its one input argument. Note that manipulators are written as *global* functions, not class methods.

Thus, the complete definition for writing an output manipulator is:

 Example 17.1

```
ostream& name(ostream& str)
{
   // Your code here using the 'str' object
   return str;
}
```

In a similar fashion, all input manipulators have the format:

 Example 17.2

```
istream& name(istream& str)
{
   // Your code here using the 'str' object
   return str;
}
```

Manipulators are "called" by an operator insertion (or extraction) function that receives the *address* of the manipulator as an argument. This implies that when you wish to invoke the manipulator, you do so by writing its name *without* the following parentheses. (This is explained in more detail later in this chapter.)

17.3   Some Simple Manipulators

As an example, here is a program that creates a manipulator called `set()` that sets the field width to 5 and the fill character to an '*'.

 Example 17.3

```
#include <iostream.h>

ostream& set(ostream& str)
{
    str.width(5);
    str.fill('*');
    return str;
}

int main()
{
    cout << set << 23 << '\n';
    return 0;
}

/* The output of this program is:

***23

*/
```

 Tip

There is nothing to prevent you from calling a manipulator just like a "normal" function. In this case you must pass the stream object as the one explicit argument. The disadvantage is that it precludes you from chaining insertion calls together.

As an example of an input manipulator, in Chapter 16 the function `Flush()` was defined to clear the system input buffer of extraneous characters. Because the function takes an `istream` object by reference, and returns an `istream` object by reference, it can be used as a manipulator.

Example 17.4

```cpp
#include <iostream.h>
#include "flush.h"

int main()
{
   cout << "Enter a number: ";
   int number;
   while(!(cin >> number).eof())
   {
      if(!cin)// Test for a bad number
         cout << "Input error!\n";
      else// Process a good number
         cout << "You entered: " << number << '\n';
      cin >> Flush;// Clear out the input buffer
      cout << "\nNext number: ";
   }
   cout << "End-of-file\n";
   return 0;
}

/* A typical run of the program would yield:

Enter a number: 12
You entered: 12
Next number: a
Input error!
Next number: 34^Z
You entered: 34
Next number: 5 6
You entered: 5
Next number: ^Z
End-of-file

*/
```

The ability to create custom manipulators allows you to eliminate the need to write the `ios::setf()` method every time the state of the output stream must be changed. For example, if you wish to turn on left or right justification, it's easy to create manipulators for these tasks.

Example 17.5

```
// File left.h

#ifndef LEFT_H
#define LEFT_H

inline ostream& Left(ostream& str)
{
   str.setf(ios::left, ios::adjustfield);
   return str;
}

#endif

// File right.h

#ifndef RIGHT_H
#define RIGHT_H

inline ostream& Right(ostream& str)
{
   str.setf(ios::right, ios::adjustfield);
   return str;
}

#endif
```

Another use of a manipulator would be to ensure that all money amounts appear right-justified, 10-position field, fixed-decimal, with 2 decimal positions.

Example 17.6

```
// File money.h

#ifndef MONEY_H
#define MONEY_H

inline ostream& Money(ostream& str)
{
   str << Right;
   str.width(10);
   str.setf(ios::fixed, ios::floatfield);
   str.setf(ios::showpoint);
   str.precision(2);
   return str;
}

#endif
```

17.4   Built-in Manipulators Taking No Arguments

Because some output (and input) stream operations are done quite frequently, the iostream library includes some pre-defined manipulators to handle these operations. They are included with all C++ compilers on the market today.

17.4.1   The Manipulator endl

For example, the manipulator endl (read: "end of line") is designed to output a new line character and flush the output buffer.

 Example 17.7

```
#include <iostream.h>

int main()
{
   cout << "Line 1" << endl << "Line 2" << endl;
   return 0;
}

/* The output of this program is:

Line 1
Line 2

*/
```

17.4.2   The Manipulators dec, oct, and hex

The manipulators dec, oct, and hex work for both input and output operations, and set the stream state to either decimal, octal, or hexadecimal, respectively.

Example 17.8

```
// Set the output state to decimal
cout << dec;
// Set the output state to octal
cout << oct;
// Set the output state to hex
cout << hex;

// Set the input state to decimal
cin >> dec;
// Set the input state to octal
cin >> oct;
// Set the input state to hex
cin >> hex;
```

Here is a test in which a hexadecimal number is input and then displayed in octal.

 Example 17.9

```
#include <iostream.h>

int main()
{
    cout << "Input a hex number: ";
    int number;
    cin >> hex >> number;
    cout << "The number in hex is " << hex << number << endl;
    cout << "The number in octal is " << oct << number << endl;
    return 0;
}

/* If you entered the number ff, you would see:

The number in hex is ff
The number in octal is 377

*/
```

17.4.3   The Manipulator ws

Recall that when using the function istream::get() or istream::getline()
with three arguments to read in a string, both leading and embedded whitespace
are retained. If you want to *bypass* the leading whitespace, and still *retain* the
embedded whitespace, then use the input manipulator ws. Note, however, that it is
effective only for the next input operation, after which another istream::get()
or istream::getline() would *retain* leading whitespace.

 Example 17.10

```
#include <iostream.h>

int main()
{
   const char quote = '"';
   cout << "Enter a string: ";
   cin >> ws;
   const int length = 100;
   char string[length];
   cin.get(string, length);
   cout << quote << string << quote << endl;
   return 0;
}

/* If you entered some spaces, the string "I like
   manipulators", the output would be:

"I like manipulators"

*/
```

17.4.4   The Manipulator ends

Another built-in manipulator that takes no argument is called ends. This causes a
null character to be output, and is useful for objects of type strstream. It is
defined as:

 Example 17.11

```
ostream& ends(ostream& str)
{
   return str << '\0';
}
```

17.4.5   The Manipulator `flush`

The last manipulator that takes no input argument is called `flush`. This is exactly the same as the member function `ostream::flush()`, and causes the stream associated with the output instance to be completely emptied. The manipulator itself is nothing more than:

Example 17.12

```
ostream& flush(ostream& str)
{
    return str.flush();
}
```

17.5   How a Manipulator Works

As stated above, manipulators really are functions, but when you write the name of a function *without* the following parentheses, the compiler generates the *address* of that function. Therefore, in the evaluation of arguments to the insertion and extraction operators via function calls (in which the order of invocation is compiler-dependent), you do not need to worry about bad side effects. In the case of a manipulator, since you are supplying the *address* of a function that takes as its one argument a reference to an `ostream` or `istream` object and returns a reference to this same object, the compiler will look for an overloaded insertion or extraction function, respectively, that conforms to this scheme.

Now, if you have a pointer-to-function variable, then you may execute the function itself by "dereferencing" that variable and enclosing the entire expression within parentheses. Since `*this` always refers to the invoking instance of any nonstatic member function call, in the case of sending output to the terminal screen it's the object `cout` which is passed to the manipulator as the actual argument. Finally, since the manipulator itself returns a reference to `cout`, this reference must, in turn, be passed back to the original statement to allow function chaining to occur.

This is how the overloaded insertion function to accommodate manipulators is written.

Example 17.13

```
ostream& ostream::operator<<(ostream& (*ptr)(ostream&)
{
    return (*ptr)(*this);
}
```

The one argument is the pointer variable `ptr` which contains the address of the manipulator function itself. The manipulator is then executed via this pointer, and at the same time `*this` is passed as the one formal argument. Then the object that `*this` represents is returned from the manipulator (by reference) back to the insertion operator which, in turn, returns it (again by reference) back to the statement that originated the call to the insertion operator. Got it?

 Tip

> *ANSI C also allows you to execute a global function through a pointer by simply writing the pointer name followed by the actual argument list.*

17.6   Manipulators Taking 1 Argument

It is possible to write a manipulator with one actual argument. This, obviously, allows you to give the manipulator much greater flexibility.

The first task you must do is to include the header file called `iomanip.h`.

 Example 17.14

```
#include <iomanip.h>
```

In Borland C++, this file automatically includes the file `iostream.h`, but this may not be true for all C++ compilers.

The generic call (assuming output) to some manipulator taking one argument would appear as:

 Example 17.15

```
cout << name(arg);
```

In order for the compiler to treat this syntax as a function call (which it is), and still avoid the problem of evaluating function calls in an unknown order, the call will be converted into a temporary instance of a class in which the insertion operator is overloaded. The details of how this works will be shown later in this chapter.

 Tip

> *The discussion of manipulators taking one argument assumes that the `iomanip.h` file utilizes templates. Borland compilers starting with version 4.0 have this feature.*

17.7   Built-in Manipulators Taking 1 Argument

Every C++ compiler also comes with built-in manipulators that take one argument.

17.7.1   The Manipulator `setw()`

Perhaps the most frequently used manipulator that takes an argument is `setw()`. Like its counterpart, the method `ios:width()`, it is used to set the field width *for the next output item only.* The one argument is, of course, the field width itself.

This example uses the `setw()` manipulator to set the field width to 5. Notice how each output line can now be written using just one statement, which was not possible with `ios:width()`.

 Example 17.16

```
#include <iomanip.h>

int main()
{
   cout << setw(5) << 1 << endl;
   cout << setw(5) << 23 << endl;
   return 0;
}

/* The output of this program is:

^^^^1
^^^23

where ^ represents a blank

*/
```

17.7.2   The Manipulator `setfill()`

Another frequently used manipulator sets the fill character. It is called `setfill()` and, as you would expect, the single argument is the fill character itself.

This example uses manipulators to set both the field width and the fill character.

 Example 17.17

```
#include <iomanip.h>

int main()
{
   cout << setw(5) << setfill('0') << 1 << endl;
   cout << setw(5) << setfill('*') << 23 << endl;
   return 0;
}

/* The output of this program is:

00001
***23

*/
```

17.7.3   Miscellaneous Manipulators

The other built-in manipulators that take a single argument are:

- `resetiosflags(long flag)`—turns off the bits specified in `flag` (input and output);

- `setbase(int base)`—sets the output base to decimal if `base` is 0 or 10; to octal if `base` is 8; to hexadecimal if `base` is 16 (output);

- `setiosflags(long flag)`—turns on the bits specified in `flag` (input and output);

- `setprecision(int prec)`—sets the number of digits displayed after the decimal point to `prec` (output).

17.8   How to Create a Manipulator with 1 Argument

The general format of an output manipulator that takes one argument is:

 Example 17.18

```
ostream& name(ostream& str, T arg)
{
   // Your code here using 'str' and 'arg'
   return str;
}

omanip<T> name(T arg)
{
   return omanip<T>(name, arg);
}
```

where `name` is the name of the manipulator, `T` is the type of the argument, and `arg` is the formal argument name itself. `omanip` is a class template defined in the file `iomanip.h`.

For example, here is a manipulator called `set()` that sets the field width to whatever the input argument happens to be, and sets the fill character to an '`*`'.

Example 17.19

```
#include <iomanip.h>

ostream& set(ostream& str, int length)
{
   return str << setw(length) << setfill('*');
}

omanip<int> set(int length)
{
   return omanip<int>(set, length);
}

int main()
{
   cout << set(7) << 123 << endl;
   cout << set(5) << 45 << endl;
   return 0;
}

/* The output of this program is:

****123
***45

*/
```

Here is another manipulator called Tab that is designed to tab to an absolute column position on some output device. This is useful when you need to do column alignment of data. If the tab position is less than the current file position marker, then a newline is performed. Note that the first position is assumed to be zero.

 Caution

Since the starting position of the terminal screen is not guaranteed to be equal to zero, you are responsible for making a pseudo call to Tab() with no argument whatsoever before any other output operation is performed. This call will force the starting position to be zero. In addition, this manipulator may not work if the output is redirected to a disk file.

Example 17.20

```
// File tab.h

#ifndef TAB_H
#define TAB_H

#include <iomanip.h>

inline ostream& Tab(ostream& str, long destination)
{
   if(destination == -1L)
      return str.seekp(0L);
   if(destination < 0)
      return str;
   long bytes_to_move = destination - str.tellp();
   if(bytes_to_move < 0L)
   {
      str << endl;
      str.seekp(0L);
      bytes_to_move = destination;
   }
   if(bytes_to_move > 0L)
      str << setw(static_cast<int>(bytes_to_move)) << ' ';
   return str;
}

inline omanip<long>Tab(long destination = -1L)
{
   return omanip<long>(Tab, destination);
}

#endif
```

(Continued)

```
// File main.cpp

#include <iostream.h>
#include "tab.h"

int main()
{
   const int array_of_tabs[] =
   {
      4, 20, 6, 25, 0
   };
   const int size = sizeof(array_of_tabs) /
                    sizeof(*array_of_tabs);
   cout << Tab();    // pseudo call
   for(int i = 0; i < size; ++i)
      cout << Tab(array_of_tabs[i])
           << "column " << array_of_tabs[i];
   cout << endl;
   return 0;
}

/* the output of this program is:

^^^column 4^^^^^^^^^column 20
^^^^^column 6^^^^^^^^^^^^column 25
column 0

(where ^ is a blank)

*/
```

 Tip

The method ostream::seekp() *is used to set the insertion point where the next character is to be inserted into the output stream. This will be discussed further in the next chapter.*

17.8.1   How It Works

A manipulator that is written with one explicit argument works by having the compiler replace the function call with a temporary instance of a class. When this instance is output, an overloaded insertion operator that was granted friendship by the class then takes control and invokes another function that performs the actual task of manipulating the stream.

This can be illustrated by the following example that is designed to emulate how the setw() manipulator works. When the expression setw(5) is evaluated, it returns a temporary instance of the class omanip<int>. This instance contains an int and a pointer to a function returning an ostream by reference and taking two

output, the overloaded insertion operator function in the class `omanip<int>` gains control and executes the function `setw()`, which then sets the proper width value.

 Example 17.21

```
#include <iostream.h>

template <class T>
class omanip
{
   friend ostream& operator<<(ostream&, const omanip<T>&);
      public:
   omanip(ostream& (*p)(ostream&, T), T x) : ptr(p), data(x) {}
      private:
   ostream& (*ptr)(ostream&, T);
   T data;
};

template <class T>
ostream& operator<<(ostream& str, const omanip<T>& obj)
{
   return (*obj.ptr)(str, obj.data);
}

ostream& setw(ostream& str, int x)
{
   str.width(x);
   return str;
}

omanip<int> setw(int x)
{
   return omanip<int>(setw, x);
}

int main()
{
   cout << setw(5) << 123 << endl;
   return 0;
}

/* The output of this program is:

^^123

(where ^ is a blank)

*/
```

Of course, there is no law that says you have to use the capabilities that `iomanip.h` provides you. In point of fact, all you really need to do is write a class similar to the one in the previous example with a constructor that takes one argument, and an overloaded insertion operator that outputs an instance of the class.

For example, here is a repeat of the `Tab` manipulator, but now written as a class (sometimes called an *effector*). Once again, you are responsible for issuing a pseudo call to the default constructor by writing the class name followed by an empty set of parentheses.

 Example 17.22

```cpp
// File tab.h

#ifndef TAB_H
#define TAB_H

#include <iostream.h>
#include <iomanip.h>

class Tab
{
   friend inline ostream& operator<<(ostream&, const Tab&);
      public:
   Tab(long d = -1L) : destination(d) {}
      private:
   long destination;
};

inline ostream& operator<<(ostream& str, const Tab& T)
{
   if(T.destination == -1L)
      return str.seekp(0L);
   if(T.destination < 0)
      return str;
   long bytes_to_move = T.destination - str.tellp();
   if(bytes_to_move < 0L)
   {
      str << endl;
      str.seekp(0L);
      bytes_to_move = T.destination;
   }
   if(bytes_to_move > 0L)
      str << setw(static_cast<int>(bytes_to_move)) << ' ';
   return str;
}

#endif
```

(Continued)

```cpp
// File main.cpp

#include <iostream.h>
#include "tab.h"

int main()
{
   const int array_of_tabs[] =
   {
      4, 20, 6, 25, 0
   };
   const int size = sizeof(array_of_tabs) /
                    sizeof(*array_of_tabs);
   cout << Tab();   // pseudo call
   for(int i = 0; i < size; ++i)
      cout << Tab(array_of_tabs[i])
           << "column " << array_of_tabs[i];
   cout << endl;
   return 0;
}

/* The output of this program is:

^^^column 4^^^^^^^^column 20
^^^^^column 6^^^^^^^^^^^^column 25
column 0

(where ^ is a blank)

*/
```

 Tip

This technique can easily be extended to accommodate two or more arguments.

Exercise 17.1

Create two output manipulators called `Uppercase()` and `Lowercase()` that cause hexadecimal numbers and floating point scientific numbers to be shown first using upper-case letters and then lower-case letters, respectively. Then write a program to test these manipulators.

 Exercise 17.2

Create an output manipulator called `Lines()` that takes an integer input argument specifying the number of new-line characters ('\n') to be output. For example, if you want to output three blank lines, you would code:

```
cout << Lines(3);
```

 Exercise 17.3

In C you may display the first x characters of a string by including a decimal point and the value for x in the format string.

```
int x = 3;
printf("%.*s\n", x, "ABCDEFG");

/* Output:

ABC

*/
```

Write a manipulator called `Substring()` that can emulate this feature. This manipulator must take two arguments: the address of the string to be printed, and an integer representing the number of characters to be displayed. (Hint: encapsulate the string and the integer into a structure object, then have the manipulator receive an instance of this structure by reference-to-`const`.)

 Exercise 17.4

Write a manipulator called `Blank_flag()` that takes one argument of type `long` and emulates the blank flag in a `printf()` function call. That is, the manipulator should output the number preceded by a blank if it is greater than or equal to zero, and precede it with a minus sign if it is less than zero.

Exercise 17.5

Write a manipulator called `Commas()` that takes one argument of type `long` and displays this number showing commas at the appropriate places.

Exercise 17.6

Write a manipulator called `Replace()` that takes three arguments—a string and two characters. The manipulator must output the string while substituting the second character every time it encounters the first character.

Exercise 17.7

Write a manipulator called `Binary()` that takes one argument of type `int` and outputs the binary representation of this number.

.

Chapter 18

File Input/Output

18.1 Introduction

File input/output in C++ using iostream methods gives you the capability to read an input file, write an output file, and both read and write the same file. To do this, classes have been derived from `istream` and `ostream` that add the capability to accommodate any legitimate file device.

18.2 File Input/Output Classes

The aforementioned classes that have already been defined for you are:

- `ifstream` (derived from `istream`). Use this whenever you wish to read a file.
- `ofstream` (derived from `ostream`). Use this whenever you wish to write a file.
- `fstream` (derived from `iostream`). Use this whenever you wish to update a file.

To use any of these classes, you must have the following statement in your program:

 Example 18.1

```
#include <fstream.h>
```

This line automatically includes the header file `iostream.h`.

18.3   Creating Instances of the Classes

There are no pre-defined instances of these classes comparable to `cin` and `cout`. Therefore, the first step in using file I/O is to create an instance of the appropriate class.

 Example 18.2

```
ifstream in;        // Input instance
ofstream out;       // Output instance
fstream in_out;     // Update instance
```

Now you may use the instance `in` with all of the member functions of class `istream`, the instance `out` with the member functions of class `ostream`, and the instance `in_out` with the member functions of both `istream` and `ostream`.

18.4   Opening a File

The first step in using a file instance is to open a disk file. In any computer language, this means establishing a communication link between your code and the external file. Each of the three file I/O classes provides the member function `open()` to do this. The declarations for these `open()` functions are as follows:

 Example 18.3

```
void ifstream::open(const char* name, int m = ios::in,
      int prot = filebuf::openprot);

void ofstream::open(const char* name, int m = ios::out,
      int prot = filebuf::openprot);

void fstream::open(const char* name, int m,
      int prot = filebuf::openprot);
```

The first argument is the external file name passed in as a constant string literal. This is analogous to the first argument that you would use in C with `fopen()`.

 Caution

If you hard-code a file name under DOS and need to specify a path, don't forget to write two backslashes (\ \) to yield one.

The second argument is the file mode, and is analogous to the second argument of fopen(). All file modes come from a public enumerated type in the class ios. There are eight possible modes, as follows:

Table 18-1 Input/Output Modes

Name	Meaning
ios::in	Input mode. (Default for input file)
ios::out	Output mode. (Default for output file)
ios::app	Append to an output file rather than update an existing record
ios::ate	Position file marker at end of file instead of beginning
ios::trunc	Delete file if it exists and re-create it
ios::nocreate	File must exist, otherwise open fails (output only)
ios::noreplace	File must not exist, otherwise open fails (output only)
ios::binary	Binary mode; default is text

Note that for an istream (input) instance, the default mode is ios::in, and for an ostream instance (output), the default mode is ios::out. However, for an fstream (input/output) instance, there is no default mode, so it is up to you to explicitly provide one. Obviously, if you need to specify more than one mode, they may be bitwise ORed together.

The third argument is the file access. Under Borland C++, the possible values are:

Table 18-2 File Access Modes

Value	Meaning
0	Default
1	Read-only file
2	Hidden file
4	System file
8	Archive bit set

For example, this is how the aforementioned three instances might be used to open some files:

 Example 18.4

```
in.open("input");
out.open("output");
in_out.open("update", ios::in | ios::out);
```

An alternate method of executing the open function is to call the constructor with the same argument(s) that you would use for the open(). Thus, instead of creating the instance and then explicitly calling the `open()` function, you can combine these two steps by writing:

 Example 18.5

```
ifstream in("input");
ofstream out("output");
fstream in_out("update", ios::in | ios::out);
```

18.4.1   Checking the Status of the File

Of course, you should always check the result of an open operation to ensure that it succeeded, and at any time you may check the state of a file object to ensure that it is still valid. The way it is done is the same way that you learned for checking the state of the `cin` object.

The following table shows the various possibilities that exist for checking for success or failure after doing an open on an instance called `file`.

Table 18-3   File Status Methods

Test	Success	Failure
if(file)	true	false
if(!file)	false	true
if(file.good())	true	false
if(!file.good())	false	true
if(file.fail())	false	true
if(!file.fail())	true	false

18.5   Closing a File

When you are done using the file, the member function `close()` in all three classes taking no arguments will close it. This function is called automatically by the destructor for the class, but you may explicitly call it if you wish.

18.6   A Simple Example of Write, Append and Read

Let's start with a simple program that accepts string input from the user and writes it to a disk file called `output`.

    Example 18.6

```
#include <fstream.h>

int main()
{
    ofstream out("output");
    if(!out)
    {
        cout << "Open failed\n";
        return 1;
    }
    cout << "Enter a line of data: ";
    const int max = 256;
    char buffer[max];
    while(!cin.getline(buffer, max).eof())
    {
        out << buffer << endl;
        cout << "Next line: ";
    }
    return 0;
}

/* A typical run of this program would yield:

Enter a line of data: This is
Next line: a test
Next line: ^Z

*/
```

Now let's give the user a chance to append more records to the file. Note that the mode of the file is `ios::out | ios::app` (although `ios::app` by itself would still have worked).

Example 18.7

```
#include <fstream.h>

int main()
{
    ofstream out("output", ios::out | ios::app);
    if(!out)
    {
        cout << "Open failed\n";
        return 1;
    }
    cout << "Enter a line of data: ";
    const int max = 256;
    char buffer[max];
    while(!cin.getline(buffer, max).eof())
    {
        out << buffer << endl;
        cout << "Next line: ";
    }
    return 0;
}

/* A typical run of this program would yield:

Enter a line of data: Some more
Next line: data
Next line: ^Z

*/
```

The mode `ios::noreplace` ensures that the file does not already exist when being opened. As a test of the open failure code, let's try to open the file with this mode specified.

Example 18.8

```
#include <fstream.h>

int main()
{
   ofstream out("output", ios::out | ios::noreplace);
   if(!out)
   {
      cout << "Open failed\n";
      return 1;
   }
   cout << "Enter a line of data: ";
   const int max = 256;
   char buffer[max];
   while(!cin.getline(buffer, max).eof())
   {
      out << buffer << endl;
      cout << "Next line: ";
   }
   return 0;
}

/* The output of this program is:

Open failed

*/
```

Finally, this program numbers and prints the records that were just written.

Example 18.9

```
#include <fstream.h>

int main()
{
    ifstream in("output");
    if(!in)
    {
        cout << "Open failed\n";
        return 1;
    }

    int rec = 0;
    const int max = 256;
    char buffer[max];
    while(!in.getline(buffer, max).eof())
        cout << "Record #" << ++rec << ": " << buffer  << endl;
    return 0;
}

/* The output of this program is:

Record #1: This is
Record #2: a test
Record #3: Some more
Record #4: data

*/
```

18.7　　The File Position Markers

So that the file I/O classes can keep track of where in a file the data is to be written to and read from, they establish what is called a "file position marker" (fpm). In Borland C++, this marker has been typedef'ed as a long integer representing an offset value from the beginning of the file. In point of fact, there are two such markers, one for reading, and one for writing.

18.7.1　　Changing the File Position Markers

The classes istream and ostream each have a member function that allows you to change these markers. In istream it's called seekg() and in ostream it's called seekp(). The function istream::seekg() is associated with the file's "get or read" pointer, and the function ostream::seekp() is associated with the file's "put or write" pointer. The declarations for these two functions are as follows:

Example 18.10

```
// class istream
istream& seekg(streampos);
istream& seekg(streamoff, ios::seek_dir);

// class ostream
ostream& seekp(streampos);
ostream& seekp(streamoff, ios::seek_dir);
```

where `streampos` and `streamoff` represent `long` integers, and `seek_dir` is a public enumerated type defined as follows:

Example 18.11

```
enum seek_dir {beg, cur, end};
```

Note that each function has been overloaded. If the one-argument form of the function is used, then the argument is the offset from the beginning of the file. If the two-argument form is used, then the first argument is the offset number of bytes (positive or negative) from the absolute `seek_dir` position. For example, a call to `seekg()` with a single argument of 0L causes the file to rewind and data to be read starting with the first record. A call with the first argument of 0L and the second of `ios::end` places the file position marker on the end-of-file byte.

18.7.2   Reading the File Position Markers

To find out the positions of these markers at any time, once again each class has an appropriate method. In `istream` it's called `tellg()`, and in `ostream` it's called `tellp()`. They are declared as follows:

Example 18.12

```
// Class istream
streampos tellg();

// Class ostream
streampos tellp();
```

The first character of a record is deemed to be in position 0. Note that for a file opened in text mode (the default), a newline character is actually stored as two characters: a newline ('\n') and a carriage return ('\r'). In binary mode, only a newline is stored (as would be the case in Unix).

To illustrate the file position marker in action, we will use an instance of the class fstream so that both output and input operations can be performed. After each record is read and printed, the file position marker (fpm) is displayed.

 Example 18.13

```
#include <fstream.h>

int main()
{
   fstream in_out("update", ios::in | ios::out |ios::trunc);
   if(!in_out)
   {
      cout << "Open failed\n";
      return 1;
   }
   cout << "Enter a line of data: ";
   const int max = 256;
   char buffer[max];
   while(!cin.getline(buffer, max).eof())
   {
      in_out << buffer << endl;
      cout << "Next line: ";
   }
   // Flush the output buffer
   in_out << flush;
   // Return to the start of the file
   in_out.seekg(0L);
   // Read and print the records, and show the file
   // position marker
   int rec = 0;
   while(!in_out.getline(buffer, max).eof())
   {
      cout << "Record #" << ++rec << ": " << buffer << endl;
      cout << "fpm = " << in_out.tellg() << endl;
   }
   return 0;
}

/* A typical run of this program would yield:

Enter a line of data: A
Next line: test
Next line: ^Z
Record #1: A
fpm = 3
Record #2: test
fpm = 9

*/
```

Let's repeat this example using a binary file just to see the difference in the file position marker.

 Example 18.14

```
#include <fstream.h>

int main()
{
    fstream in_out("update",
         ios::in | ios::out | ios::trunc | ios::binary );
    if(!in_out)
    {
        cout << "Open failed\n";
        return 1;
    }
    cout << "Enter a line of data: ";
    const int max = 256;
    char buffer[max];
    while(!cin.getline(buffer, max).eof())
    {
        in_out << buffer << endl;
        cout << "Next line: ";
    }
    // Flush the output buffer
    in_out << flush;
    /  / Return to the start of the file
    in_out.seekg(0L);
    // Read and print the records, and show the file
    // position marker
    int rec = 0;
    while(!in_out.getline(buffer, max).eof())
    {
        cout << "Record #" << ++rec  << ": " << buffer << endl;
        cout << "fpm = " << in_out.tellg() << endl;
    }
    return 0;
}

/* A typical run of this program would yield:

Enter a line of data: A
Next line: test
Next line: ^Z
Record #1: A
fpm = 2
Record #2: test
fpm = 7

*/
```

18.8   Using the Line Printer

The line printer is just another output file insofar as DOS is concerned. To redirect output to a printer from within your program, use the predefined name `prn`, as shown in the following example.

 Example 18.15

```
#include <fstream.h>

int main()
{
    ofstream printer("prn");
    printer << "This line appears on the printer\n";
    return 0;
}
```

 Tip

The actual condition of the printer (device time out, selected, out of paper, etc.) must be tested by the function biosprint() *which is prototyped in the file* bios.h. *This is specific to DOS.*

Exercise 18.1

Write a C++ program that writes all 256 characters in the collating sequence to a disk file in character, decimal, hexadecimal, and octal formats, and then reads each of the 256 records back in and displays it. (Caution: you may not be able to write number 26, the end-of-file character.)

Exercise 18.2

Given the following class definition:

```
class File
{
      public:
    int open(int argc, char* argv[]);
    void read();
    void write();
    void beginning();
    void end();
    void print();
    void close();
      private:
    fstream in_out;
};
```

write the definitions of the member functions so that the user of the class has complete flexibility as to the name of the external file to be manipulated, and modes to be used. All such variables are entered from the DOS command line. The first argument is the disk file name, and the remaining arguments represent the various open modes, exactly as specified by the enumerated types, e.g., "in" for input, "out" for output, etc.

Bibliography

AT&T Library Manual, C++ Stream Library, 1989

Atkinson, Lee and Atkinson, Mark, Using Borland C++, Que Corporation, 1991

Barkakati, Naba, Object-Oriented Programming In C++, Sams Publishing, 1991

Becker, Pete, Template notes

Berry, John, C++ Programming, Howard W Sams & Company, 1988

Borland C++ 3.0 Programmer's Guide

Budd, Timothy, An Introduction To Object-Oriented Programming, Addison-Wesley Publishing Company, 1991

Cargill, Tom, C++ Programming Style, Addison-Wesley Publishing Company, 1992

Chirlian, Paul M, Programming in C++, Merrill Publishing Company, 1990

Coplien, James O, Advanced C++, Addison-Wesley Publishing Company, 1992

Davis, Stephen R, Hands-On Turbo C++, Addison-Wesley Publishing Company, 1991

Dewhurst, Stephen C and Stark, Kathy T, Programming in C++, Prentice Hall, 1989

Dlugosz, John, The C++ Test of Knowledge, 1995

Eckel, Bruce, Using C++, Osborne McGraw-Hill, 1989

Eckel, Bruce, C++ Inside & Out, Osborne McGraw-Hill, 1993

Eckel, Bruce, Thinking in C++, Prentice Hall, 1995

Ellis, Margaret A and Stroustrup, Bjarne, The Annotated C++ Reference Manual, Addison-Wesley Publishing Company, 1990

Flamig, Bryan, Turbo C++, A Self-Teaching Guide, John Wiley & Sons, 1991

Gorlen, Keith E and Orlow, Sanford M and Plexico, Perry, Data Abstraction and Object-oriented Programming in C++, John Wiley & Sons, Inc., 1990

Graham, Neill, Learning C++, McGraw-Hill, 1991

Harbison, Samuel P and Steele Jr, Guy L, C: A Reference Manual (third edition), Prentice Hall, 1991

Horstmann, Cay S, Mastering C++, John Wiley & Sons, Inc., 1991

Hughes, Cameron and Hamiton, Thomas and Hughes, Tracey, Object-Oriented I/O Using C++ Iostreams, John Wiley, 1995

Ladd, Scott Robert, C++ Techniques & Applications, M&T Books, 1990

Lippman, Stanley, C++ Primer (2nd edition), Addison-Wesley Publishing Company, 1991

Lucas, Paul J, The C++ Programmer's Handbook, Prentice Hall, 1992

Mancl, Dennis, "Inline functions in C++", The C++ Report, February 1990

Meyers, Scott, Effective C++, Addison-Wesley Publishing Company, 1992

Murray, Robert, "The C++ Puzzle", The C++ Report, September, 1991

Murray, Robert, C++ Strategies and Tactics, Addison-Wesley Publishing Company, 1993

Pappas, Chris H and Murray, III, William H, Turbo C++ Professional Handbook, Osborne McGraw-Hill, 1990

Papurt, David M, Inside the Object Model, SIGS Books, 1995

Perry, Greg, Moving From C To C++, Sams Publishing, 1992

Plum, Thomas and Saks, Dan, C++ Programming Guidelines, Plum Hall, Inc., 1991

Pohl, Ira C, C++ for C Programmers, The Benjamin/Cummings Publishing Company, 1989

Prata, Stephen, C++ Primer Plus, Waite Group Press, 1991

Rudd, Anthony, C++ Cpmplete, John Wiley & Sons, Inc., 1994

Saks, Dan, "Standard C++: A Status Report", Supplement to Dr, Dobb's Journal, December, 1992

Schildt, Herbert, Turbo C/C++ The Complete Reference, Osborne McGraw-Hill, 1990

Schildt, Herbert, Using Turbo C++, Osborne McGraw-Hill, 1990

Shapiro, Jonathan S, A C++ Toolkit, Prentice Hall, 1991

Skinner, M T, The Advanced C++ Book, Silicon Press, 1992

Stevens, Al, Teach Yourself C++ (Fourth Edition), MIS: Press, 1995

Stroustrup, Bjarne, The C++ Programming Language (Second Edition), Addison-Wesley Publishing Company, 1991

Wang, Paul S, C++ with Object-Oriented Programming, PWS Publishing Company, 1994

Weiner, Richard S & Pinson, Lewis J, The C++ Workbook, Addison-Wesley Publishing Company, 1990

Weiner, Richard S & Pinson, Lewis J, An Introduction to Object-Oriented Programming and C++, Addison-Wesley Publishing Company, 1988

Weiskamp, Keith & Flamig, Bryan, The Complete C++ Primer, Academic Press, 1990

Weiskamp, Keith and Heiny, Loren and Flamig, Bryan, Object-Oriented Programming with Turbo C++, John Wiley & Sons, Inc., 1991

Index

Symbols

`#define`
    vs. `const`   23
`*this`
    definition of   178
    dereferencing   178
    used to make a copy of invoking
        instance   178
`/*` token   2
`//` token   2
`__cplusplus` macro   3, 243

A

abstract base class
    how to create   314
    used to implement specification   314
abstract data typing   95
access privileges
    with a private derivation   288
    with a protected derivation   288
    with derived classes   288
access specifiers
    definition of   100
    how to write   101
    `private`   100
    protected   288
    `protected`   100
    `public`   100
    with derived classes   286
ADT. See abstract data typing
`Amortizd` class   316
array
    initialization of   12
    of constant data members   164
assignment
    vs. initialization   8, 150
assignment operator
    inherently supplied   249
    overloading   255
    with inheritance   300
AT&T Bell Laboratories   1

B

base/member initialization list
    order of initialization   160
    purpose of   151
    syntax of   151
    throwing an exception from   396

when mandatory   153
with a constant   156
with a reference   156
with inheritance   298
with pointers   157
`bool` type
    backward compatibility   29
    conversions to type `int`   27
    definition of   27
    how to display   448
    how to input into   465
    input of   29
    value of `false`   27
    value of `true`   27
    with Boolean expressions   28
    with Boolean operators   28
    with relational operators   28

C

C++ keywords   36
`calloc()` function   75, 77
cast
    C++-style   146
    C-style   146
    function-style   146
        to create unnamed object   148
        when returning by value   146
    new style
        description   29
        generic format   30
    vs. a conversion   30
catch block. See exception handling
`catch` keyword. See exception handling
`cerr` object   429
`char**` types, how to support   21
`cin` object
    condition of   459
    declaration of   44
    definition of   44
    flushing   463
    testing for errors   460
    use to access members   47
    with `operator>>()`   45
class
    as a namespace   416
    components of   96
    creating instances of a   111
    data
        nonstatic   96
        static   96

Companion disk for Learning C++ A Hands-on Approach (2nd edition)

All of the examples contained in this book may be obtained on diskette by sending $15.00 for each diskette to the following address:

Eric Nagler
P O Box 2483
Santa Clara, California 95055-2483

The price includes all shipping, handling, and sales tax. Please add $5.00 for each foreign order.

✂ – ✂ – – – – – – – –

Companion disk for Learning C++ A Hands-on Approach (2nd edition)

Quantity	Price each	Foreign order	Total enclosed
	$15.00	+ $5.00	

Name: _____

Company or school: _____

2nd address line: _____

Street: _____

City : _____

State: _____

Country (if not U.S.): _____

Zip code: _____

Please send a check or money order. For foreign orders, please use a check in U.S. funds drawn on a U.S. bank.

PWS Publishing Company assumes no responsibility for this offer.